NEVER ENOUGH

JOE McGINNISS

SIMON & SCHUSTER

NEW YORK LONDON TORONTO SYDNEY

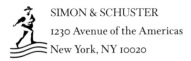

SIMON & SCHUSTER
1230 Avenue of the Americas
New York, NY 10020

Grateful acknowledgment is made to the following for permission to use illustrative material: photo 11: Douglas Healey/Polaris; photos 12 and 18: *Sing Tao Daily*; photos 13 and 19: *The Standard*; photo 16: *Eastweek*; photo 17: William Farrington/Polaris; photo 21: Patrick Andrade/Polaris.

Designed by Joel Avirom and Jason Snyder

Manufactured in the United States of America

ISBN-13: 978-0-7394-9655-8

For Nancy

Always remember others may hate you but those who hate you don't win unless you hate them. And then you destroy yourself.

–RICHARD M. NIXON (1913–1994),
IN HIS WHITE HOUSE FAREWELL SPEECH

PROLOGUE
THREE DAYS IN NOVEMBER 2003

IT WAS 8:00 P.M. MONDAY IN HONG KONG, 6:00 A.M. MONday in Chicago when Nancy Kissel called her father, Ira Keeshin. She was crying.

"Rob and I had a huge fight last night," she said. "I'm pretty badly beaten up. I'm sure he broke some of my ribs. And I'm afraid. I'm afraid he's going to come back and hurt me more."

"Wait. He *hit* you?"

"He was drunk. It was horrible . . ." She started crying so hard she couldn't talk.

"Where is he now?"

"I . . . I don't know. He left. He could be anywhere."

"How are *you*? Have you been to a doctor?"

"I'm going in the morning. My ribs are killing me. I'm all beat up."

"And you don't know where Rob is?"

"He could be anywhere. I'm scared he'll come back."

"How are the kids?"

"They're fine. They don't know anything."

"Are Connie and Min there?"

"Yes, they're here."

"Make sure they stay with you. And keep the door locked. Double-bolt it. This is awful. What the hell happened?"

Instead of answering, Nancy broke down in tears again.

"Never mind. Listen, I'll get down there as fast as I can. If he comes back, call the police. Stay safe. That's the most important thing. Don't go out anywhere he might be able to grab you. Keep Connie and Min with you. Call some friends to come over. I don't want you alone until we know where he is."

She was sobbing.

"Maybe he just lost it for a minute Maybe he's ashamed, that's why he left."

"No. This wasn't the first time."

"What—"

"Just *get here*, please. I don't know what to do."

Ira was sixty years old, five seven, physically active, physically fit. He thought fast. He talked fast. He was impulsive. He was not a long-term planner. He had a quick sense of humor. He had a temper. He had a heart. He didn't have much contact with his first ex-wife, Nancy's mother, but he'd stayed on good terms with his second, even after he'd married for a third time.

He was the number two man at a specialty bread company that supplied bread and rolls of the highest quality to many of Chicago's finest restaurants and huge quantities of lesser-quality product to such national chains as Chili's, Cheesecake Factory, and TGIF.

He arrived in Hong Kong on Wednesday night. He had visited Nancy and Rob there before. Nancy had said she'd have a car and driver meet him at the airport, but he found no one waiting for him. He took a taxi to Parkview, the multitower luxury apartment complex where Rob and Nancy lived. He checked into the hotel on the grounds, walked to their building, and took the elevator to the twenty-second floor.

Nancy was thirty-nine but looked younger. She was short and blond, flashy and feisty. She had lively eyes and a brilliant smile. Her shapeliness did not suggest that she'd borne three children. Heads still turned when she entered a room. Normally. Now she looked haggard and scared.

"Has he come back?"

"No."

"Has he called?"

She shook her head.

He started to hug her.

"*Don't!* Didn't I tell you he broke my ribs?"

Ira smelled scented candles. He glanced around the living room. Dozens of candles were burning. He thought he smelled lilac and vanilla. But he was too tired to smell straight, too tired to think straight, almost too tired to stand.

"Will you be okay overnight?"

"I'll be fine."

"Then I'll see you in the morning after I've had a little sleep. We'll go to the police, file a missing persons report."

"And an assault and battery complaint."

"That, too."

After kissing each of his three grandchildren as they slept, Ira went back to the hotel and to bed.

Isabel was nine, Zoe six, and Ethan three. Rob and Nancy had arrived in Hong Kong in 1997 when Zoe was an infant. Ethan had been born there. Rob had been sent to Hong Kong to make money for Goldman Sachs and for himself. He'd done both. Three years later, he'd moved to Merrill Lynch to make more.

Ira had breakfast with the children while Nancy got dressed. He took the girls down to their school bus. They were thrilled by Grandpa Ira's surprise visit. Connie, the nanny—or *amah*, as nannies are called in Hong Kong—would take Ethan to his preschool later.

The morning was cool, the sky clear. November marked the end of Hong Kong's summer. In November, the daytime temperature dropped into the seventies and the humidity eased. The air pollution lingered—the pollution never went away anymore—but it was slightly less oppressive than in summer.

Ira and Nancy took a taxi to the Aberdeen Division police station on Wong Chuk Hang Road, near the Ap Lei Chau Bridge. As soon as they arrived and stated their business they were led to a conference room and joined by Sergeant Mok Kwok-chuen, who was ready to write down the details.

But instead of speaking, Nancy started to tremble, as if on the verge of a seizure. Then she closed her eyes and began to rock back and forth, her arms crossed tightly in front of her, moaning.

Ira tried to calm her. She quivered and sobbed. Sergeant Mok was attentive and solicitous. Ira told him that Nancy had been badly beaten by her husband, who had then gone missing and who was still missing after three and a half days.

Eventually, Nancy was able to stutter a brief account of what had happened. She said her husband had been drunk and had begun hitting and kicking her when she'd resisted his attempts to have sex. Then he'd left their apartment and she didn't know where he'd gone. The account came out in fits and starts. Nancy would speak a few coherent sentences, then slip back into a state in which all she did was tremble, moan, and cry.

Sergeant Mok explained that he could issue a missing persons report, but that before Nancy could press assault and battery charges a police doctor would have to examine her and record her injuries. He said that could be done at Queen Mary Hospital in nearby Pok Fu Lam, not far from the University of Hong Kong. Ira and Sergeant Mok helped her to a waiting patrol car.

It was almost noon when they arrived. Queen Mary, the teaching hospital for the medical school of the nearby University of Hong Kong, was one of the largest and busiest acute-care facilities in the territory. The lobby was overflowing with patients waiting to be seen. The Hong Kong patrolman who brought Ira and Nancy to the hospital explained to a receptionist why they had come. The receptionist told him that Nancy would have to wait her turn. They sat and they waited. And they sat and waited. Nancy did not like to sit and wait under any circumstances. She didn't see why she should be made to now. This was the sort of thing she'd been putting up with for six years. The Chinese did not seem able to grasp the obvious fact that certain people should not be made to sit and wait.

Ira asked the patrolman how much longer the wait would be. He didn't know. Nobody knew. Nancy had already been waiting for two hours. She said enough was enough. She was a busy woman. The children would soon be getting out of school. She and Ira left. Maybe she'd come back tomorrow.

That evening, Ira and Nancy brought Isabel, the nine-year-old, back to school for a dance lesson. Like most children of wealthy expatriates in Hong Kong, the Kissel girls attended the Hong Kong International School, the territory's most costly and prestigious day school.

After Isabel ran inside, Ira suggested that they drive down the hill to Repulse Bay. He thought the quiet beach, the peaceful waters, the open air, and sense of space—space being Hong Kong's most precious commodity—might comfort his daughter. On the way she stopped at a 7-Eleven and bought a pack of cigarettes. Ira had never seen her smoke. "I've been smoking for a while," she said. "Rob hated it. Fuck him."

They found a gazebo at the edge of the beach and sat down. They talked about how sad it was that everything had fallen apart. Rob and Nancy had been married for fourteen years. They'd been in Hong Kong for six. At first, Rob had worked for Goldman Sachs. After three years, he'd moved to Merrill Lynch. He had an important job. He made a lot of money. He was planning to make a lot more. Nancy enjoyed the royal lifestyle of the wealthy expat. She liked to spend. Suddenly, all that seemed over.

Ira was perplexed by Rob's disappearance. Nancy said Merrill Lynch had told her he hadn't been in his office all week. He found that hard to imagine. Rob was obsessed with his work. He was driven. He'd often said he could not rest as long as anyone he knew was making more money than he was. But now? Ira sensed that divorce was inevitable. Nancy said she'd been living a nightmare all year. No matter how sorry Rob might be, she couldn't forgive him this time. She'd take the children and move back to the United States and let lawyers hammer out the details. Ira, an emotional man, began to weep. So did Nancy. They sat together at the edge of the bay, his arm gently around her because he did not want to hurt her ribs, and cried together.

They met Isabel in the parking lot after the lesson. They could not talk about Rob in front of the children. Nancy had told them he was on another business trip. He traveled everywhere from Mumbai to

Manila, and he was gone more than he was home, so the children didn't question the explanation.

Isabel climbed into the backseat of Nancy's Mercedes and asked her to play the Avril Lavigne CD. Her favorite song on it was "Complicated." On the way back to Parkview she and Nancy sang along.

Why'd you have to go and make things so complicated?
I see the way you're actin' like you're somebody else . . .

They dropped Ira at the hotel. He was still jet-lagged and worn to the nub by emotional strain. He went to his room and fell asleep.

The phone woke him at 11:00 p.m. It was Nancy.

"You've got to come over! *You've got to come over right away!* The police are here. They're asking me questions. There's just so many police. *You've got to come over right away!*"

PART ONE
CASTING THE DIES

1. GROWING UP KISSEL

ROB KISSEL WAS NOT ONLY THE RICHEST AND BEST-LOOKING kid in his class at Pascack Hills High School in Montvale, New Jersey, he was also the most unselfish and considerate. He never spoke ill of anybody. He was as sweet to the plainest girl as to the prettiest. He never kicked anyone when he was down.

But the quality for which he was best known was competitiveness. Rob did not merely have a will to win: he had a need that bordered on the desperate. Anyone who'd ever met his father knew where it came from.

Bill Kissel, a New Jersey native, had graduated from the Case Institute of Technology—now Case Western Reserve University—in 1951 with a degree in chemistry. For twenty years, he worked for Sun Chemical in Fort Lee, New Jersey. Then he realized his true talent was entrepreneurial. He left Sun in 1972 to start a company that manufactured dry toner for printing cartridges.

The dry toner field was one of the many whose lack of glamour defined New Jersey. The state was the dry toner capital of America, if not the world. Dry toner is composed of tiny plastic particles blended with carbon. The smaller the particles and the more uniform their size, the better the result from the copying machine. The conventional method of making dry toner was called pulverization. It involved grinding the dry plastic from which the toner was made into particles of the smallest possible size. But that size wasn't small enough for a new generation of copying machines. Xerox spent millions of dollars in the 1960s trying unsuccessfully to produce a toner of smaller and more uniform particle size by chemical processes.

Where Xerox failed, Bill Kissel succeeded.

By jiggling a few molecules, he developed—and quickly patented—a means of creating dry toner particles chemically, instead of by brute force. His method created particles less than half the size of those produced conventionally. In the world of dry toner it was as if a new continent had been discovered. The companies who used toner-based print systems beat a path to Bill Kissel's door. For a few halcyon years, his company, Synfax, was the name of the game. By the time the big boys caught up, his fortune was made.

Bill's vigor was impressive. He played to win and he won. Acquaintances admired his tenacity and durability. He could be charming and gracious in social situations and he knew how to catch flies with honey, but he was not an easy man to grow close to. The moment he sensed a lack of acquiescence in a subordinate—and Bill considered almost everyone a subordinate—his eyes turned steely and his voice grew harsh. He was five eight, slim, and irascible. He had a reputation for vindictiveness. People said, "You don't want to cross Bill Kissel." He took pride in that.

He'd married a woman quite his opposite in every way. Elaine Kissel was warm and welcoming and a testament to the likelihood that Bill possessed virtues not readily apparent to outsiders. She was the velvet glove on Bill's fist of steel. Elaine nurtured while Bill harangued. She offered safe haven and solace.

They had three children: Andrew, born in 1960; Robert, born in

1963, and Jane, born in 1968. Elaine made the family while Bill made the money that gave the family a standard of living he approved of.

For many years, the Kissels lived in a comfortable house on a quiet street in the pleasant northern New Jersey town of Woodcliff Lake. But when Bill struck it rich he wanted more. He bought a grandiose mansion in Upper Saddle River. It was built on two acres of land and contained 7,500 square feet of living space. It was so big that family members spoke to one another by intercom. Visiting friends got lost in its maze of corridors.

Richard Nixon lived around the corner. He would come down to the bottom of his driveway on Halloween and hand candy to trick-or-treaters through the gate.

Bill acquired a yacht, a Cadillac Seville, a Mercedes-Benz convertible—and the list went on. But they were mere toys. The possession he cared about most was his multimillion-dollar vacation house at the Stratton Mountain Ski Resort in Vermont.

Bill was a skier, so he determined that the family would ski. And they would learn to ski well enough to please him. Every winter weekend he put his wife and his children in his Cadillac and hauled them up to Stratton Mountain, whether they liked it or not. Except for Andrew, they learned to like it.

To Bill, no offense was minor. For reasons no one ever understood—he didn't like to talk about his own childhood in a second-generation Austrian-Jewish immigrant family—there was more vengeance than forgiveness in his heart. He had come to believe early on that a man did things for money, not for love, and that he had better do them right the first time. Someone had taught him that second chances were for sissies. Someone had taught him that the father set the standards and that it was the job of the sons to measure up without complaint. Someone had taught him that failure must be greeted with contempt. Elaine tried to shield the children from Bill's anger, but the oldest, Andy, bore the brunt.

He started out as a bright little boy but grew into an angry, sullen teenager, almost as hard to live with as his father was. Rob would be in the living room with a girlfriend when Andy would come into the house. Rob would say hello. Andy would say, "Fuck you," and walk into his bedroom and slam the door. His favorite song in high school was Harry Chapin's "Cat's in the Cradle," about a father who never had time for his son: *I'm gonna be like you, Dad. / You know I'm gonna be like you . . .*

There had been no family meeting at which Bill announced that he was stripping his hopes and dreams from Andy's chest and pinning them on Rob's instead, but by the time Rob entered high school everyone in the family had no doubt that this had occurred. Somehow, Rob shouldered the burden. His competitive instinct—primal in its force—drove him on.

In the classroom, however, Rob's killer instinct slumbered. Bill blamed the school. He withdrew Rob from Pascack Hills and sent him to the Saddle River Day School for senior year. Rob improved his academic record at Saddle River, but his transcript still lacked the preternatural sheen that might have caught the eyes of Ivy League admissions officers. At Bill's urging, he went to the University of Rochester to prepare for a career in engineering.

Rob did well at Rochester. He pledged Psi Upsilon, which had been Horatio Alger's fraternity. Even there, his competitiveness set him apart. He never did anything casually. If scores were being kept, Rob's had to be highest. His favorite song was Neil Young's "Old Man." *Old man, look at my life, / I'm a lot like you were . . .*

He graduated in 1986, having decided on a career in finance, not engineering. Finance meant Wall Street, which meant New York. For anyone who grew up on the Jersey side, New York was Xanadu. It was the land of hopes and dreams, the fast track, the big league, the epicenter. It was where you went to find out who you were and to discover what you might become. Rob looked across the river with longing. It was the late 1980s and Wall Street was overflowing with young men making millions before the ink on their grad school diplomas was dry. When the wind was blowing in the right direction, Rob thought he could actually smell the money.

He was the kid with his face pressed against the glass of the candy store window. But Rob didn't just want to buy candy. He was Bill's son. He wanted to own the store. In 1987, after a tense year spent working for his father at Synfax, he enrolled in New York University's Leonard N. Stern School of Business. Two weeks before classes started, he and a Psi U brother named Mike Paradise flew to the Club Med Turkoise in the Caribbean Turks and Caicos islands.

Turkoise was not for the prim and proper. Club Med's brochures explained that it had been designed for "travelers in their twenties and thirties who enjoy making friends on vacation and value communal fun." The message seemed to be: clothing optional, drugs permitted, sex guaranteed. Rob was twenty-three, handsome, and single. What could be better than that?

2. GIRL OF THE GOLDEN WEST

ON A WARM AND SUNNY SATURDAY IN THE SPRING OF 1966, a young couple from the nearby suburban town of Wyoming, Ohio, drove into downtown Cincinnati to have lunch, stroll a bit, and do some shopping.

Cigarettes had begun to carry warning labels, John Lennon had said the Beatles were more popular than Jesus, and the United States had started bombing North Vietnam with B-52s. *The Sound of Music* had just won the Academy Award for Best Picture, and *Bonanza* was the most popular program on television. In Cincinnati, despite another dazzling display from Oscar Robertson, the Royals had been eliminated in the first round of the NBA playoffs. In baseball, with young Pete Rose nearing his prime, the Cincinnati Reds were hoping for another first division finish.

Ira Keeshin and his wife, the former Jean Stark, were not much older than Pete Rose. They had met as students at Grinnell College in Iowa in 1960, when Ira was a sophomore and Jean a freshman. Jean got pregnant. They got married. They transferred to Michigan State, from which Ira graduated with a degree from the School of Hotel, Restaurant, and Institutional Management.

Jean Stark came from one of Cincinnati's wealthiest families. Her mother was a Lazarus, as in Lazarus department stores, which dominated the retail market in the Midwest. Lazarus stores had been around for more than a hundred years. They were the first department stores in the country to install escalators. Later, they were first to become air-conditioned. In 1939, Jean's grandfather, Fred Lazarus, Jr., persuaded President Franklin D. Roosevelt to fix the date of Thanksgiving as the fourth Thursday in November rather than the last, in order to assure a longer Christmas shopping season. Eventually, Lazarus would merge with the Federated chain, which would drop the Lazarus name in favor of Macy's, but in the mid-1960s it was hard to find a department store in Ohio that the Lazarus family did not own.

Ira and Jean moved to Cincinnati in 1966 so Ira could join the family business. They made an attractive couple. The Lazarus family had high hopes for them. Ira was revitalizing the department store restaurants and Jean, despite what the family considered some worrisome liberal tendencies, was about to become the first Jewish member of the Junior League of Cincinnati. They had two young daughters, Laura and Nancy, and they saw no clouds on their horizon.

On this particular Saturday, Ira and Jean were shopping at Closson's, a Cincinnati institution almost as integral to city life as were the Lazarus stores. For almost a hundred years, Closson's had housed the city's finest art gallery. Among Cincinnati's moneyed classes, there was a feeling that if it didn't come from Closson's, it wasn't art. Ira and Jean were looking for a Mother's Day present for Ira's mother. They were drawn to a grouping of lead statuettes created by a local artist named Lattimer. One, in particular, caught their eyes.

It was eight inches high, weighed eight pounds, and portrayed two young girls sitting face to face, as if in a garden. Rising from a two-inch base of solid lead, the figurines suggested both the closeness of sisters and the innocence of childhood.

To Ira and Jean, the two girls on the statuette represented their own two daughters, Laura and Nancy. They bought the statuette and gave it to Ira's mother for Mother's Day. It became the object she cherished most for the rest of her life.

Like a lot of marriages begun with an unplanned pregnancy, Ira and Jean's eventually ran aground. They divorced in 1977. Laura was fourteen and Nancy was twelve, and the divorce sent the two girls tumbling out of the world of privilege and stability, the only one they'd ever known.

By then, Ira owned the Wheel Café, which was even more of a downtown Cincinnati landmark than Closson's. The Wheel Café had anchored Fountain Square for longer than anybody could remember. Generations of politicians had clustered around its varnished tables to share their dreams and plot their schemes. Although Ira was proud to own this piece of Cincinnati history, after the divorce he worried that Jean's family might cast a pall on its future. He sold the restaurant and went to Minneapolis to become concessions manager at the new Hubert H. Humphrey Metrodome.

Jean felt liberated by the divorce. Despite her Junior League membership, she had the heart of a hippie. Her family's wealth oppressed her. She found Cincinnati society suffocating. She yearned for space in which she could develop her artistic sensibility and her inner self. She moved to California with Laura and Nancy, eventually settling in the small town of Piedmont, in the hills just beyond Berkeley. She left behind all the Lazarus family money and support.

Jean's first problem as a single mother was finding work. It was not one she ever fully resolved. She had not graduated from college, nor had she ever developed marketable skills. Women in the Lazarus family had not been encouraged to do either. Aware that she could not support herself and her daughters as an artist manqué, she tried repeatedly to plug herself into the workforce. She either quit or was fired from countless office jobs. She had a brittle nature not well suited to the give and take of an office environment. She quarreled easily and often. She was intelligent and articulate, but neither equanimity nor resilience was among her strengths.

She developed an anxiety disorder. She slumped into debilitating periods of depression. She came to recognize that she was not a very good mother. Her own mother had been so disabled by alcohol and had collapsed in so many public places that the family had put the word out that she was epileptic. Jean herself had never experienced mothering, and found that she had little aptitude for it.

Despite her best efforts, she didn't cope well with Laura and Nancy's teenage years. In search of stability herself, she wasn't able to provide it for her daughters, and her attempts to bond with them never got beyond smoking pot in the kitchen. The girls started building their own lives. Laura married young and moved away. Nancy had a hard time at Piedmont High. She acted out. She snorted coke. She slept around. She was effusive one minute, angry the next. She found it difficult to channel her energies. She was bossy and loud, lewd and crude. She was either the leader of a group or she quit it. It was her way or the highway.

What Nancy had going for her were her looks. She was a knockout. She stood a full-breasted five foot four, dyed her hair blond, and made ample portions of her firm and shapely legs available for viewing. Her manner fluctuated between brash and insouciant. She was quick, sharp, and funny. She did not shy from attention and she paid attention to the impression she made. She had a provocatively dirty mouth and talked as if there was nothing she was afraid to try.

She had artistic talent but little discipline. She was no more likely to last through four years of college than she was to fly to the moon. She made a pass at junior college, followed by a halfhearted attempt to enroll in a Los Angeles art school. She and her mother reached the conclusion that they'd both be better off if Nancy left home. She moved to Minneapolis to live with her father. He'd remarried and had a five-year-old son. His new wife welcomed Nancy with genuine warmth.

Ira encouraged her to try college again. Without enthusiasm, she enrolled at the University of Minnesota, where winter arrived on the heels of Labor Day. Students wrapped in parkas and scarves walked through tunnels to get to class because it was too cold aboveground. Bob Dylan had lasted only a semester at the University of Minnesota, and Nancy did not outdo him. She disliked her classes, her classmates, the darkness, the cold, and the snow. Midway through her second semester, she put together a portfolio of her artwork and sent it to the Parsons School of Design in New York. To her surprise and delight, she was accepted.

Parsons, with its campus in Greenwich Village, is one of the top design schools in the world. Nancy arrived in the fall of 1984, when she was twenty. She brought with her an inquiring mind, an adventurous soul, swelling ambition, and a body that was nothing short of luscious. What more did a newcomer need?

Bored by routine, she quit Parsons after a year. It had served its purpose—introducing her to New York City. She got a job at Caliente Cab Company, a trendy Tex-Mex restaurant on Waverly Place. Her first job was as a "border guard," a hostess who escorted customers from the Mex side to the Tex side and vice versa.

It was a business where quitting time was after midnight in a city where a lot of people considered that late afternoon. Though the work pace was hectic, it couldn't compare to the cocaine-fueled after-hours social life.

Nancy had the looks, the energy, and the attitude to flourish, and she did. When she called home, her mother detected a hard new edge in her voice, which Nancy said was the sound of street smarts. She was flamboyant. She dyed her hair red, then blond, then red again, then back to blond. She partied fervidly. She attracted attention and reveled in it. New York didn't faze her. She felt it was the stage she'd been born to perform on.

Many of her dates were out-of-work actors. One had appeared briefly in *Full Metal Jacket*. Another had an intermittent role in a soap opera. They struck her as glamorous, but at least one of them actually struck her. It may have been two. Nancy seemed to enjoy telling friends that she could provoke men to the point of violence.

She had not yet mastered her own short temper. Often, it showed itself at work. Like her mother, she was frequently hired and fired. She'd win a quick promotion with her charm, then provoke a spat and get sent packing. From Caliente Cab Company she went to El Rio Grande on Thirty-eighth Street, from there to brief stints at three or four other places, and finally to Docks on the Upper West Side (where, to her delight, she once catered a birthday party for Imelda Marcos).

Wherever she was, Nancy came alive at closing time. She moved with what in earlier times might have been called a fast crowd: men with more plans than money, but always enough for cocaine; women who were smart, sexy, and unattached. In New York in the mid-1980s, she was living *Sex and the City* before it was born.

Although she tended to pick up and drop companions as often as she changed jobs, Nancy maintained her friendship with her ex–Parsons classmate Alison Gertz. Alison was the genuine article—a Park

Avenue socialite and an heiress. She came from a department store fortune, too—and her relevant parent had not been disinherited. Gertz (later Stern's) had been the Lazarus of Queens and Long Island. Eventually, like Lazarus, the Gertz/Stern's chain was absorbed by Federated, leaving Ali's father even wealthier than Nancy's mother might have been.

In late summer of 1987, Nancy decided to take a vacation. She'd seen a Club Med brochure. The spot that caught her eye was the Turkoise in the Turks and Caicos. She persuaded Ali—not that Ali needed much persuading—that the two of them should fly down for a week of uninhibited fun. They arrived on a separate flight but on the same day as Rob and Mike Paradise.

3. YOUNG LOVE

THEY MET ON THE NUDE BEACH. ROB SAID, "I BET YOU'D look great with your clothes on." It was lust at first sight.

To Rob, Nancy personified everything hip and stylish and daring and free. She *was* New York, in all its sophistication, glamour, and allure. She was sparkly and saucy and had the street-smart veneer she'd been striving for. She was also gorgeous enough to make his pressed-against-the-glass-storefront, Jersey-guy eyes fall out. Plus, she was Jewish.

To Nancy, Rob personified everything she wanted in a husband. He was good-looking and hard bodied, clever and ambitious, well educated and smart. And, she soon intuited, from a family that was—at least by New Jersey standards—filthy rich. Plus, he was Jewish.

Neither of them ever looked back.

But neither did they charge ahead recklessly. Nancy may have been impetuous, but Rob was as methodical as a Swiss watchmaker. His heart had leapt impulsively, but his mind soon assumed full control. There was passion and romance and there were dreams of the splendor yet to come, but he laid out their future systematically.

They would date each other exclusively for a year. Then he'd move to an apartment big enough for both of them. Then they'd get engaged. By then he would have his master's in finance from NYU. Once it was clear that his future was assured, they would marry.

His first job was with a small, staid New York investment bank named Ladenburg Thalmann. This was not the glamour end of the spectrum. Ladenburg was a perfectly respectable establishment, with impeccable roots in German-Jewish society. But its heyday had come in the nineteenth century. By the second half of the twentieth it was no longer a first-rank player on Wall Street.

But Rob was now an investment banker and determined to live as much like one as his salary permitted. The first thing he did was move to a landmark building: La Rochelle, on Columbus Avenue and Seventy-fifth Street, where Mike Paradise and his wife were already living. Nancy moved in with him as soon as they were engaged.

Bill disapproved of Nancy from the start. He thought she was common because she didn't have a college education. He referred to her as "that waitress." Nonetheless, Rob and Nancy married in September 1989, only a few months after his mother died.

Nancy chose Ali Gertz to be her maid of honor. The year before, Ali had learned that she was dying of AIDS. The news reverberated throughout the Upper East Side. AIDS was for drug addicts and homosexuals; Park Avenue socialites did not get AIDS. Ali told friends that she must have been infected by a Studio 54 bartender with whom she'd gone to bed at the age of sixteen. The bartender, a bisexual, had later died of the disease.

Knowing she was dying, Ali made a choice. Instead of retreating to her Park Avenue apartment or her family's summer home in the Hamptons, she stepped into the limelight, hoping that awareness of her fate would jar others into taking precautions. Barbara Walters interviewed her. *People* magazine put her on the cover. *Esquire* named her Woman of the Year. She was privileged, beautiful, and articulate. Her speaking out about AIDS triggered a quantum jump in awareness that no one who had unprotected sex was immune. She would continue to speak until the last of her strength deserted her. She died in 1992. ABC broadcast a movie about her called *Something to Live For*, which featured Molly Ringwald as Ali and Lee Grant as her resolute and loving mother.

Nancy's choosing Ali to be her maid of honor seemed an act of love: letting a dying friend share in a commitment to life. A few ungenerous souls among the guests, however, viewed it as a grasp at Ali's celebrity coattails. On the morning of the wedding, Nancy and Ali and Nancy's second-closest friend, Bryna O'Shea, went to the Essex House on Central Park South to have their hair done and to put on their gowns.

As they were dressing, Ali began to recite a list of the pills she had to remember to take. There were uppers for energy, downers to take the edge off the uppers, dozens of high-potency vitamins, and, most important, AZT. She had to take four hundred milligrams every four hours and she wanted to be sure she wouldn't forget amid the excitement of the wedding reception. She started to explain that AZT was most effective in combating the HIV virus that was the precursor to full-blown AIDS, but that her doctor had said—

"Just shut up, Ali," Nancy said. "This is my day. Nobody wants to hear about your fucking pills."

The wedding took place at the East River Yacht Club, across the East River from Manhattan. Nancy wore a gown she had selected at Victoria Falls in Soho. The reception was held at the club's restaurant, Water's Edge, which offered an unrivaled view of the skyline.

The weather that day was glorious. A warm September sun shone from a clear blue sky. Guests crowded onto the restaurant's outside deck. The Manhattan skyline dominated everyone's field of vision. To Rob and Nancy, it represented limitless promise. A magnetic field seemed to emanate from it, drawing them into its mysteries, tempting them with its riches, thrilling them with its range of possibilities.

The bride and groom were radiant. They danced with élan. Their smiles were illuminated by joy. But Nancy later complained to friends that Ali Gertz ruined the day. All through the reception she talked to the other guests about AIDS. Whether she meant to or not, she stole the spotlight. She was beautiful, she was a celebrity, she would die young. Nancy felt that more attention was paid to her than to the bride. Nancy had no time for her after that.

Nancy was not a forgiving person. She took offense at the most innocuous of remarks and found disparagement in the most neutral of comments about her. Her reactions were swift and extreme. If she felt a friend, or even a relative, had slighted her, she would cut them out of her life without a further word. And it was permanent. Nancy did not relent. In this, she was similar to Bill. No Amish church practiced shunning with more rigor than Nancy.

Rob and Nancy remained at La Rochelle on West Seventy-fifth Street. Rob liked living in the same building as Mike Paradise, his old college roommate, who by then was married and practicing law in midtown Manhattan. The two couples socialized frequently. One evening the foursome had made a dinner date, but Mike's wife canceled at the last minute, saying she was not feeling well. An hour later, Nancy looked out her window and saw Mike and his wife laughing happily as they climbed into a taxi in front of La Rochelle.

She felt as if she had been spat upon. She told Rob that not only was she never going to speak to either Mike Paradise or his wife again, but that Rob was not to do so either. So in thrall to her was he that for the next two years he did not say so much as good morning to his old college friend.

For their first anniversary, Rob bought Nancy a mink coat. Bill paid for it. Unable to express love in other ways, Bill sometimes compensated by bestowing expensive gifts. Rob made sure Nancy never found out that he'd bought the coat with his father's money. She was thrilled to receive the coat. It seemed to change her personality. For the first time, she acted truly proud of herself—as if the gift were a reward for accomplishment. She glowed when she wore it and she wore it everywhere, nine months a year. At restaurants, she did not check it. Instead, she draped it over the back of her chair. The Madonna song had been written for her:

You know that we are living in a material world
And I am a material girl.

4. LAZARD FRÈRES

ROB GLOWED LIKE NEON AGAINST THE DRAB, GRAY LADEN-burg Thalmann sky. He viewed his time there as an apprenticeship. It lasted a year; then Lazard Frères hired him. This was his big step up, even if by 1990 Lazard had entered a period of genteel decline.

Lazard traced its roots to the California Gold Rush, but its corporate culture reflected old-world—some said outmoded—attitudes shaped by the French billionaires who controlled it. In the 1960s and '70s, Felix Rohatyn's brilliance and flair carried the U.S. division of Lazard into the front ranks of American investment banking, but as larger, more aggressive, and more technologically advanced competitors muscled their way onto the scene, Lazard witnessed a dimming of its luster. Even Rohatyn wondered aloud whether the jaguar that was Lazard could survive among a herd of elephants.

Rob did not concern himself with such metaquestions. What he cared about was advancement. His competitive instinct had not waned. Even in a field where everyone worked preposterously long hours and where everyone was single-mindedly focused on the one goal that mattered—making money—Rob stood out. He knew that money—enough money—could buy his father's respect. This mattered more to Rob than he liked to admit. It might even have mattered more than he recognized.

Rob didn't have the polish needed for mergers and acquisitions. M&A, as it's called in the investment banking business, required an element of salesmanship in addition to the necessary number-crunching skills. Rob found his niche in the more predatory realm of distressed debt. The idea with distressed debt was to make money from failure, not success. It worked like this: you find a bankrupt company or one on the verge of bankruptcy, buy the company's bonds at a penny on the dollar, and use the resulting leverage to force reorganization. Then, instead of taking cash payment on the bonds, you take shares of the company's stock. As your reorganization turns the company around and it starts showing a profit, your shares rise a few thousand percent and everybody is happy, especially your bosses. At the end of the year, when you get a bonus ten times bigger than your salary, you're even happier.

The M&A stars and the ballsiest, craftiest, luckiest traders wore the crisp white uniforms adorned with epaulets and scanned the horizons from the top deck. The distressed-debt boys worked the engine room, out of sight. This was where Rob discovered his true talent: he could plow through thousands of pages of red ink and spot the single spark of life. He could find—among the halt and the lame, the sick and the dying—those few companies worth a bet. The work was more tedious than glamorous, the hours it demanded not merely unreasonable but grotesque. "I laugh when I think about forty-hour weeks," Rob would say. "I'm putting in forty-hour days." But he got results. He got such good results that he didn't even notice that he'd begun to cross over: he was becoming an investment banker, not a mere man.

The only reason people become investment bankers is to get rich. Not only do they have no problem worshipping Mammon to the exclusion of all else in life, they also lose the ability to understand people who don't. They tend to believe that the only reason other people don't become investment bankers is either because they're not smart enough or they're afraid of hard work.

It's a unique perspective.

In his splendid novel *A Ship Made of Paper*, Scott Spencer describes the breed. He writes that in lieu of happiness they experience "the grim, burnt comfort of thriving in a world that is, for the most part, brutal and uninhabitable." The investment banker, Spencer writes, "spends the best part of nearly every day surrounded by people who make money, not houses, or soup, not steel, not songs, only money, and who quite openly will do anything for financial gain. . . . He has made an alliance with these squandered souls, these are his people, his teammates, and among them he feels the pride of the damned. His friends are the guys who will fly halfway around the world to convince someone to take a quarter of a point less on a deal. Everyone else is a civilian, all those fruits and dreamers who do not live and die by that ceaseless stream of fractions and deals that is the secret life of the world."

This was now Rob's world. He'd been drawn to it by the promise of outrageous wealth, but his years at Lazard added a twist: no longer was it enough to earn millions per year, or even to earn more millions this year than last. The only way to really succeed was to earn more millions each year than anyone else.

"What good does it do me to make ten million a year," he would ask friends rhetorically, "when the guy down the hall is making twenty?"

Rob had been at Lazard for three years when he and Nancy had their first child. They named her Isabel. Her birth meant they had to find a bigger apartment. Nancy spent months looking for the right place. She found her dream flat in the mid-Manhattan district called Chelsea.

Then Bill entered the picture. He came across the river to inspect. He walked up and down the street in front of the apartment. Trash blew across his path. Glass from broken bottles crunched beneath his feet. He saw winos, panhandlers, and people who looked like drug addicts. He saw women who must have been whores. With even more distaste, he found himself gazing upon people of indeterminate gender.

"It's a slum," he told Nancy. "It's a filthy slum filled with perverts. How could you think I'd let my grandchild be raised in that kind of squalor? I won't permit you to live in that apartment." Nancy asked Rob to try to talk some sense into his father.

"Are you kidding? Find someplace else," Rob said.

Eventually, they moved to Mercer Street in Greenwich Village. Isabel's room was in a basement down the stairs. The only outside light came through barred, street-level windows the size of manila envelopes. They needed an intercom to hear Isabel cry. Nancy liked it because the upstairs rooms were large and bright. She said Isabel would be fine. Rob was spending a hundred hours a week at the office, so he wasn't much affected by where they lived. Soon enough, they'd have their multimillion-dollar condo—as long as he never slowed down.

Nancy showed great affection for her daughter, but she had inherited her mother's lack of aptitude for parenting. In the right mood, she could spend hours playing happily with the baby on the floor, but the tasks of motherhood bored her. Feeding a toddler three times a day— *every day*? Doing laundry? Taking the child out for fresh air? Such chores annoyed her. They dampened her carefree spirit. She felt they were depriving her of her right to remain irresponsible.

The apartment was only two blocks from Washington Square Park, where neighborhood toddlers played. Before wheeling Isabel there for the first time, Nancy girded herself for the banal chitchat she expected from the other young mothers—women, no doubt, who'd never partied from closing time until dawn. What she found floored her: there *were* no other young mothers there. The dozen or so toddlers running around were all in the care of their *nannies*. Rob got an earful that night.

———————————

Nancy had always worn a hard shell. She was easy to meet, but not easy to know. Even women who considered her a good friend sensed that she did not want to be known. You could talk to Nancy about what she'd bought, not how she felt. You could ask about the baby's outfit, not how she and the baby were. Nancy didn't simply have boundaries; her friends suspected she had built castle walls around her heart. It must have gotten lonely inside.

One of the few people to whom she felt close was Ira's mother. Throughout her childhood and adolescence, both before and after the divorce, Ira's mother had been a gentle, caring presence in Nancy's life. In 1996, when Ira's mother was dying in a hospice in Evanston, Illinois, Nancy flew out to be with her.

The lead statuette that Nancy's mother and father had bought in Cincinnati thirty years earlier was by the old woman's bedside when she died. Nancy, too, had come to treasure the statuette. In the figures of the two young and innocent little girls—so trusting, so seemingly full of sweetness, hope, and love—Nancy felt a link to something ineffable and precious and lost. Her older sister, Laura, reeling from her own rocky adolescence, had married and had moved to Oregon, severing all contact with the family. But on the statuette, Nancy believed, the two of them could stay forever linked. To Nancy, the statuette symbolized the capacity for closeness so lacking in her life.

She brought it back to New York from Evanston. It became her most valued possession, even more than the mink coat.

5. GOLDMAN SACHS

IN THE 1990s, THE POACHING OF INVESTMENT BANKING stars became the rule rather than the exception on Wall Street. Cadres of headhunters roamed the canyons like guerrilla bands. If you were an investment banker and you weren't regularly offered a higher-paying job at a more prestigious firm, there was something you weren't doing right.

Rob had been performing brilliantly at Lazard. And Lazard, though slowly sliding from the first tier of investment banks, remained a land of plenty for headhunters. In 1996, Rob's was among the heads hunted and delivered to Goldman Sachs. If boys of an earlier era had dreamed of one day wearing a New York Yankee uniform, rookie investment bankers in the 1990s yearned for the day when they could hold in their hand a business card that said Goldman Sachs. By almost any standard of measurement, Goldman Sachs was the leading investment bank in the world.

"Money is always fashionable," Henry Goldman, son of the bank's founder, said late in the nineteenth century. For the next hundred years, Goldman set the standard for haute couture in the banking world. It achieved its preeminence by being, as senior partner Gus Levy said in 1969, "long-term greedy." As a private partnership, Goldman did not have to answer to shareholders who expected spectacular earnings growth every quarter. Instead, the bank could formulate strategies that would play out over years.

The corporate culture at Goldman stressed teamwork. The slogan "At Goldman Sachs we never say 'I'" was taken seriously. Nonetheless, the bank rewarded individual performance with salary and bonus packages that were stupendous even by the lavish standards of the industry. Rob was at the point in his career when promising young bankers were given three- to four-year tours of duty overseas. The world of finance was global, and banks wanted their rising stars to gain experience in nerve centers other than Wall Street.

In 1997, the most dynamic, hypersensitive financial nerve center in the world was Hong Kong. The myth of the "Asian miracle" still carried the force of doctrinal truth. For more than a decade, led by Japan, Asian societies had been honing their economic systems to the finest of points. The region had it all: the strong work ethic, the focus on education, the thrifty populace, and the ability to manufacture cheaply and export products that other countries were hungry to buy. Asia would own the twenty-first century—all the magazines and TV news shows said so. Everyone in the financial realm rushed to stake his claim. Banks loaned money, mutual funds bought stocks and bonds, investors built factories and office buildings, currency traders sold deutsche marks and dollars to buy baht and won and rupiah. On the receiving end, men who'd been driving motorbikes all their lives were suddenly debating the merits of various models of Mercedes-Benzes.

This *was* the future, the experts agreed. Asia ruled. The good times were rolling and they were here to stay. The first ones now would always be first. If it was already too late to get in on the ground floor, there was plenty of space on the mezzanine. The world's leading financial journals spoke with one voice: any dollar not invested in Asia might as well stay under the mattress.

Hong Kong seemed the perfect place for a rising star like Rob Kissel to perfect his skills. He rejoiced when he learned he'd be heading there. "They only send winners," he told friends. "This means I'm on the fast track to make partner. Hong Kong is the key to the mint."

Hong Kong also offered temporary respite from the Kissel family's intramural wars. Rob was ready to take a break. The extended Kissel family raised dysfunctionality to an art form. Family gatherings became emotional bloodbaths. Between engagements, members sharpened their elbows—and teeth—for the next.

In 1992, Andrew, who had graduated from Boston University and gone into the real estate business, married Hayley Wolff, a former world-class competitive skier whom he'd met at Stratton Mountain. She'd worked part time as an instructor, and Jane Kissel had been one of her pupils. Hayley was smart and tough and fashionably blond. She could turn from charming to acerbic on a dime. After graduating from the University of Pennsylvania, she'd obtained her master's degree in finance at Columbia and was advancing toward a position as an entertainment-industry stock analyst at Merrill Lynch.

Bill admired her accomplishments but was miffed that she'd married Andrew instead of Rob. It didn't matter that Rob had never even sought to date her. Bill felt that Rob deserved the Ivy League heiress with the steel-trap mind, while "the waitress" would have been good enough for Andrew. Hayley, on the other hand, though she respected his intelligence and drive, thought Rob was a one-dimensional bore. She saw Andrew as a witty, wounded, vulnerable work in progress, battling bravely against the low self-esteem caused by his father's contempt. She was convinced she could find his hidden better side.

But it was Hayley's pedigree—her "heiress" status—more than her attitude or personality that first caused problems with Bill. She was the daughter of Derish Wolff—Phi Beta Kappa at Penn, MBA from Harvard, and since 1982 president/CEO of Louis Berger Group of East Orange. Louis Berger was an international engineering firm that had designed everything from Burma's Mandalay Road and the Bangkok International Airport to the Trans-Amazon Highway, the East Pakistan Road in Bangladesh, and the Stockholm subway system, to name but a few. Louis Berger Group made Bill Kissel's Synfax look like a high school chemistry experiment, and Derish Wolff's wealth made Bill's look like chump change. Bill's envy and resentment were predictable. He was a man to whom wealth and worth were synonymous. And Hayley didn't even have to say anything. The look in her eye said it all: my father's is bigger than yours.

A new front opened in the intramural war in 1994 when Andrew borrowed $500,000 from Rob to launch his own real estate company, which would focus, he said, on buying small apartment buildings in what he called "under the radar" neighborhoods in Bayonne, Hoboken, and Jersey City. He called the company Hanrock: "h" for Hayley, "a" for Andrew, "n" for Nancy, "r" for Rob, and the "ock" at the end to make "rock," which would show that the company was rock solid. To Nancy, who often referred to Andrew as a "lizard," the only "rock" in Hanrock was the one he'd crawled out from under. "You give half a million to your slumlord brother, while I have to go without a nanny," she groused to Rob.

Andrew had been working for W&M Properties, a midtown real estate firm that according to *The New York Times* specialized in "identifying and acquiring distressed but potentially profitable properties and renovating them in a style that attracts first-class tenants." There was no shortage of "distressed" properties in Jersey City. The trick would be to make them profitable.

But Andrew had another trick. In 1992, he and Hayley had bought a one-bedroom condo at 200 East Seventy-fourth Street. Within three years, he became treasurer of the co-op board. He viewed the position as a license to steal. Starting in January 1996, he regularly wired funds from the building's reserve account into personal and corporate accounts of his own. His early success as an embezzler made him both edgier and more arrogant than he had been.

Meanwhile, Hayley manufactured excuses to avoid socializing with Nancy and Rob. "I hate it when she comes here," she told Andrew. "She walks around the whole apartment, *pricing* everything I've just bought." At the same time, Nancy complained to Rob, "Their house at Stratton is twice as expensive as ours."

Bill remained the catalytic agent. He and the lady friend from Florida who'd been living with him since soon after his wife had died would arrive for a holiday dinner. Invariably, Andrew and Hayley would be the hosts, because Nancy simply wouldn't do it. Just as invariably, within the first five minutes, Bill would make a caustic remark. He'd say something snide or belittling, then take a drink into an adjacent room and close the door behind him. Neither Nancy nor Hayley could understand his behavior: why the need to hurt and humiliate? Andrew and Rob were not perplexed. They'd never known him to be any other way.

The two brothers reacted as they had since childhood. Rob

gamely endured it, while Andrew replied with bitter insults of his own as soon as they all sat down to dinner. For Andrew, the difference was that alcohol and cocaine now dulled his feelings and sharpened his tongue.

Little sister Jane opted out of the wasp's nest as soon as possible by marrying a gentile and moving west. Rob and Nancy and three-year-old Isabel and a second child, six-month-old Zoe, left for Hong Kong in June 1997. Nancy was looking forward to a surge in Rob's earnings and to the opulent lifestyle described by Goldman Sachs wives who'd returned from their tours of duty in Hong Kong. Rob was looking forward to these also, but equally to having half a world's worth of insulation from the corrosive bickering that seemed the only way of life the Kissels knew.

6. HONG KONG

THROUGH MOST OF ITS HISTORY, HONG KONG PERCHED ON the southeast coast of China like a diamond at the edge of a rice paddy. Even now, with China in the midst of the most explosive economic growth in world history, Hong Kong continues to dazzle.

Hong Kong is a city, an island, and, as of 1997, a special administrative region of China. SAR status means the Chinese government can allow Hong Kong's rampant capitalism to flourish unfettered without feeling that they've spit on Mao's grave. The SAR consists primarily of Hong Kong Island, Kowloon on the mainland (a seven-minute ferry ride across Victoria Harbor), and beyond Kowloon, the New Territories (which were new to Hong Kong more than a hundred years ago when England acquired them). The New Territories stretch north ten miles to the Shenzhen River, which forms the border with mainland China.

Hong Kong's population is almost seven million, of which more than 95 percent are Chinese, almost all of them Cantonese. The urban core has a population density of more than 100,000 per square mile, which makes it the most densely populated area in the world. In Hong Kong, nobody lives on the ground floor. Of its 8,000 buildings, 7,500 are high-rises. A small percentage are luxury apartment towers. The rest, stretching to the horizon in all directions, are featureless, identical blocks of concrete jammed so close together that you could reach out your window and eat your neighbor's dinner. Nine months a year the humidity has the kick of a horse. Twelve months a year the air is so polluted it could choke the horse that just kicked you.

But there is another Hong Kong: the Hong Kong of legend and postcards. This is the Hong Kong built by billions of dollars of foreign investment. This is the Hong Kong whose wealth is incalculable, the Hong Kong with the most spectacular skyline in the world.

In the last decades of the twentieth century multinational corporations flocked to Hong Kong, in part because of its location—half the world's population can be reached by a flight of five hours or less—but more because its government not only lets them have their cake and eat it but assures that they don't have to pay for it.

Hong Kong imposed no financial restrictions on corporations. All the world's money was welcome there and encouraged to turn itself into more. There was a laughably low tax on corporate profit and no limit on what that profit could be. Taxes taken for granted elsewhere in the world—on capital gains, for example, or on interest earned—were nonexistent. There wasn't even a sales tax, and individual income was taxed at only 15 percent, no matter how large the income was. For expat citizens of countries such as the United States and England, employment in Hong Kong was the gift that kept on giving.

Hong Kong became, in the words of writer P. J. O'Rourke, "a stewing pandemonium: crowded, striving, ugly, and the most fabulous city on earth."

The grandest offices in the most spectacular of Hong Kong's skyscrapers were occupied by the mercenaries whose efforts produced the highest return on the investments their companies made in posting them to Hong Kong in the first place: in other words, investment bankers.

Throughout the 1990s, these bankers descended on Hong Kong by the thousands, bringing with them their Porsches and Mercedes-Benzes, their Rolexes and Movados, their Gucci shoes and cuff links, their Zegna and Armani suits, their Versaces and Valentinos, and, if they had them, their wives and children. What they did not bring they bought, for the only pleasure in an investment banker's life that can rival the thrill of making money is the orgiastic joy of spending it.

Each morning, swift, silent elevators whisked these predators to their hushed offices and sacred conference rooms, from which they plotted their assaults on the summits of capitalism. A thousand feet below them, hundreds of restaurants and gleaming fast-food stalls dotted the air-conditioned lobbies and the stunningly modern shopping malls that adjoined their palaces. A maze of elevated and air-conditioned walkways permitted them to go weeks on end without ever setting foot on a Hong Kong street, without ever hearing the din, feeling the humidity, or choking on the filthy air.

The expat investment banker in Hong Kong—and more of them came from the United States than from anywhere else—could indulge himself in feelings of superiority every bit as grandiose as those displayed by England's colonial masters of the nineteenth century. Plus, the modern banker had air-conditioning.

The highest priority of his employer was to assure that none of the untidy business of actually *living* in a foreign country would distract him from the avid pursuit of riches. He was in Hong Kong to work at least a hundred hours a week. He was there to make gargantuan sums of money—fantastic, outlandish, inconceivable *gobs* of money—for his company. In the process, he could expect to enrich himself even beyond the limits of socially acceptable greed, while living like the sultan of Brunei.

He could also shield himself from contact with those who might not recognize his primacy. In Hong Kong, this meant the 95 percent of the population that was Chinese. In their eyes, no matter how much power you wielded in your own world, no matter how much wealth you had accumulated, you were and always would be a *gweilo*.

Literally, the term meant "white ghost," but usage had expanded the definition to "foreign devil." It was not dissimilar to *farang* in Thai. There was no way to construe it as a compliment. *Gweilo*, in fact, was one of those wonderful words that conveyed a host of complex and subtle attitudes but that, at the end of the day, left the individual to whom it had been applied feeling ever so slightly diminished. That was not the way a master of the universe was supposed to feel.

It was much in the employer's interest, therefore, to make Hong Kong seem, insofar as possible, to be simply a postcard. You could gaze upon the panorama from a skyscraper window and marvel at the human energy being expended down below, but you wouldn't have to hear it, smell it, taste it, or have it undermine your absurd but indispensable sense of self-worth. For what good to the firm was an investment banker with an inferiority complex?

———

Rob and Nancy and their two children arrived in Hong Kong in June 1997 and moved into a 3,500-square-foot apartment in the most grandiose of all the expat banker havens: Parkview. Parkview was an eighteen-tower residential complex set high atop a hill in the green and leafy Tai Tam district on the more verdant south side of Hong Kong Island. It didn't have the tallest towers in Hong Kong, nor did it boast the newest, but it sat in the middle of a 3,000-acre park in which no other construction had been or would be permitted.

"All things are possible here," promised Parkview's advertisements, and the claim seemed only slightly overstated. The complex, which had opened in 1989, contained more than a thousand apartments. Only a fifteen-minute drive from the skyscrapers of Central that housed the brain trusts of Hong Kong's multinational corporations--the Goldman Sachs offices were on the sixty-eighth floor of the Cheung Kong Center on Queens Road–Parkview offered unpolluted air above the toxic brown sheet that covered the island.

Parkview was not so much a luxury apartment complex as it was a self-contained world. Within its walls were a hotel, eight restaurants, four tennis courts, three squash courts, two swimming pools, two driving ranges, a three-story health club with personal trainers and nutritionists on hand, a preschool, a children's playground, and daily supervised activities for children, as well as a theater, an art gallery, a beauty salon, a supermarket, a formal garden, and a "Lifestyle Shop" that sold everything from paperweights to silk slippers branded with the Parkview logo. Its parking lot was so chock-full of Rolls-Royces, Bentleys, Mercedeses, and Porsches–with even the odd Lamborghini– that it at first appeared to be the world's most expensive used car lot. But what put Parkview furthest over the top were its Roman baths. These, said an illustrated brochure, "reflect the luxury and debauchery of the Roman Empire perfectly."

The towers themselves—as graceless from the outside as concrete fire hydrants—formed an oval that suggested a circling of the wagons. This backside-to-the-world arrangement sent an unmistakable message: at Parkview you could live as if the world outside did not exist.

One of Parkview's idiosyncrasies was that social status was determined by tower: the higher the number, the loftier the resident's standing inside the walled city. (Within a given tower, of course, the higher the floor, the higher the status.) If a man failed to deliver the results his company expected, his housing allowance was cut, necessitating an embarrassing move to a lower-numbered tower. This was known as "downtowering," and those who had to do it soon learned that their uptower friends no longer had much time for them.

Rob and Nancy started on the sixteenth floor of tower 14, which pleased Nancy immensely—until she learned that everybody who was anybody lived in tower 17.

She quickly hired the requisite live-in Filipina nanny, or *amah*, Conchita Pee Macaraeg (Connie) and live-in Filipina housekeeper, Connie's cousin, Maximina Macaraeg (Min). They lived in a converted pantry behind the kitchen and worked six days a week.

With Rob working sixteen hours a day, six and a half days a week, and traveling frequently to Taipei, Seoul, Bangkok, Singapore, Ho Chi Minh City, and mainland China, and with Connie taking care of the children and Min taking care of the apartment, Nancy found herself with nothing to do. Every expat wife in Hong Kong faced the same situation upon arrival. No matter how grand her lifestyle, she was suddenly both redundant and isolated. Her husband didn't need her except for sex, and he was usually either too tired or too busy for that, or possibly enjoying it in more exotic fashion with the bar girls who flocked to the investment banker hangouts in the section of Central called Lan Kwai Fong.

She had no friends or family within reach. The city at whose edge she found herself was home to a society that seemed not so much exotic as impenetrable. Not to mention suffocating, nerve-jangling, and entirely indifferent to her presence. For the adventurous woman, the resourceful and imaginative woman with a richly textured inner life, the woman who committed herself passionately to social or environmental causes, Hong Kong was a challenge to be met. These women could survive and even flourish. But for those who, like Nancy, had little within themselves to fall back on, Hong Kong often proved destructive. Consumed by his work, the man would thrive. Disabled by the difficulty of adjustment, the woman would founder. Not for nothing did expats call Hong Kong "the graveyard of marriages."

For Nancy, these stresses were compounded by knowing that she'd lost control of her life. Control—of both people and situations—had always been essential to her. No matter the proximate cause, the worst of her fights with Rob had been fundamentally about control: who set the agenda, who dictated the terms of the relationship. With the move to Hong Kong, Rob had trumped her. Suddenly she was a stranger in a strange land, controlling only two Filipina domestic helpers. She could no longer shape circumstance, she could only be shaped by it.

There was no way Nancy would adjust to that.

Rob and Nancy had arrived in Hong Kong only days before the most epochal moment in its history. At precisely midnight on June 30, 1997, upon expiration of the ninety-nine-year lease that had made the territory a British colony since the Opium Wars of the nineteenth century, England ceded control of Hong Kong to China. The event had been anticipated, debated, longed for, dreaded, and obsessed over since 1984, when the British and Chinese had agreed on the change in sovereignty. The handover was accompanied by an emotional elegy from Chris Patten, the last British governor of the colony, a few stilted words from Prince Charles, and the most spectacular fireworks display of the twentieth century.

At the stroke of midnight, the Scots Guards band played "God Save the Queen" for the last time on Hong Kong soil and the Union Jack was lowered to make way for the Chinese flag. For millions of Chinese and British citizens, not only in Hong Kong but around the world, the peaceful transition was a historic event of vast significance that they would remember for the rest of their lives.

But investment bankers view the world through a different lens, one shaped by the prism of profit. For Rob, the change in sovereignty was not the big news. The big news came two days later when the government of Thailand allowed the baht to float freely in currency markets. It sank like a stone, triggering one of the most sudden and dire economic collapses in the history of modern Asia. The Asian currency crisis of 1997–98 (also known as the Asian financial crisis of 1997–98, the East Asian financial crisis, the Asian economic crisis of 1997, the East Asian economic collapse, et cetera) had begun.

7. MOMMY DEAREST

BOOKS HAVE BEEN WRITTEN, CONFERENCES HAVE BEEN convened, and opposing analyses have clashed like swords as researchers and theorists have sought to explain the East Asian crisis: what caused it, what exacerbated it, what finally brought it under control. Rob spent scant time pondering the abstractions. What he wanted to know was which companies among the dozens suddenly going belly-up could be resuscitated (and later controlled) by Goldman Sachs.

The crisis started in Thailand in late June when the government announced it was removing the props from under one of the country's largest financial services companies, Finance One. This meant that creditors would face losses from which the government had previously protected them. Foreign money was sucked out of the country overnight. The government had no choice but to try to float the baht. Within days, a pandemic of what *New York Times* columnist and Princeton economist Paul Krugman called "bahtulism" swept across East Asia.

The Malaysian ringgit, the Indonesian rupiah, and the Philippine peso fell in tandem with the baht. Multinational banks yanked massive sums from the region as fast as their cursors could fly across their screens. There was no precedent for the crisis that ensued. Over the next twelve months the U.S. dollar value of most East Asian currencies fell by more than 50 percent and most regional stock market indices lost more than half their value.

Not in his wildest dreams could Rob Kissel have envisioned such a delightful scenario to greet him upon his arrival in Hong Kong. Cries of corporate anguish were music to his ears. The greater the pain, the greater his gain.

By the time of the '97 collapse Rob had been a distressed-debt specialist for almost ten years. He'd learned to consider the field's perverse mind-set not only rational but morally palatable, much as a military commander could speak of an "acceptable" number of casualties. Rob's Hong Kong was one very long branch on which hundreds of vultures perched. They pushed and pulled and elbowed one another as they jostled for the best position from which to view the fresh carcasses below. When one flapped its wings to begin a descent, dozens followed. And there was no shortage of carrion to pick over. For a distressed-debt specialist based in Hong Kong, the East Asian financial crisis was the opportunity of a lifetime. Suddenly, there were *trillions* of dollars worth of distressed assets scattered all over the continent. It was a bonanza beyond belief.

Rob was constantly in motion, taking close-up looks at the companies he'd flagged as possible targets for Goldman's ministrations. One week he'd be in Seoul, Taipei, and Singapore; the next in Jakarta, Bangkok, and Kuala Lumpur. On occasion, he'd take a meeting in Shanghai or Beijing. No one counted the hours they worked, nor the far fewer hours per week that they slept. It was a vultures' feeding frenzy. Rob had never experienced such exhilarating, exhausting times. He knew he was in the middle of something historic. He also knew that if he slowed down somebody else would beat him to the next pot of gold.

Rob and Nancy established a presence in the expat community. They joined the United Jewish Congregation, whose membership, a brochure said, consisted of "business and professional people who will be in Hong Kong for two to five years." It was, in other words, an investment banker's synagogue. They joined the Aberdeen Marina Club, which described itself as "a privileged haven" for expats. They sent Isabel to the Hong Kong International School—the most prestigious day school in Hong Kong—where she'd be surrounded by other wealthy expat children.

And still Nancy felt lost and isolated, reluctant to venture beyond the bars of her gilded cage. When she did, it was to shop at stores such as Gucci, Hermès, Dolce & Gabbana, Louis Vuitton, Versace: places that did not seem foreign, because she knew them well from New York.

One of her problems was transportation. Yes, Parkview was only fifteen minutes from Central, but how to get there? She had the Mercedes in the Parkview garage, but she was terrified of taking it on Hong Kong's narrow, twisting secondary roads or on the spanking new urban highways where she so easily could get lost. Public transportation was not an option. Hong Kong's public transportation system was considered among the world's best: swift, safe, reliable, and clean. But there was no way Nancy was going to crowd onto a bus or subway car with all those jabbering Chinese who would look at her and see not the gorgeous, wealthy young wife of a Goldman Sachs investment banker, but merely a *gweilo*. Eventually, she worked up the courage to grit her teeth and drive. Until then, she spent almost as much on taxi fares as she did in the shops that were her destination.

In the summer of 1998, at the start of Rob and Nancy's second year in Hong Kong, Nancy's mother, Jean, had cancer surgery. She lost half a lung but received a favorable prognosis. By fall, she was well enough to fly to Hong Kong with her new husband, a travel agent. Jean had two days to visit Nancy before boarding a cruise ship bound for Singapore. She was taken aback—very aback—by her first glimpse of Parkview. Nothing had prepared her for its scale, nor for its vulgar excesses, its ostentatious opulence.

The thought of her daughter living in such a place worried Jean. She feared that Nancy would lose herself amid the pretension, would vanish into Parkview's sumptuousness only to reappear as a stranger dripping baubles, unrecognizable even to herself.

But Jean knew better than to say this. She knew how Nancy reacted to anything she perceived as criticism even in the best of times, which Jean sensed these were not. Nancy spoke of Rob only to complain about him. He was almost never home. When he was, all he did was criticize. He was constantly scolding her for not paying enough attention to the children.

On the second and last day of Jean's visit, Nancy was in the middle of explaining how unreasonable and demanding Rob was when two-year-old Zoe, who had been playing on the floor nearby, began to scream. Zoe was more temperamental than Isabel. She would melt down at the slightest provocation, sometimes apparently for no reason at all.

Jean was full of grandmotherly love, but screaming children had always set her teeth on edge.

"Can't you make her be quiet?" Jean said.

"Connie will deal with it. If she ever gets out here. *Connie! I need you right now! Hurry up!*"

Still screaming, Zoe started to punch and kick at her mother.

"Can't you control her?"

"Stay out of this, Mom."

Zoe was now writhing on the living room floor. Connie raced in from another part of the apartment. She carried Zoe to her room and closed the door. Slowly, the screaming subsided.

"Nancy," Jean said, "I think it's time that you learned to take care of your children yourself."

Nancy gasped.

Then—and even years later Jean didn't know another way to say it—Nancy went berserk. She charged at Jean and grabbed her and yanked her off the couch. Never robust, Jean had been especially frail since her surgery. Screaming even louder than Zoe had—and using language that Zoe wouldn't learn for years—Nancy propelled her mother down the hallway.

"Don't-you-ever-tell-me-how-to-handle-my-own-children!"

She squeezed Jean's shoulders and pushed her up against the door.

"Get out! Get out! Get out of my house! I never want to see your fucking face again!"

Nancy opened the door and gave Jean a shove hard enough to make her stumble into the hallway and slammed the door in her face.

Jean pounded on the door, begging Nancy to let her back in. There was no response. She pounded and begged until she was too exhausted to continue. She took a taxi to the cruise ship in tears.

She let an hour pass, then phoned the apartment. Nancy picked up. The instant she heard Jean's voice she was possessed by another fit. She yelled things into the phone that Jean could not imagine a daughter ever saying to a mother. Jean hung up but called again an hour later. This time, Connie answered. She said Nancy was lying down and did not want to be disturbed.

Jean was still crying when the cruise ship left the harbor in late afternoon.

8. THE PERFECT COUPLE

THE MORE MONEY ROB MADE, THE MORE NANCY SPENT. SHE bought clothes, jewelry, and perfume. Then more clothes, jewelry, and perfume. Then scarves and shoes and cosmetics. It was so easy to spend vast sums of money in Hong Kong, where shopping was the national pastime. In fact, if it weren't for the 6.5 million Chinese who lived there, Hong Kong could have become Nancy's kind of town.

She shopped out of boredom. She shopped out of anger at Rob. She shopped so she could talk about her shopping. She shopped because the stores were open. She shopped because she never felt she had enough.

While she shopped, Connie took care of the children. That's what Connie was for. Connie had turned out to be smart, conscientious, and caring—the perfect *amah*. But even with Connie, Nancy felt oppressed by motherhood. It never stopped. There were no fixed hours, there were no days off. Children needed to be clothed and fed and cleaned and cleaned up after; they needed to be entertained and educated and disciplined. Nancy was perfectly happy to get down on the floor and play with them when in the mood—she delighted in her children then—but not even Connie's round-the-clock service spared her the burden of responsibility. She loved to be a third child with her children; it was parenting she found so hard to cope with.

Nancy brooded about her body. She'd always known her looks

were something special, but she would turn thirty-five in the spring of 1999, and it alarmed her to think—and of this she was convinced—that in terms of physical attractiveness she would soon enter an irreversible period of decline. She'd look so much better, she thought, if only she hadn't had children. Her two pregnancies had taken a toll. It galled her to see her breasts begin to sag, to see the slight padding on her hips, to spot incipient cellulite on her thighs. That was the main reason she didn't want to have the third child that Rob had begun to insist on. He wanted a son. Easy for him to say, she told her friend in San Francisco, Bryna O'Shea, it wouldn't cost him the last of his looks.

She learned she was pregnant in February 1999. The baby was due in October. Ultrasound showed it was a boy. Rob was delighted. Nancy was not.

———————

By the spring of 1999, the East Asian financial crisis was starting to wane. There were signs of stabilization, if not recovery. For Rob, it had been a hell of a ride. He had established himself as one of the distressed-debt stars of Hong Kong. Because he was at Goldman, he couldn't say "I," but everyone who counted knew he'd become a powerful force.

He was a natural. He had a nose for big game and the ruthlessness to chase it until it dropped. He could spot a company in dire straits in the Philippines from as far away as the Strait of Malacca. And he had a jeweler's eye for discerning the hidden strengths and weaknesses in a bankruptcy filing or annual report.

He and Nancy celebrated his success like true children of Parkview: they uptowered. They went, in fact, all the way up to tower 17, the most coveted and expensive of Parkview's residential buildings.

Tower 17! For two years, Nancy had dreamed of tower 17. She'd seen the wives who lived there flaunting their self-importance—as if they had gotten there on their own. She'd marveled at their ability to patronize and condescend. She'd observed the cars they drove and the clothes and jewelry they wore. She'd envied them. Every woman in Parkview envied the wives of tower 17. Now she would be one of them, pregnant or not.

Nearly a year had passed since Nancy had thrown her mother out of the apartment. Jean and her husband lived in Sebastopol, California, an hour and a half north of San Francisco. One day in late spring of 1999, Bryna O'Shea called her from San Francisco to say she was about to fly to Hong Kong to visit Nancy. Jean asked her to deliver an heirloom necklace that she knew Nancy coveted almost as much as she did the lead statuette she had gotten from Ira's mother.

"Frankly, Bryna, it's a peace offering. Maybe you could let her know how hurt I am that she still refuses to have anything to do with me."

"I'll do what I can," Bryna said.

When she got back from Hong Kong a week later, Bryna called to say that Nancy and the children were fine and that Nancy was delighted to have the necklace.

"Did she say anything about me?" Jean asked.

Bryna hesitated. "She did give me a message to pass on, but I don't think I should."

"Why not?"

"I don't want to tell you, Jean. It's only going to hurt."

"Never mind that. What did she say?"

Bryna took a deep breath. "She said it's a shame you'll never get to see your grandchildren again."

In October 1999, Nancy gave birth to a son. He was named Ethan. Rob was thrilled. Nancy went into what her tower 17 friends said was postpartum depression. Rob had his doubts. To him it looked suspiciously like an excuse to be lazier than ever and to neglect her duties to their growing family. No matter how hard he worked, no matter how much he traveled, Rob remained concerned about his children. He had great respect and admiration for Connie, but he wanted the children raised by their mother.

He told Nancy to start preparing nutritious food instead of letting Isabel and Zoe stuff themselves with fast food day and night. She could also teach them some table manners. And some manners in general. And she could teach them to clean up after themselves instead of hollering for Min to come do it.

At an even more basic level, she could start to take an interest in her children. She could give them their baths once in a while instead of letting Connie do it. She could put them to bed at night instead of letting Connie do it. She could read to them and encourage Isabel to read on her own and get Zoe started. She could make sure Isabel did extra arithmetic, instead of assuming that the Hong Kong International School was doing enough. She could get Zoe away from the television set and start teaching her about numbers, instead of assuming *Sesame Street* would suffice. Rob had high expectations for his children and he didn't want them undermined by his wife. And it wouldn't hurt if she took a bit more of an interest in him.

He didn't like arriving home from Taiwan late on a Friday night, knowing he'd have to fly out again on Sunday night or Monday morning, and being treated as if he were an uninvited guest. But when he tried to talk to her about performing the duties of a wife and mother—and, yes, on occasion he might seem impatient, or even annoyed—she would erupt. Connie and Min could hear her from the other end of the apartment.

"Don't you *dare* talk to me like that, you fucking five-minute father. You're the one who turns this household into chaos. You come in late, the girls are asleep, you wake them up and get them all excited and then you lose interest and sit in your armchair and drink your fucking single-malt scotch and leave me to pick up the pieces. Don't you *dare* tell me how to raise my children. Don't you *dare* tell me how I should be spending my days."

Rob couldn't understand it. The more money he made, the less happy she was. That seemed illogical, and Rob was a logical man.

But they made it a point to show no trace of discord in public. Expat life was all about façade. At the United Jewish Congregation, at the Aberdeen Marina Club, at Goldman Sachs functions, and at Parkview, Rob and Nancy had appearances to maintain. He was the brilliant banker, devoted husband and father. She was the loyal wife and energetic mother with the sparkling smile and the look of mischief in her eye. To others, they seemed the perfect couple. "We all envy you," a Parkview neighbor told them one day. "You two have the best marriage in Hong Kong."

9. THERE'S NO SUCH THING AS ENOUGH

FROM THE MOMENT ROB WENT TO WORK FOR GOLDMAN Sachs in 1996, his eyes were on a single prize: making partner. No other position on Wall Street offered anything approaching either the cash or cachet of a Goldman Sachs partnership. A PMD (partner managing director) could count on an annual bonus of $10 million or more, adjusted for inflation, until retirement. He (or she, although almost 90 percent of Goldman partners were male) was also eligible to invest in Goldman ventures that were closed not only to the public, but to the firm's non-PMD executives. In addition, a PMD could buy Goldman stock at a 25 percent discount.

That was the cash part. As for cachet, becoming a Goldman Sachs partner was the equivalent—in the closed-end world of investment banking—of becoming a made man in the Mafia. Suddenly, you could get whatever table you wanted at the New York restaurant of your choice—the firm would handle your reservation. And to assure that you got to keep as many of your millions as the tax code allowed—and to save you time that could be better spent working on a new deal for Goldman—the firm took care of your tax returns. Plus, you were guaranteed the envy, if not necessarily the admiration, of your erstwhile peers.

Goldman, which employed more than twenty thousand people worldwide, named new partners—about a hundred of them—once every two years. Rob had been too new to the firm to be considered in 1998, but after kicking sand in the faces of the boys from Morgan Stanley, Deutsche Bank, Credit Suisse, UBS, JP Morgan, and others for the two years that followed, he fancied his chances for 2000.

Unfortunately, some of the silky-smooth senior managers in the Hong Kong office perceived his aggressiveness as abrasiveness. Yes, one had to be greedy, that was a given. But one should not appear to be. Whereas at most investment banks the bottom line was all that counted, at Goldman attention was still paid to appearances. One was expected to keep one's naked avarice cloaked, or at least coated with a genteel veneer.

Also, one was expected not to cut into line. Hierarchy was to be respected. It was fine to let the competitive juices flow when one was trying to beat the competition, but open combativeness was to be checked at the office door. Rob paid less attention than he should have to the maxim "At Goldman we never say 'I.'"

He also—unwisely—tried to elbow his way past a PMD who had been instrumental in bringing him to Hong Kong. Without the PMD's support, Rob had no chance of making partner. It became clear to him—and to Goldman—that his future lay elsewhere. Once again, his head was available to be hunted. In short order it was: this time on behalf of Merrill Lynch.

Merrill had been slow to make an Asian footprint and was in a hurry to catch up. His new firm didn't have the Goldman Sachs aura, but it offered what Rob coveted most: limitless opportunity. Between Mumbai and Manila there remained many blank spaces on Merrill's map of distressed-debt opportunity. Rob would be given the mandate of filling them in. Taking his top assistant, David Noh, with him, he jumped ship virtually overnight. The new century would bring with it new horizons. And at Merrill Lynch, Rob would be able to say "I."

Nancy was the only possible downside. She'd had her fill of Hong Kong. Rob had told her it would be for three years and the three years were almost up. "I've been looking online at houses in Westport," she told him in the early spring of 2000. "There's not much for five million, but there are a couple in the seven to eight range that might be worth checking out."

"I don't think so," Rob said.

"Why not? Don't you want to live in Connecticut?"

"Plans have changed."

"What are you talking about?"

"I'm leaving Goldman. I've received a terrific offer from Merrill Lynch. They're going to make me Asia-Pacific managing director of Global Principal Investments. I'll be in charge of everything except Japan. The money is going to be unbelievable."

"Are you telling me you're staying in Hong Kong?"

"*We* are. Probably for another three years."

"No, Rob. *You* are. I can't take any more of Hong Kong. I'll take the children and leave."

"I won't let you do that. You have to stay here."

The fiercest battle for control they'd ever had ensued. It involved many ugly scenes and threats of divorce. In the end, Rob won, but at a cost. Andrew and Hayley had bought a multimillion-dollar house high up on Stratton Mountain, while Rob and Nancy remained stuck in a condo in the village at the base of the ski lift. Nancy said she'd stay in Hong Kong, but in return Rob would buy a $2-million Stratton home and give Nancy a million dollars for renovation. She got the project started during a long summer vacation in Vermont. She told friends she'd never forgive Rob for keeping her in Hong Kong against her will, but she gloated that she'd made him pay $3 million for her acquiescence. And she proudly said she'd make the home a work of art: something that Andrew and Hayley would have to envy.

They went to Phuket for a week's vacation at Christmastime. Ira and his wife flew out to join them. All of them had been there before. The beaches were fabulous. But Phuket was not the place to go if you were trying to kid yourself about your body.

Fully clothed—and considering the clothes she bought, not surprisingly—Nancy still made heads swivel. But she had not gotten her body back in the shape she wanted, although it had been more than a year since she'd given birth to Ethan. She blamed this on her self-diagnosed postpartum depression.

Ira could see she wasn't happy. She complained incessantly about Hong Kong. She exchanged sharp words with Rob as never before. When she fell silent, she seemed morose. As a veteran of two divorces, Ira was quick to pick up bad marital vibes. He couldn't ask Nancy directly how she was feeling. That would have crossed her line in the sand. Instead, "as one ex-restaurateur to another," he reminded her there was no such thing as a free lunch.

"What's that supposed to mean?"

"It means that if you care so much about the lifestyle Rob's money buys you, you should suck it up and stick it out for the next three years." These were bold words to speak to Nancy. Ira quickly sought to soften them. "But maybe it's not worth it. Maybe it's too much to handle. You always have the option of getting out." Instead of jumping down his throat and telling him to mind his own business, as Ira had expected she would do, Nancy simply lapsed into silence.

Ira found Rob much more voluble and, except when he was carping at Nancy, more congenial than ever before. Rob told Ira he'd named him—not his own father or brother—as executor of his will. "It only seems logical," he said, "since everything I have would go to Nancy." Ira was grateful for Rob's trust.

Otherwise, the talk focused on business, in particular about how well Rob was doing at Merrill Lynch. Smoking a Cuban cigar at poolside, Rob told Ira that his income was growing exponentially. He was doing more deals and bigger deals than he'd ever done at Goldman Sachs, even at the height of the crisis.

But he was dissatisfied. No matter how much money an investment banker made—and bonuses of $25 million a year were not unheard of—there would always be an upper limit. And there would always be someone, somewhere, making more. But not if you ran your own hedge fund, Rob said. He was fascinated by the "two and twenty" approach to compensation, whereby the fund manager received, as a management fee, 2 percent of all money invested and 20 percent of the annual profit.

As his cigar smoke spiraled toward the clear blue sky, Rob tossed out examples. If he started with $100 million from investors—and he knew he could start with more than that—he'd receive only $2 million in management fees (plus expenses, of course, and his expenses would be strictly five-star), but there was no limit to what 20 percent of the profits could be. Given his expertise and his energy, Rob could foresee returns of at least 50 percent per year. Say he had $500 million in the fund; his management fee would be $10 million and at 50 percent profit for a year, he'd earn $50 million. That would be $60 million per year, which was approaching the level of real money. And he knew he could do even better than that.

"But when does it stop, Rob?" Ira asked. "When do you realize you've got enough?"

Rob laughed.

"You are kidding, aren't you? There's no such thing as enough."

10. COMING UNDONE

IN HIS BOOK *HONG KONG WATCHING,* LONGTIME RESIDENT George Adams notes that the surest sign an expat wife is not adapting is if she finds herself "teaching part-time at an international school . . . for the purpose of having something to do."

Nancy began to fill her days by volunteering at the Hong Kong International School. She didn't teach, but—feeling a surge of energy by the spring of 2002—she became active, almost hyperactive, in school affairs. She more or less appointed herself school photographer and, despite trampling a few toes in the process, she became director of fund-raising for school events.

Nancy didn't serve on committees, she formed them. She didn't work on a project, she directed the work. "Once she got rolling, she was unstoppable," a friend said. "Sometimes it got a little scary." She told school officials that the work she was doing entitled her to her own parking space. She got it. It made her feel appreciated.

Even from Hong Kong, Nancy directed the early phase of the Stratton renovation. She told Bryna O'Shea that she was going to make the house *her* house. Rob's name would remain on the title, of course—it was the money he'd earned that paid for the house—but in every other way he'd never be more than a visitor. "It's going to be all me," she told Bryna. The house would be her revenge against Rob for having made her stay in Hong Kong. It would reflect *her* taste, *her* judgment, *her* personality. She told Bryna that whenever she was there and Rob was not she wouldn't even hang his picture on the wall. He might control their relationship in Hong Kong, but Vermont would be another story.

Then the bills from Stratton subcontractors started to arrive at Parkview. Rob was shocked. To end an argument he might have said she could spend a million dollars on the renovation, but he had second thoughts once he began to see the actual costs. He told Nancy all estimates would have to be submitted to him for advance approval henceforth. Her response left him in no doubt about what "ballistic" meant.

Their fights about the cost of the renovation became the most furious they'd ever had. They soon went past the point of reasonable discussion. No decision was made without lengthy argument conducted with voices raised. Nancy was in a constant rage, sometimes suppressed, sometimes not. She felt Rob wanted only to thwart her. They had enough money to spend twice what she proposed. For a million dollars—or not much more—she could turn their home into a showplace that would make not only Andrew and Hayley, but also Bill sick with envy. So what was the problem? As always, it came down to control. She fought for it, but she was learning the hard way that the source of the money would always have ultimate control.

She started to smoke. It calmed her; it gave her a chance to be alone for a few minutes; it reminded her of her days of youth and freedom in New York. She knew how much Rob hated smoking, except when he had one of his big fat cigars in his mouth. He asked her to stop; she defied him. He told her that smoking made her smell so awful that he didn't want to be near her, not even in bed. Nancy considered that a plus. Ever since Ethan had been born, she'd been recoiling from his touch.

As the time for their 2002 summer vacation approached, she told Rob she wanted to return to the United States a few weeks ahead of time. She said she wanted to supervise the renovation personally, but really, she needed to get away from him. Even though his travels reduced their time together to a minimum, it seemed too much. She felt she was suffocating, and not only from Hong Kong's air pollution.

She flew to New York in early June with Connie and the children, but instead of going directly to Vermont, she installed them all at the Surrey, an elegant residential hotel on East Seventy-sixth Street between Central Park and Madison Avenue. Rob's draconian attitude toward the renovation budget had left her seething. The surest way to get back at him was by spending. She was going to pillage the boutiques of upper Madison Avenue. By the time the credit card bills arrived in Hong Kong she'd be laughing up her designer sleeve in Vermont.

Her routine was simple. Connie would take care of the children all day while she shopped. Then Connie would put the children to bed while Nancy rested up for the next day's spree. At first, she shopped by category. She might decide it was a perfume day. She could start at Bond No. 9, then go to L'Occitane and maybe, just for fun, Penhaligon's, where besides the perfume she could pick up a sterling silver compact mirror. She'd always had a thing for eyeglass frames. She'd bought dozens over the years, but there was no harm in adding to her collection. That meant Alain Mikli, Oliver Peoples, Morgenthal Frederics, and Robert Marc. She could buy a few at each store and then see which ones Bryna liked best when she flew in from San Francisco for a visit. Getting more expensive, she could pick up a Rikiki shirt and a snap cardigan or two from agnès b. Then head for BCBG Max Azria—what fun that was!—

then Davide Cenci, which had that marvelous lambs' wool suit with the fur collar. Which was not to denigrate Gianfranco Ferré. She could devote loads of time—and money—to all the new shoe collections. Sonia Rykiel always had something outrageous. To go with a new pair, that embroidered tulle and cotton eyelet dress from Luca Luca would be perfect. For pure whimsy, what could beat a quilted leather cell phone case from Juicy Couture?

After a few days, she'd get bored with shopping by category and switch to shopping by location. She would choose one block per day, say the block between Seventy-second and Seventy-third streets, and buy something in every store on the block. That was the kind of challenge she enjoyed, plus it gave some structure to her days.

The intensity of the shopping experience would exhaust her. She would return to the Surrey at midday to nap, usually for two hours or more. She had an increasing need for time alone, periods of the day when she had no responsibilities. Sometimes she wanted to climb into bed and never come out. Even though Connie—dear, tireless Connie—mothered the children day and night, taking care of their every need and want, Nancy found their presence stressful.

For one thing, they had to be fed. Connie could shop for the basics—corn dogs, Pop-Tarts, frozen waffles, potato chips, ice cream, M&M's—but she had never learned how to cook. The Surrey was a residential hotel and did not offer room service, but luckily the deli downstairs delivered. In the morning, Nancy would call down for breakfast and within fifteen minutes a boy would bring bacon and eggs, toast, apple juice, coffee, and pastries to the door. At lunchtime Connie could hail a taxi and take the kids to the nearest McDonald's. And Nancy could order dinner—hot dogs and French fries—from the deli.

The children ate their meals in front of the TV set. Watching television was their major activity, to the point where the first word Ethan ever spoke was "remote." Television kept them quiet, and it was important to keep them quiet, because if one of them blew, that might be it for the next few hours. Their tantrums didn't wind down. When they got hysterical, they stayed that way. And anything could set them off. The potatoes were touching the meat. There wasn't enough chocolate in the chocolate milk. The ice cream was too hard or too melty. The Coca-Cola didn't fizz enough. Each of them had a personal flashpoint when it came to food hysteria.

Those were the mealtime hazards. There were others. Telling them to put on shoes and socks could trigger a bout. Running the bathwater could mean they wouldn't stop screaming until midnight. And no one—not even Connie—ever tried to persuade them to brush their teeth. As for picking up their clothes or toys or their dirty dishes from in front of the TV set, it didn't occur to Nancy to ask them or to model such behavior. She herself never picked up, and Min, the housekeeper, had not made the trip. Soon unspeakable messes clogged every room. Old friends from New York were appalled when they visited, but Nancy didn't seem to notice, and she certainly didn't seem to care.

Bryna O'Shea arrived from San Francisco to help with the shopping and to laugh about old times. Bryna had remained Nancy's best friend by never opening the door that led to feelings. The friendship was warm but superficial. But Bryna was an astute woman of keen insight. She took in a lot more than she let on. The change in Nancy's personality since Ethan's birth worried her, even if she couldn't mention it. She was also concerned about the change in Nancy's attitude toward Rob. Nancy had gloried in talking about their physical passion for each other. She'd always spoken about Rob with affection. No longer. She now portrayed him as a coldhearted martinet. Bryna knew him at least as well as she knew Nancy, and the Rob Nancy described was not the Rob Bryna knew.

One evening she and Nancy went to the movies. They saw *Unfaithful*, featuring Diane Lane, Richard Gere, and Dominic Chianese. In *The New York Times*, Richard Holden wrote that the film was a graphic demonstration of how "sex, especially reckless adulterous sex, can rock people's lives and have catastrophic consequences."

Nancy identified with the Diane Lane character, a beautiful, affluent, and seemingly content suburban housewife who felt a void where passion should have been. Another man, whom she met by chance in New York City, filled the void to overflowing.

"*That's* why people have affairs," Nancy said.

The movie plays out with the husband learning of the affair and killing the lover. Then he must dispose of the body. First, he must carry it out of the apartment undetected. He rolls it up inside a carpet and carries the carpet away. He doesn't get caught.

That summer at Stratton was even more contentious than usual. Bill had sold the original family house, so he and his lady friend had to stay either with Andrew and Hayley, which tended to be explosive, or in the condo that Rob and Nancy and the three children and Connie were living in as renovations continued on their house.

Andrew's behavior was more erratic than ever. The others were convinced that cocaine and alcohol abuse were the causes. Hayley advanced the theory that Andrew suffered from bipolar disease and needed therapy and medication. Bill scoffed at this. He told Andrew to his face that he'd always been a worthless embarrassment to the family and told

Hayley she'd made a mistake in marrying him, besides which she'd made a fool out of herself on MSNBC the previous week by recommending Bally's and Six Flags, and that she should have worn more makeup. He also said she should have married Rob, so Rob wouldn't have been stuck with a waitress for a wife. Rob defended Andrew and Nancy, causing Bill to turn on him. Nancy told Bill that no matter how many bedrooms they'd have in the new house there would never be one for him. Andrew told Rob he didn't need his little brother sticking up for him, and he told Bill to go fuck himself because he'd already made $20 million from dealing in New Jersey real estate and now Hanrock—in which Bill had no part—was expanding into New York and Connecticut. Hayley blamed Bill for Andrew's problems. Nancy told Hayley she'd overpaid for the new sofa, besides which the color clashed with the wallpaper. Andrew poured himself another drink and told them they were all pathetic and stormed upstairs. Bill poured himself another drink and took the family dog into the study and slammed the door shut. Bill's lady friend told the others they should try harder to get along. Hayley told Nancy it was a shame her new diet wasn't working. Rob slammed his fist on the table, then stood and stalked out to the porch. And that was only one dinner.

The Kissels—except for Jane and her husband, Richard, who was a prince of a fellow—seemed prisoners of their own masochistic dysfunction. Even living in Hong Kong, Rob and Nancy got swallowed up by it every summer and every Christmas vacation. For Christmas of 2002 they descended on the British Columbia ski resort at Whistler Mountain. It offered the highest lift-serviced vertical slopes in North America, and the two-bedroom deluxe suite at the Four Seasons was only

$2,950 per night. Rob and Nancy brought the kids, but not Connie. When they arrived, Ethan was sick with aches, chills, and a fever.

Nancy said she'd stay with Ethan while the others skied. This annoyed Rob. He accused her of snubbing the rest of the family. The hotel could arrange for someone to stay with Ethan, he pointed out. Nancy said no. At least during the day, she was going to stay in the room with Ethan. Assuming the hotel could send someone up for a couple of hours in the evening, she'd join them for dinner.

For the next two nights, Nancy sat at the large dinner table and listened to the others bicker. She didn't feel like talking to any of them. In particular, she didn't feel like talking to Rob. Their mutual hostility was a new addition to the group vitriol. Since returning to Hong Kong from Vermont, they'd waged a pitched battle for control. Each felt there could be only one person directing the relationship and heading the family. Rob's criticisms of Nancy's reckless spending and increasing irresponsibility in regard to the children were matched by her attacks on him for being both physically and emotionally absent from her life and for ordering her around like a servant whenever she was in his presence.

On their third night at Whistler, Nancy left the table in the middle of dinner, saying she could not take any more acrimony. Rob went after her to tell her to come back. No one in the family knew what happened next between the two of them. Much later, Nancy would claim that Rob had hit her and had pushed her down a flight of stairs. But Nancy said a lot of things. At the time, she didn't look like she'd been hit and pushed down a flight of stairs.

In any event, on that third night she went to the room and got Ethan and had a Four Seasons limousine take her to the Vancouver airport, and she flew back to Hong Kong with her son. That was a serious breach of Kissel protocol: you weren't supposed to run away from a fight.

11. SARS

THE EASIEST WAY TO GET TO MAINLAND CHINA FROM HONG Kong is to take a KCR East Rail train from Kowloon to Shenzhen. The trains run from 6:00 a.m. to midnight. It's a forty-minute trip. KCR stands for Kowloon-Canton Railway. Canton was the name of the capital of Guangdong province before the Chinese made everything harder to spell.

Today, Canton is called Guangzhou. It's still the province capital, but Shenzhen, a hundred miles closer to Hong Kong, has become Guangdong's biggest city. In 1979, Deng Xiaoping turned Shenzhen from a fishing village into the fastest-growing city in the world by designating it as the country's first special economic zone.

Special economic zones are places within China where everybody is allowed to make as much money as they want. The population of Shenzhen went from about eleven in 1980 to almost ten million by the turn of the century. Its motto was "A new high-rise every day and a new boulevard every three." It had its own stock exchange and its own skyline and it was the busiest port in China. Shenzhen was where iPods were made. In Shenzhen, people called Hong Kong a suburb.

But there was more to Shenzhen than met the iPod.

There was, for example, the Dongmenwai wet market, where local chefs browsed daily among the thousands of cages and crates containing the raw materials, so to speak, that gave Cantonese cuisine its special flair.

At Dongmenwai it was possible to buy almost anything that could be cooked and eaten, from basics like dogs and cats and fresh fish intestine to monkeys, scaly anteaters, bamboo rats, and even—on certain days—rare delicacies such as the *Deinagkistrodon acutus*, the snake that was the main ingredient in Hundred-Pace Viper Soup.

Year in and year out, however, Dongmenwai's most popular item was the masked palm civet. This was a harmless and unprepossessing animal about the size of a weasel. Tens of thousands of them roamed the forests and brushlands of Guangdong province. In appearance they closely resembled the Chinese ferret badger, but as anyone who had eaten both would testify, the similarity ended there.

In Shenzhen and Guangzhou and throughout Guangdong province, masked palm civet was a delicacy nearly as coveted as shark fin. The fresher the better, of course, which meant the chef would either have his civets killed in the market while he watched, or bring a few live ones back to the restaurant to kill in the kitchen himself as customers placed orders. Not infrequently, a group preparing to feast on civet would require the chef to bring to their table the live civets he'd be cooking for them.

There was only one problem with the masked palm civet. As health officials determined only after the worldwide epidemic had run its course, the cute and tasty civet harbored in its saliva and feces a virus that, when transmitted to humans, caused the previously unknown and potentially fatal disease that came to be called severe acute respiratory syndrome, or SARS.

No one knows why the virus suddenly jumped across the species barrier in 2002 and began to infect humans in Guangdong province—at first, mostly chefs and workers in the wet markets—but by February 2003 doctors in Guangzhou found themselves trying to treat a disease they'd never before encountered.

Early symptoms—fever, chills, aches, cough, headache—mimicked those of influenza, but instead of easing after a week to ten days they grew suddenly more severe and were accompanied by difficulty breathing. At that point, pneumonia developed, proving fatal in about 10 percent of cases.

At Zhongshan Hospital, a teaching hospital recognized as one of the best in Guangzhou, perplexed doctors called in Dr. Liu Jianlun for consultation. At sixty-four, Dr. Liu, a pulmonary specialist, had essentially retired from both his teaching and clinical positions, but he quickly answered the call. Ten days after he'd started seeing patients with the disease, he started to experience symptoms of it himself. Dr. Liu would have strongly recommended complete bed rest for a patient feeling as sick as he was, but he had made a commitment to attend a nephew's wedding in Hong Kong on February 22.

Liu and his wife traveled to Hong Kong on February 21 and checked into room 911 at the three-star Metropole Hotel in Kowloon. They set out on a sightseeing trip with his brother-in-law, but by then he was so ill that he had to turn back. At the Metropole, Liu took to his bed. Overnight his symptoms worsened dramatically. As his breathing became more labored, his wife called the nearest hospital, the Kwong Wah Hospital, to say he would be coming in, but that he was suffering from a highly contagious and potentially deadly disease that had not yet been identified. Liu himself got on the phone to say he should be placed in an isolation ward and that no one should examine or treat him without wearing full protective clothing.

Liu never left Kwong Wah Hospital. He died on March 4. His wife escaped infection, but his brother-in-law died a week later. Because of Liu's insistence on being treated as dangerously contagious, none of the medical personnel who had contact with him were infected.

At the Metropole, however, Liu had neither taken nor urged such precautions. As a result, seven other guests, all with rooms on the ninth floor, contracted the virus. The method of contagion was never determined, but it could have been something as innocuous as Liu sneezing in the elevator or even simply pressing the ninth-floor elevator button after coughing into his hand.

The symptoms of SARS did not manifest themselves for three to seven days after the onset of the infection. Thus, feeling fine, the seven virus-bearers from the ninth floor of the Metropole continued on their ways. Three flew to Singapore, two to Toronto, and one to Hanoi. The seventh, a twenty-six-year-old airplane mechanic who lived in Hong Kong and had gone to the hotel only to visit a friend, went back to work.

By March 5, however, the day after Liu died at Kwong Wah Hospital, the mechanic was sick enough to be admitted to Prince of Wales Hospital. Unlike the doctors at Kwong Wah, no one at Prince of Wales had been forewarned of the special danger their new patient represented. He was placed not in isolation, but in a ward. When his breathing difficulties grew worse, he was treated with a nebulizer, thereby dispersing contagious droplets from his lungs throughout the ward.

The first sign of anything out of the ordinary came on the morning of March 10, when a dozen nurses and orderlies called in sick. By the end of the day another fifty members of the Prince of Wales medical staff—all displaying the same symptoms—had reported that they were ill. The next morning, March 11, Prince of Wales officials notified the Hong Kong Department of Health, which immediately contacted the

World Health Organization representative in Beijing to report the onset of a possible epidemic.

Within twenty-four hours of receiving the information from Hong Kong, WHO issued a global alert about this unfamiliar and potentially fatal disease of unknown origin. On March 15, WHO put a name to it: severe acute respiratory syndrome. By then, the virus had been carried to Singapore, Canada, and Vietnam. One hundred forty-three patients and employees of Prince of Wales Hospital had been infected. And the virus had made its capricious way to block E of the Amoy Gardens housing estate, where it would trigger the largest SARS outbreak in the world.

One of those infected at Prince of Wales was a thirty-three-year-old Shenzhen man who came to the hospital regularly for kidney dialysis. He began to display symptoms on March 14, during an overnight visit to his brother, who lived in block E. His was one of the 20 percent of SARS cases in which the symptoms included diarrhea.

Amoy Gardens was a typical Hong Kong housing estate. It had been built more than twenty years earlier, and its twenty thousand residents were crammed into eight-to-a-floor, five-hundred-square-foot apartment units in a cluster of towers each thirty stories high. From a public health standpoint, it was not an ideal place for someone infected with the SARS virus to have diarrhea.

Later investigation showed that a design defect in the U-shaped water traps connected to the bathroom floor drains permitted sewage droplets contaminated with the virus to be sucked into the bathroom when the exhaust fan was used. The fan then blew the droplets into a narrow air well between buildings, from which they entered neighboring apartments through open windows. Within ten days of the infected man's overnight stay, more than three hundred Amoy Gardens residents—most from block E and the neighboring block D—grew ill with SARS. At that point, the government of Hong Kong abandoned its attempts to downplay the seriousness of the outbreak and ordered the shutdown of all schools and day care centers within the territory.

That was enough for Rob Kissel. During the last week of March, he put Nancy and the children and Connie on a plane to New York.

12. HOMES SWEET HOMES

THEY HAD ONLY BEEN GONE A FEW DAYS WHEN ROB CALLED Bryna O'Shea in San Francisco.

"Bryna, I've got a problem."

"Yes?"

"It's my marriage. I'm afraid it's falling apart. I need someone to talk to about it. I figured someone who knows Nancy would be best. That is, as long as I can talk to you in confidence. As long as you won't tell Nancy what I say."

"I don't know, Rob. I'd be in a tough position. I'd feel weird keeping secrets from Nancy, especially about her own marriage. And suppose Nancy tells me something about you? I wouldn't be able to share it."

"I understand. Please, Bryna. I'm afraid I'm losing her and I don't know what to do about it."

"Rob, I don't think I'd be comfortable—"

"Bryna, *please.*"

Bryna worked in public relations in San Francisco. She was good at her work. But private relations were a different matter, especially relations between two people she knew as well as Rob and Nancy. On the other hand, over the years she had known him, she'd come to appreciate Rob more and more—his earnestness, decency, and genuine love for Nancy and his children.

"Please, just let me cry on your shoulder once in a while? I don't think anybody else could understand."

"Okay," Bryna said. "But I'm not ever going to become a messenger between you two."

Rob told her he was watching the marriage crumble before his eyes and he didn't know what to do. He said Nancy was changing in ways he didn't understand. Her words and actions were making it clear that not only didn't she love him, she didn't even like him anymore. He said this was breaking his heart.

Then he started on his list of complaints. Nancy had no interest in raising the children. He loved them and hated to see them being both neglected and spoiled when he wasn't around. Then there was the matter of money. "Her spending is out of control," he said. "But there's more to it than that. It seems like an act of aggression, as if she's spending primarily because she wants to piss me off. I bitch at her about it and she gets huffy and defensive. Then she accuses me of trying to control her, to show her who's boss. I feel like she's trying to manufacture reasons to despise me. Bryna, I don't know how to reach her anymore. I don't know how to bring her back."

Bryna couldn't give him any answers. She'd already heard about the child-rearing and money problems from Nancy, who had rather a different point of view. According to her, Rob was a tight-fisted bastard who was humiliating her by treating her as less than an adult in money matters, an absentee father who burst onto the scene intermittently, whining that nothing was being done properly and throwing a fit for two or three days before rushing off again to the world he really cared about.

"I have no advice to give you, Rob, but I'll be here if you really need to talk."

He began to call her three or four times a week. For the first time in his life, he was facing a problem that money couldn't fix.

The first thing Nancy did when she arrived in New York was to call her former pediatrician. He refused to examine the children, saying he could not risk having the SARS virus infect his office.

Nancy's intention had been to put Isabel and Zoe in a private school in New York City for the rest of the term, while Connie took care of Ethan. But no private school would enroll them after hearing they'd just arrived from Hong Kong. She could see no alternative but to head for Vermont, where the schools were not so persnickety. She rented a Ford Explorer SUV–not at all pleased that she couldn't rent a Range Rover on short notice–and drove to Stratton amid light snow on April 3. It snowed five more inches the next day and three inches the day after that.

The contractor had completed most of the interior remodeling, but the exterior work had just begun and could progress only as quickly as the fickle Vermont spring permitted. The house sat on a steeply canted hillside lot on Stone House Road, overlooking the Stratton Mountain Country Club golf course. A mason had persuaded Nancy that she needed an extensive new system of retaining walls. She'd also been sold on the idea of regrading the driveway to make it less steep. And then there was landscaping, a lot of landscaping. New trees and shrubs started to arrive by the truckload. Work on the multilevel rock garden began.

In Vermont, as was standard for April, the winter winds subsided only gradually. Snow still flurried from hostile gray skies. The air resisted the intrusion of warmth. Trees had not yet started to bud. But Nancy's days were filled with talk of dogwoods that would flower in May, hemlocks, yews, and red-osier dogwood shrubs. She had to decide on the placement of the perennial gardens and the annual beds and choose plants. Did she want the traditional hostas and bleeding hearts for the shady spots? Pink impatiens or violet? As for lamium in the rock garden, wouldn't 'White Nancy' be perfect? And would periwinkle suffice as ground cover to supplement the fine fescue grass, or did she want pachysandra as well?

Around the corner and up the hill, Andrew was spending a lot of time at his Stratton Mountain vacation home. But he was in no mood to socialize. Over the winter, members of the co-op board at 200 East Seventy-fourth Street had begun to scrutinize the transactions that Andrew, in his capacity as treasurer, had been making with residents' money during the preceding six years.

He and Hayley had bought two apartments adjacent to their first and had renovated them into a $3 million duplex that was the building's showplace. Andrew listed his net worth as $20 million. He drove a Mercedes so loaded with electronic gadgetry that neighbors joked about his national security clearance. He'd been calling himself "The King of Seventy-fourth Street" until a lawyer hired by the co-op board's finance committee bearded him in his Stratton den in January to discuss discrepancies in the building's accounts.

Andrew admitted he'd been stealing. He begged for mercy. He asked if there might not be some way for his two little daughters to avoid the trauma of seeing their father hauled off to prison. He paid a million dollars in restitution and resigned from the co-op board. He rented a $15,000-per-month house in Greenwich and put the Seventy-fourth Street duplex up for sale. But the co-op board didn't think he'd come completely clean. They hired outside auditors who discovered that since 1996 Andrew had surreptitiously siphoned more than $4.5 million from co-op accounts.

During the first week of April, as Rob arrived for a short visit, Andrew found himself not in Stratton contemplating the onset of spring, but at 305 Madison Avenue in New York City, in the office of his new criminal attorney, Charles Clayman, of Clayman and Rosenberg, trying to negotiate a settlement with the co-op board that would allow him to escape prosecution.

––––––––

Nancy saw Rob's visit as an intrusion. Their phone calls had been curt and brief. She didn't reply to his e-mails. He said he hadn't seen his children for almost a month and he missed them. Nancy told him she didn't believe that. She said she knew he'd come only to check on the renovation and, insofar as he could, on her spending. On his first morning there, she put a pair of white gloves on his breakfast place mat. "I'm sure you'll need them for your inspection," she said.

A few days later, on April 21, Rob turned forty. He felt it was a significant milestone. He waited all day, expecting a celebration, or at least some acknowledgment, from Nancy and the children. There was none. She never told the kids it was Daddy's birthday, and she completely ignored it herself.

He returned to Hong Kong nursing hurt feelings. Nancy hadn't kissed him hello or good-bye, she had not let him hug her, and, worst of all, she'd insisted that he sleep in the basement. He'd been too shocked and hurt even to argue about it. Once again, he told Bryna, he didn't know what to do.

"I can't keep shrugging this off as postpartum depression," he said. "I'm sure some of it is my fault, but I'm starting to think it might be a good idea for her to see a shrink."

"Don't dare suggest *that*," Bryna said.

"What can I do?"

"I don't know, Rob. She hasn't been in touch with me. I'm not sure there's anything you can do. It sounds to me like she's jumped the track."

He was back in Hong Kong for only a week when he had to turn around and make another grueling sixteen-hour flight to JFK, because Merrill Lynch had summoned him to New York. But it was worth it: they offered him a job in Tokyo, supervising all of Merrill's distressed-debt investing throughout Asia. It was by far the biggest promotion he'd ever received. It would make him one of the most important and influential investment bankers in the world. He was so excited he sped to Vermont to share the good news with Nancy. They would be leaving Hong Kong! He was sure she'd fall in love with Tokyo! But ten minutes after walking into the house on Stone House Road he decided not even to mention it. As he said late that night in an e-mail to Bryna O'Shea:

So I walk in from New York tonight and get crushed by the dog and all the kids. Jumping, screaming, licking. Very nice welcome. Nancy is sitting at the table, saying nothing. I didn't see her when I came in. She says something to the kids and I turn around and saw her and said, "Hello, nice to see you." I had to shake off the kids and get up and go over and give her a kiss. Not much effort on her part. Never much effort. Is she jealous that I get a big hello from the kids and the dog? Wouldn't that be ridiculous?

Merrill Lynch had suggested that he keep himself available for short-notice meetings about Tokyo. He decided to spend most of May working from Vermont. David Noh, the brilliant and tireless assistant he'd brought with him from Goldman, could step in for him in Hong Kong. As in April, Rob slept in the basement. This so perturbed Connie that once she actually raised her eyebrows at him in puzzlement. He merely shrugged. He brooded his way through the nights. He worried that he couldn't trust Nancy up in Vermont all alone. She told him nothing about what she did or whom she saw. But that was a problem he'd come prepared to deal with this time.

In Hong Kong, Rob had bought the Spector Pro and eBlaster computer spyware programs. They would allow him to monitor the Web sites Nancy visited, the search terms she used, and, more important, the e-mail she sent and received. He didn't know what she was up to, but with Spector Pro and eBlaster he was going to find out.

The second week in May, as the renovation neared completion, Rob called Prime Focus Communications in Brattleboro. He'd spoken to them the previous summer about home theater installation. The owner, Lance Del Priore, and his brother, Mike, had come to the house to sketch out preliminary plans. Now Rob called to say he was ready to proceed.

Mike Del Priore came by the next day. He spent more than two hours with Rob, reviewing component choices and installation options. Rob decided on a $35,000 system. Two weeks later, on Thursday, May 22, Prime Focus phoned. They'd received all the components and would be able to install the system the following week. "I'll be back in Hong Kong by then," Rob said. "But my wife will have my phone numbers, so call me if something unexpected comes up. And don't change anything without talking to me directly. My wife does not have the authority to approve any further expense. I want that to be absolutely clear."

On Tuesday, May 27, the day after Memorial Day, Mike Del Priore called to say he'd be out to install the system the next day. Nancy said she looked forward to seeing him.

Wednesday morning was humid, with gentle rain falling occasionally on the newly landscaped hillside outside the house. The sky was only shades of gray, but the air was rich with the honeyed smell of spring growth and flowering. Nancy was finishing a cup of coffee in the kitchen shortly after 9:00 a.m. when she heard the Prime Focus truck come down the driveway.

Michael Del Priore rang the doorbell.

Nancy answered. She was wearing denim shorts that rode high and tight on her thighs and a sleeveless yellow top with a scooped neckline. She flashed her most dazzling smile.

"Hi, Michael," she said. "Wow, you look terrific. You must have started really working out."

Nothing would ever be the same.

PART TWO

THE SUMMER OF LOVE, THE AUTUMN OF DISCONTENT

Summer

13.

Rob

FRANCIS XAVIER SHEA GREW UP IN THE BOROUGH OF Queens in New York City. After graduating in 1965 from Rice High School on 124th Street in Harlem, where the Congregation of Christian Brothers taught him discipline the old-fashioned way—with paddles and leather straps—he joined the U.S. Marines. Parris Island was almost a vacation after four years at Rice.

He spent a year in Vietnam with the First Marine Aircraft Wing, stationed outside Danang. Then he became a New York City policeman. Over the next thirteen years, he received sixty-seven department medals, including the Medal of Valor, the department's third-highest commendation, awarded "for acts of outstanding personal bravery intelligently performed in the line of duty at imminent personal hazard to life under circumstances evincing a disregard of personal consequences." In Frank's case, this involved a Sunday-morning shootout with two Jamaican drug dealers on Sutter Avenue in Brooklyn in April 1977. As Frank and his partner approached their parked car, one of the dealers fired a shot that hit Frank's partner in the leg. Frank returned fire with a shotgun. One of the dealers survived, one did not.

Frank wound up as a homicide detective, working out of the Seventy-fifth Precinct in the East New York section of Brooklyn. One night in 1986, shortly after midnight, he and his partner, the late Larry Daniels, were rushing to Baptist Medical Center on Linden Boulevard to interview four shooting victims in the emergency room. At the intersection of Sutter and Euclid, they were broadsided by a car driven by a woman speeding to the hospital with her baby, who was having a seizure. Frank was injured badly enough to take early disability retirement.

He founded a private investigation firm named Alpha Group in 1996, with headquarters in Farmingdale, Long Island. Alpha Group was a full-service, high-tech agency. They did internal corporate investigations, corporate security assessments, computer data retrieval, installation (and removal) of electronic surveillance devices, and vehicle tracking by GPS. By 2003, Alpha was doing a lot of international work. Frank was becoming as familiar with the streets of Istanbul, Mumbai, and Mexico City as he'd once been with Francis Lewis Boulevard.

He had just returned from Hong Kong on June 4, 2003, when Rob Kissel called him. Had Rob called twenty-four hours earlier, they could have met face to face. Rob said Frank had been recommended to him by a corporate lawyer familiar with Alpha's work. But then Rob stopped.

"What is it we can help you with?" Frank asked.

"This is personal," Rob said. "It doesn't involve Merrill Lynch."

"I understand."

"It's, ah, it's actually kind of a delicate matter. It's something—look, it's a little bit awkward to talk about, but it's a matter involving my wife."

"Are you talking about what we refer to as matrimonial work?"

"Yes, yes, exactly. It's . . . she . . . I'm not sure about this, but I think she may be in the early stages of . . . of . . ."

"A relationship?"

"Yes. Sorry. I don't normally have such a hard time expressing myself, but this situation is . . . well, embarrassing."

"You don't have to be embarrassed with me, Mr. Kissel."

"Rob. Please call me Rob. What I want to ask about is, well . . . is there some way you could sort of keep an eye on her, and on this guy? His name is Mike Del Priore."

"Surveillance. Yes, we can do that."

"Right, surveillance. You know, I can't believe I'm actually having this conversation."

"The first call is the hardest, Rob. But believe me, this is nothing out of the ordinary. Can you tell me why you've become suspicious of your wife?"

"Well, I did something I probably shouldn't have done. I installed a spyware program on her laptop. Are you familiar with spyware?"

"What did you use, Spector Pro and eBlaster?"

"Yes, exactly. How did you know that?"

"I figured a guy like you, Rob, investment banker, you'd want the best."

"She's been e-mailing this guy. He's a stereo guy. About a week ago, he installed some home theater equipment in our house in Vermont. She's been writing to him ever since. And I don't like the tone of what I'm reading. I want to know if she's seeing him."

"I can put a man on her, Rob. Let's say for a week?"

"I . . . I guess so. I don't know. It's probably nothing. Look, I'd better think about this. Can I call you tomorrow?"

"You can call me anytime. Let me give you my home number and my cell."

Frank Shea didn't know whether he'd hear from Rob Kissel again or not. Some people called back, some didn't. It wasn't as if Frank was eager to run a surveillance. He didn't like matrimonial work. For the most part, Alpha operated at a higher level and on a larger stage. But Robert Kissel was with Merrill Lynch in Hong Kong. Frank already had clients in Hong Kong and wouldn't mind adding Merrill Lynch to the list. Corporate security for the Hong Kong offices of a multinational like Merrill would be a tasty cherry to pick. He'd seen it happen before: do some personal work for a corporate executive and wind up with the whole corporation.

Rob did call back the next day. All traces of hesitancy were gone. Crisply and authoritatively, he said he wanted to initiate the surveillance immediately. The fee of $12,500 per week, plus expenses, did not faze him.

Forty-eight hours later, at 4:00 p.m. on Saturday, June 7, investigator Rocco Gatta, a former Nassau County policeman and, like Frank Shea, an ex-marine, was sitting in a Ford Taurus parked in the driveway of the unoccupied house adjacent to the Kissel home at 702 Stone House Road in Stratton Mountain, Vermont. A hard rain was falling and fog was starting to form. Nonetheless, when a blue Chevy van pulled into the Kissel driveway an hour later, Gatta could see clearly that it bore New Hampshire license plate 910-153.

He called Frank Shea with the number. Twenty minutes later, Frank called back to say that the van was registered to Michael Del Priore, thirty-nine, of Ferncroft Drive, Hinsdale, New Hampshire. The van was still there five hours later when Gatta returned to his sixty-nine-dollar-per-night room at the Stratton Mountain Village Inn, eight miles away.

Nancy

On the day of the installation, Nancy spent a lot of time in the living room, talking to Michael Del Priore while he worked. He wore a tight sleeveless T-shirt. He had big shoulders, big biceps, strong pecs. By the time he was finished, she'd learned that he had two teenaged sons from a first marriage and a five-year-old daughter from his second, which was ending in an exceptionally nasty divorce.

His wife had accused him of inappropriate physical contact with the daughter, and until recently he'd only been able to see her under supervision. But that was behind him, he said, and now he saw her, unsupervised, every other weekend.

In the living room, the children were wrestling over the new remote. They wanted to get rid of the high-definition National Geographic channel and find some cartoons to watch on the just-installed fifty-eight-inch Panasonic plasma TV. The rain had tapered to a drizzle and pockets of mist were forming on the hillside above the house.

"So you're finished. Does that mean I'm not going to see you anymore?"

"I guess not until your husband buys something else."

The children had found *SpongeBob SquarePants* on Nickelodeon. They were playing with the volume control on the remote, seeing how loud it would go. Connie appeared from the back of the house to quiet them down.

"Let me know how to reach you," Nancy said. "I'm sure I'll have some questions about this stuff."

"Just call the store and leave a message. I'll get back to you right away."

"No. I want to know how to reach you directly. Give me your cell phone number. And your number at home. Why not give me your e-mail address, too?"

Del Priore offered Nancy his warmest smile. "You know, maybe— oh, I shouldn't ask you that," he said.

Nancy offered her dazzling smile in return. "Of course you should. What is it?"

"I just thought maybe—see, my daughter gets a little lonely just with me and she doesn't know any kids in my neighborhood. I was thinking maybe sometime I could bring her over here to play with your kids."

"Of course you can." Nancy gave him her devilish smile. "As long as you stay, too."

"Sure. I'd stay."

"Then it's a date. I'll e-mail you and we'll figure out the best day. Probably a weekend, because you're working. You can come in late af- ternoon and stay for supper."

And so at 5:00 p.m. Saturday, June 7, in a downpour, Michael Del Priore—accompanied by his five-year-old daughter Amity—made his first nonworking visit to the home of Rob and Nancy Kissel. He didn't notice Rocco Gatta sitting in the Taurus in the driveway of the house next door.

Amity was introduced to Isabel, Zoe, and Ethan and they all went off to watch television. The picture on the new Panasonic was bright and sharp. Nancy fed them corn dogs on sticks, potato chips, and ice cream. Amity was delighted. Usually her father made her eat a salad with her dinner.

Nancy found talking to Michael—from the start, she always called him Michael, never Mike—very different from talking to Rob. For one thing, she could control the conversation. With Rob, conversation, like

everything else, had turned into a contest that could have only one win-
ner. Michael didn't seem like much of a talker, but she liked the sound
of his voice. She also liked the trace of southern accent he'd brought
back with him from his seven years in Alabama and Arkansas. But
what she liked most was the look in his eyes that said he knew he was
more than just a poor man in a rich woman's house.

They went into the recreation room with the kids to play darts.
Michael stood behind Nancy as she aimed at the board. He put his hands
on her shoulders. She didn't ask him to remove them.

Michael and Amity left at 10:30 p.m. The rain had slowed to a
drizzle. Rocco Gatta had already gone back to his motel. Nancy walked
out to the driveway with Michael.

"Do you know what I did?" she said. "I did the craziest thing. I've
always wanted a tattoo. My uptight husband, of course, has strictly for-
bidden me to get one. He thinks I'd look like a biker chick instead of the
perfect little banker's wife. I told him I wanted one for my birthday in
April. Instead, he gave me a Mercedes. But I decided this week, fuck
him. My FedEx man has a tattoo so I asked him where he'd got it. He
told me from Blackbear Tattoo in West Brattleboro. I made an appointment for two o'clock next Friday. Only now—and I know this sounds
silly—now I'm a little nervous about it."

"How come?"

"I don't know. It's just—I've never even been *near* a tattoo parlor,
and . . . I mean, I know it's not like a drug den, I know there's not going
to be a bunch of Hells Angels waiting around to grab me and drag me
into the back, but—would you come with me?"

"To get a tattoo?"

"To get *my* tattoo." She had a cocky little look in her eye. "Unless
you think we should have matching tattoos."

"Yeah, I could go with you."

For a moment he thought she was going to stand on tiptoe and kiss him on the cheek. Instead, she tossed him another radiant smile, accompanied by a wave good-bye. "See you Friday," she said. "Be here by noon."

"Yes ma'am."

They both laughed.

"She's pretty nice," Amity said as they drove away. "Do you like her, Daddy?"

"Yeah," Michael replied slowly. "I think I do."

14.

Rob

FOR THE NEXT THREE DAYS, ROCCO GATTA FOLLOWED Nancy everywhere she went: to the Crossgates Mall in Albany; to the Stratton Mountain School, where she dropped off and picked up Isabel and Zoe; and to Manchester, Vermont, forty minutes away, where she shopped at a store called the Jelly Mill.

The Jelly Mill advertised "gifts for every interest in a festive atmosphere highlighted by a 1914 nickelodeon . . . fine collectibles, toiletries, essential oils, candles in every shape and color, bubbling garden fountains, cards, and some of the most appealing sculptural pieces you'll ever see." It was somewhat downscale by Nancy's standards, but after all, she was in Vermont, not Hong Kong.

Gatta captured her on video as she entered the store, but he did not follow her inside. With his dark glasses and a face that looked as if it had been carved, none too skillfully, out of granite, Rocco Gatta was not the sort of guy who would have blended easily into the background at the Jelly Mill. He just followed her back to Stratton.

Nancy was getting more and more nervous about her tattoo. Although she'd been planning to meet Del Priore Friday morning, she invited him for supper on Thursday, telling him his duty would be to prevent her from chickening out. Rocco Gatta noted his arrival at

5:45 p.m. and his departure at 10:30. Two confirmed sightings seemed enough. Gatta returned to New York the next morning and compiled his report. Frank Shea called Rob that night, which was Saturday morning in Hong Kong.

"I'll fax you the full report early next week," he said, "but here's the headline: she is definitely seeing Del Priore. He was over there twice, and not during regular business hours. He was there last Saturday for several hours in the evening and again last night. He didn't stay overnight."

Rob received the news calmly. He thanked Frank for a job well done. He said they should try to get together socially the next time he came to New York. Then he called Bryna O'Shea.

"You're not going to believe this," he said, "but I think Nancy's fucking the stereo boy."

"What are you talking about?"

"The way she's been acting," he said. "I started to wonder. I started thinking there might be something going on. So I hired a private detective to surveil her."

"You did *what?*"

"I know it sounds melodramatic. But this fellow came highly recommended. Very experienced, very upscale. He's in New York."

"You've been having her followed?"

"Only for a week. It just ended."

"Wasn't that a little extreme?"

"I need to know what's going on, Bryna. And I can't trust Nancy to tell me. It's now clear I can't trust Nancy at all."

"Wait, Rob. Let's take it from the top. What's this about a stereo boy?"

"The guy who just installed our new home theater at the house. He's been back. Twice. After the installation was finished."

"Maybe there's a problem. Maybe the wiring?"

"There's a problem, Bryna, but it's not with the system. He comes over at dinnertime and he stays until late at night. Do you get what I'm saying? He's still there after the kids have gone to bed. He's there after Connie's gone to bed. He's there with Nancy, just the two of them."

"Have you asked her about him?"

"What good would that do? She'll only lie. Besides, I just found out. The detective just called me. Bryna, she's having an affair."

"You don't know that."

"I'll tell you something else. They've been sending e-mails back and forth. I've been reading them."

"How have you been doing *that*?"

"Spyware. I hooked it up to her computer when I was up there in May. I know it's wrong, but what was I going to do? I'm in Hong Kong and she's balling some blue-collar asshole up there and I need to know what's happening."

"Are you sure that's what's happening?"

"I don't have any videos of the two of them in bed together, but these e-mails are much too friendly and cute. And now I know for a fact that she's seen him at least twice. In the house. At night. Bryna, don't be naïve."

"I've been called a lot of things, Rob, but never naïve. Okay, suppose it is true? What are you going to do about it?"

"What do you think I should do?"

"Ask her what the hell is going on."

"But I can't, don't you see? I can't tell her I put spyware on her computer. I can't tell her I've been having her watched and followed."

"Why not?"

"Because that would be the end of everything. If she finds out about that, the marriage is over."

"Which you don't want?"

"Of course I don't. You know what I want. I want things back the way they used to be. I don't even know why they went so wrong."

"Well, you've got two choices, Rob: either confront her or don't. But just sitting there tearing yourself up about it isn't going to do anybody any good."

"I don't know. I don't know what to do. Maybe you're right. Maybe it's nothing. Maybe I'm overreacting."

"I didn't say it was nothing. It doesn't sound like nothing. But I'll say this, Rob: before you do anything drastic, you'd better be absolutely sure you know what's happening. No guesswork. No assumptions."

"You're right. I need hard evidence. In the meantime, I'm going out of my fucking mind."

Nancy

It was raining on Friday, June 13. It seemed as if it had rained every day since the end of April. The ground was saturated. Seeds drowned. Farmers moaned. People made jokes about how maybe they should start planting rice.

As Rocco Gatta headed back to New York, Michael and Nancy were driving down Route 30 to Brattleboro in the rain. She drove. She wanted to be in control. She'd upgraded her rental car from a Ford Explorer to a Lincoln Navigator. There was also a Corvette in the garage, but she thought a Corvette would attract too much attention in Brattleboro.

They wound their way down Stratton Mountain to Jamaica, which had a population of about one thousand, and on to Townshend, which also had a population of about one thousand (plus the longest covered bridge in Vermont), and through Newfane, which had a population of about fifteen hundred. Fewer people lived in the thirty-five-mile area between Stratton Mountain and Brattleboro than lived in a single tower of a Hong Kong housing estate.

They talked about music. She liked the Backstreet Boys. He liked Rascal Flatts. They both liked Brian McKnight. They talked about movies. Her favorite movie of all time was *Bonnie and Clyde*. Her recent favorite was *Unfaithful* with Diane Lane. Michael hadn't seen it. She told him he should.

"Do you know what kind of tattoo you want?"

"I want the Chinese characters for the years my three kids were born."

"I don't think they do Chinese at Blackbear."

"They'll do whatever I tell them to do."

Brattleboro was a river town. Like Rutland and Bennington and Bellows Falls, it was nitty and gritty, a brick and mortar town that smelled of fresh tar and fast food, not maple syrup. There were postcards of Brattleboro, population twelve thousand, but nobody bought them.

Once, it had been a thriving railroad and mill town. Even in 2003, down by the river—in the section that the locals called the Brat—many of the abandoned factories and shut-down hotels were still standing. Rudyard Kipling had lived there a hundred years earlier, but by 2003 the only writers to be found were in the Brattleboro Retreat, a drug and alcohol rehab center that had become the town's biggest employer.

Still, remnants of a counterculture remained. Sixties hippies who wanted to renounce bourgeois values but who hadn't quite been ready to live on a farm had settled in Brattleboro. Echoes of their music, faint whiffs of pot smoke, and some of their offspring survived. The Blackbear Tattoo and Jewelry Company served their needs.

It was not quite as easy as Nancy had expected to find the right designs for her tattoos. She'd brought a drawing of the Chinese characters she wanted, but she and the tattooist had to spend an hour on the Internet before she was sure they had it right.

"Don't fuck it up," she told the tattooist. "I'm not going through this again."

Michael waited patiently, easing himself into his new role as Nancy's escort.

———————

She was excited when it was over. Three tattoos—Chinese characters, each about the size of a quarter—adorned her bare left shoulder.

"Wait until my uptight husband sees these," she said. "He'll totally freak out."

"Do you really think he won't like them?" Michael asked.

Nancy laughed. "If you knew him, you wouldn't be asking that question. He doesn't like anything I do unless it's something he's told me to do. But a tattoo? It'll be like I'd acted in a porno film. You don't understand, Michael. You couldn't understand, which is one reason why I like you so much. My husband is all about appearances. All that matters is how it looks, not what it is. But fuck him. Let's go into town and take a walk and then we'll find someplace where I can buy you dinner. I don't want to go home yet. I'm having too much fun."

It was only a five-minute drive from Blackbear to the center of the Brat. The rain had stopped, leaving the air heavy and the sidewalks wet. Nancy was so delighted by her tattoo—or by the fact that she'd finally shown the courage to get it—that she almost broke into a trot.

They wound up at the Riverview Café on Bridge Street and got a table by the window.

"That's where I live," Michael said, pointing across the river at New Hampshire. "Five miles that way."

"Do you want to show me your house?" Nancy asked.

"No, ma'am. I'd be embarrassed to after being in yours. It's a mobile home."

"You'll show it to me. Not tonight, but soon."

Nancy ordered a shot of tequila before dinner. "I don't drink much," she said, "but it seems like a girl with a tattoo ought to drink a shot of tequila."

She seemed about to call him Clyde and to tell him to call her Bonnie. Michael, who didn't drink or smoke or swear, ordered a root beer.

After dinner Nancy had a Jägermeister, a seventy-proof herbal liqueur. She was giggling by the time she finished it and she told Michael he'd better drive back to Stratton. She gave him the car keys as they walked across the parking lot.

But before he could put the key in the ignition, she started to cry. She put her face in her hands and she cried. She put her hands by her sides and she shook her head back and forth and she cried. She bawled. Tears streamed down her cheeks. She cried and she cried and she cried.

Michael always kept close track of time. So he knew she cried for twenty-two minutes as he sat next to her, saying nothing.

Finally, she looked at him.

"Don't you see how conflicted I am? For years, I've had to pretend. I've had to act like the perfect wife, the perfect mother, the perfect woman in the perfect marriage. But it's all been bullshit. You're the first man who's ever accepted me as I am, without judging. I have such strong feelings for you, Michael, but I don't know what to do."

One of Michael's attributes was that when he didn't know what to say he said nothing.

"My marriage . . . my husband . . . oh my God, Michael, you have no idea what a hell it is. You can't know what it's like to live with someone you're afraid of. Someone who cuts you to pieces with every word."

He listened.

"It's the money, it's the kids, it's this and it's that and it's everything. Everything I do is wrong. Everything I say. It's how I dress. It's how I talk. It's how I look. He hates it all. He cuts me down to nothing. I'm living in hell and nobody knows it and I can't tell anyone because I'm afraid."

She put her face back in her hands and cried again. She cried for another twelve minutes. Fog from the river spread slowly across the parking lot. She stopped crying. As soon as she stopped crying, she fell asleep. Michael drove back to Stratton. He drove with one hand. His other hand was on Nancy's leg. When she finally woke up, sniffling, she didn't move her leg away. Instead, she put her hand on his and left it there all the way home.

She had weekend plans with the children and couldn't see him. But on Monday she disconnected a few wires behind the television and said she needed him to come to the house to fix it. He came the next day, Tuesday, June 17, in late afternoon.

She'd finally finished the renovation. Her goal, she had written to Bryna O'Shea after a long e-mail silence, was to make the house "all me. I want the kind of comfort that's healing to my soul and inner spirit . . . my private retreat . . . an environment of solitude. Each time I walk through the door I want to be greeted with warmth and love." Nowhere was her vision more fully realized than in the guest room. She named it the "Blue Room." The walls were painted blue, the bedspread and sheets and pillowcases were blue, the nightstands and the armchair were blue. She called it "a place of extra comfort . . . to find rest . . . and bring peace."

She brought Michael to the Blue Room after he'd finished reconnecting the wires. It was there that they became lovers. It was "a perfect place to share with the man I was falling in love with," she wrote in a computer journal she updated intermittently. And it seemed even more perfect when Michael told her that his favorite color was blue.

"Two people from different worlds," she wrote to him in an e-mail the next day, "brought together . . . feeling an overwhelming connection . . . discovering that one is truly the other's soul mate . . ."

Michael brought Amity over again on Saturday. While Connie was watching the children, Nancy brought him up to the Blue Room again. This time, they stayed for three hours.

They quickly established a routine. They would see each other only on weeknights, after 9:30 p.m., after Connie put the children to bed. No more weekends: if she started to leave the children with Connie on weekends, Rob would surely find out. They talked by phone ten times a day. On nights when Michael didn't come over, they would stay on the phone for hours. Fortunately for them, they had little need to e-mail.

15.

Rob

ROB HAD TO FLY TO NEW YORK FOR ANOTHER SERIES OF meetings about Tokyo at Merrill Lynch. He met Frank Shea for breakfast at Le Parker Meridien on West Fifty-seventh Street, on Thursday, June 26. Merrill Lynch had booked Rob into a room overlooking Central Park. He and Frank met at Norma's, the hotel's breakfast restaurant, which was famous for its thousand-dollar omelet filled with lobster and sevruga caviar, known informally as the "investment banker over easy." But Rob restricted himself to orange juice, oatmeal, and whole wheat toast. He didn't even eat much of that. His anguish over Nancy's affair had taken his appetite away.

Frank's first impression of Rob was of a tense, driven, but essentially gracious man who'd been confronted for the first time in his life by a situation that resisted quantification. No amount of number crunching could reveal what was inside a woman's heart. Rob seemed tormented by uncertainty but very much in love.

He had called Nancy from Hong Kong just before leaving for New York. His daughter Zoe had answered the phone.

"Daddy," she said, "Mike keeps bringing Amity over to play and I don't like her."

"Mike, the man who put in our big TV?"

"Yes. I don't like Amity, she's a pain."

"When was the last time she came over?"

"Last night. And Mike sits in your special chair. I told him he shouldn't sit there because it's your chair, but Mommy says it's all right because Mike's her friend."

"I'll talk to Mommy about that, sweetie. In fact, why don't you get Mommy now."

When Nancy picked up the phone, Rob said, "I understand the stereo boy has been hanging around."

"Michael? Oh, he's brought Amity over to play a couple of times."

"Michael? Since when did the stereo boy become 'Michael'?"

"That's his name, Rob. And he's not a boy, he's a man."

"Who the hell is Amity?"

"His daughter. She's five years old and very sweet and very lonely. Michael's in the middle of a horrendous divorce and I suggested that he bring Amity over once in a while to play with the kids. They all adore her."

"That's not what Zoe says. Zoe just told me she's a pain in the ass. And why is Michael sitting in my chair?"

"Wait a minute, Rob. Who the fuck do you think you are, Papa Bear? Michael can sit anywhere he wants in my house."

"How about when he wants to lie down?"

"What are you talking about?"

"Don't play dumb, Nancy. You're fucking the stereo boy."

"Stop calling him 'the stereo boy.' You sound pathetic."

"You're having an affair with that asshole!"

"How could you even think something like that, much less insult me by saying it?"

"How many times has he been over?"

"Twice. Big fucking deal."

"Don't invite him again."

"It's my house and I'll invite anybody I want. You're such an asshole. Michael is my friend and that's that."

"Your friend? The last time I saw him he was the guy from Prime Focus who was going to install the home theater."

"If you could only hear how fucking ridiculous you sound. I've had enough of this conversation. Good-bye."

———————————

Now, over breakfast at Norma's, Rob said, "I don't know what to do next, Frank. I wish I believed her, but I don't. And the e-mails—they're damaging, but they don't *absolutely* prove anything."

"My only word of advice, Rob, is you'd better be sure you really want to know what's in her e-mails. I've seen plenty of cases where that's caused more problems than it's solved. Sometimes you're better off not confirming every suspicion. Especially if you're trying to hold the marriage together."

"No, Frank. I've got to know. But once I *have* proof, what do I do?"

"A lot depends on your level of tolerance. Assume the worst: assume she has slept with the guy a couple of times. Is it worth busting up the marriage for that?"

"Maybe not. But who says it's only going to be a couple of times?"

"Rob, she needs the lifestyle you make it possible for her to have. She's not going to throw that away to go live in a trailer park. You can lay it on the line: 'Stop seeing him or start seeing my lawyers.' If it comes to that. I hope it doesn't."

Nancy

While Rob was having breakfast with Frank Shea, Nancy was driving into New York City with Connie and the children. Once again she'd booked connecting suites at the Surrey. Bryna O'Shea would be arriving from San Francisco the next day.

It had become Bryna's tradition to vacation in late June and come back to New York to visit friends and relatives. Nancy was the friend with whom she spent the most time. They shopped in expensive stores and ate in expensive restaurants and stayed out late going to clubs, and they talked about how much fun they'd had when they were single.

Bryna got into New York only hours before Rob left. For once it wasn't raining, but the first heat wave of the summer had arrived, bringing temperatures in the nineties and rendering the New York air as stagnant and gritty as Hong Kong's. Rob was at the Surrey when she got there. He looked drawn and wan. She was shocked by how thin he was. Rob had always been fit. He'd even competed in a Hong Kong triathlon. Now he seemed almost frail. Even more than his words to her over the previous two months, Rob's appearance made clear to Bryna the extent of his distress.

They had only the briefest chance to talk.

"You look like shit," Bryna said. "What's happening? Confrontation? Open warfare?"

Rob shook his head. "Nothing like that. We've barely talked. I just stopped by to see the kids. I'll try to figure it out once I get back to Hong Kong, but it's really weird to look at her and imagine her screwing some illiterate handyman."

Bryna raised her eyebrows.

"All right, he's not illiterate. And he knows how to stick a plug in a socket. And he's sticking his plug in Nancy's socket. And if I don't get out of here right now I'm going to say or do something I'll regret."

"Stay in touch," Bryna said.

It was only after Rob had left for the airport that Nancy told Bryna that she'd be going back to Vermont the next morning. She had to get back, she said. There was just so much to do, getting the girls ready for camp.

Bryna knew that wasn't true. She knew Nancy never did anything to get the girls ready for camp. Connie did it all. There was another reason why Nancy was in such a hurry to get back to Vermont, and because Rob had been confiding in her Bryna knew what it was, *but* because Rob had been confiding in her she couldn't let Nancy know that she knew.

For their one night out, Nancy wanted to go to the Odeon. In the mid-1980s, when Nancy and Bryna had been working and playing in the sandbox of the lower Manhattan restaurant and club scene, the Odeon had been the destination of choice for hip young martini-drinking, coke-snorting New York yuppies.

Without the Odeon, there might not have been a TriBeCa. Without the Odeon, the area surrounding West Broadway between Duane and Thomas streets might always have remained Washington Market. Jay McInerney set many a *Bright Lights, Big City* scene at the Odeon. After midnight, when those who'd come only to dine had been cleared out and the Bolivian marching powder was thick as pollen in the air, one might see not only McInerney, but John Belushi or Mary Boone or Bret Easton Ellis at the Odeon. It had been the epicenter from which had radiated the Wall Street greed and excess that defined the eighties and that lured Rob Kissel into the honeyed trap of investment banking.

Those glory days were long gone by the summer of 2003, when

Nancy and Bryna ate dinner at the Odeon, but maybe it was a lingering aura of licentiousness that emboldened Bryna to ask the sort of personal question she knew Nancy despised.

"Are you having a fling?"

"God, no. Why would you ask something like that?"

"You seem different, sort of jittery, as if you wished you could be somewhere else. I know things have been rough with Rob. And I remember how we talked after we'd seen that movie with Diane Lane."

"That's just crazy," Nancy said. "You should know I'd never do anything like that."

And back in Vermont, Nancy decided she could not continue. Rob was already too suspicious. Nancy knew how obsessive he could be. He'd been hostile at the Surrey. She'd put nothing past him. She could even imagine him having her followed. And she was afraid of what he'd do if he ever found out the truth.

"I can't see you anymore," she told Michael in a phone call on June 27. "Rob's too suspicious. I feel like he's been spying on me. And who knows what else he might do? He has power, Michael. He has money. He might even come after you."

"Don't worry about me. I can take care of myself."

"Well, I'm frightened. There was a look in his eye that really spooked me. It's like he already knows and he's just waiting to spring the trap."

"We'll be careful. We'll be even more careful than we have been."

"No, Michael, I can't do it. I won't be able to see you anymore." And then she broke down in tears. Before long, Michael began to keep track of how many times Nancy told him they could not continue their affair and how much time passed before she told him it was on again. This first time, it was three days.

"I've got to see you. I don't care if he knows. He's never let me do anything I've wanted to do, but I'm not going to let him keep me from seeing you." But three days after that Rob called from Hong Kong to remind her that he didn't want her seeing Del Priore anymore. She said she wouldn't. He warned her that she'd better not. She got scared and called Michael.

"I *really* can't see you anymore. We shouldn't even talk. Suppose he's tapping the phone? That's the kind of thing he would do. He can be dangerous, Michael. And I'm getting the creeps."

"I wouldn't let anybody hurt you, baby doll."

She loved it when he called her baby doll. "The phone is too risky. Even the cell. We'll have to stay in touch by e-mail."

Then Rob hurt his back and wound up in traction in a Hong Kong hospital. She called Michael the day she heard the news.

"It's okay! He's in the hospital. You can come over tonight!"

16.

Rob

ROB HAD HAD A BAD BACK FOR YEARS, PRIMARILY FROM IN-juries suffered while skiing too aggressively at Stratton Mountain. The Irish-born Park Avenue spinal surgeon Patrick O'Leary had operated on him in 1995, performing a laminotomy and discectomy between lumbar disks four and five on the right side. Five years later–in support of the theorem that the most likely outcome of back surgery is more back surgery–Dr. O'Leary did a revision laminotomy at L4–5 right and an excision of recurrent disk herniation in the same region.

But on his first weekend back in Hong Kong in the summer of 2003, Rob blew out another disk playing tennis. This was at L3–4, right, just above his earlier injury. He was crippled in an instant and in excruciating pain. At the hospital doctors admitted him immediately and put him in traction.

He remained there for a week. To be lying flat on one's back in paralyzing pain in Hong Kong while reading secret e-mails between one's wife and her new lover in Vermont was a distinctly twenty-first-century form of torture: electronic waterboarding, more or less. The exchanges he read were hardly pornographic, but they removed any lingering shred of doubt about the nature of Nancy's relationship with Del Priore.

Discharged from the hospital, Rob spent the second week of July doing physical therapy three times a day. But even with that, and even using a cane, he wasn't able to walk more than twenty yards at a time and found it almost impossible to go down a flight of stairs. He had no strength in his right thigh and, except for the pain he felt when he tried to walk, he was numb between his right knee and ankle. It seemed clear he would need another spinal operation.

He flew to New York to see Dr. O'Leary in mid-July. After all the X-rays and MRIs and ultrasounds and scans were completed and their results scrutinized by some of the highest-priced doctors on the Upper East Side of New York City, Dr. O'Leary scheduled surgery for early August. Although barely able to drive—he could only brake and accelerate with his left foot—Rob managed to get himself to Stratton the same day. He was motivated. He was angry. He was hurt. He was obsessed. He'd memorized dozens of lines from Nancy's e-mails to Del Priore. He now knew she'd been lying to him. He now knew the truth.

He arrived at the house on the evening of July 18. It had been a perfect Vermont summer day: the sky clear, the humidity low, the temperature in the upper seventies. The loveliness of the weather could not have been more at odds with Rob's mood.

That night, he called Bryna from the basement. "I confronted her," he said. "Point blank. I told her I knew she was having an affair. I said her computer had a virus and for some reason it was copying me on her e-mails. I'd read them. So I knew. But it was over, I told her. She had to go back to Hong Kong right away. That item was not negotiable. Back to Hong Kong. Immediately."

"What did she say?"

"First, she went ballistic about me being sneaky and spying on her. I said I wasn't the issue: she was. Her and her affair."

"What did she say?"

"She didn't admit it, but she didn't deny it, either. She said, 'It's not black and white. It's not what you think. It's complicated.' I told her it wasn't complicated, it was simple: she'd been having an affair and I'd caught her and now she was going back to Hong Kong."

"Is she?"

"No. She told me Zoe is in day camp, Ethan has his playgroup, Isabel's still up at Camp Vega, and she wasn't going to disrupt their summers just because I was throwing a fit."

"But those aren't the real reasons."

"Of course not. But I can't just abduct her. Besides, she promised she wouldn't see him again. She promised she wouldn't even talk to him. And she's certainly not going to be sending him any more e-mails."

"Do you believe her? Do you really think she'll stop seeing him? Even though you're back in Hong Kong?"

"I don't know. But at least I know how to find out."

Rob flew back the next day. His back was killing him. He could still barely walk. On Sunday, July 20, he e-mailed Frank Shea: "Can you get someone up to Vermont for Monday night? There may also be afternoon situations. Nancy will be more aware, because I've asked her to come home early. I want her back here because I believe she's having an affair. I told her that on the basis that her computer has a virus I've read a bunch of e-mails from her to Mike. I asked her not to see him nor talk to him and just come back to Hong Kong. This is a critical week to determine if she spends any meaningful time with him."

An hour after sending the e-mail, he called Shea.

There was a fresh edge of panic in his voice.

"Can you do it, Frank? Can you have someone up there tomorrow night?"

"It's already in place. Rocco Gatta will be going up tomorrow."

"Look, Frank, my oldest girl is away at camp—that's Camp Vega, up in Maine, I think I told you about it when we had breakfast—and the other girl is going to day camp. Nancy can easily arrange to have the nanny take the youngest out of the house all day, so it's not just night-time, do you understand?"

"Loud and clear, Rob. We'll be watching all day."

"And you've got to let me know, all right? I can't wait for a summary at the end of the week. If they're together, I need to know right away. You've got all my numbers, don't you? My cell, the office, the Parkview number?"

"I've got 'em all, Rob. We're on top of this. I've told Rocco to call me the minute something happens and I'll call you the minute I hear from him."

"It's getting worse, Frank. The whole thing is getting more serious. I want to catch them in the act."

Nancy

For two whole weeks, before Rob came to New York to see Dr. O'Leary, they had felt free. Nancy still kept weekends reserved for the children, and Amity didn't come over again, but during the week the affair filled not only their nights, but, increasingly, as Rob would come to suspect, their afternoons.

Nancy called Michael just after July 4 and told him to take the afternoon off from work. He arrived at the house at 2:00 p.m. She was waiting in the driveway in full Bonnie and Clyde mode: reckless, thrill-seeking, ready to cut loose. "Let's go for a ride," she said.

This time he drove. "Where do you want to go?" he said.

"I don't know. I don't care. Let's go somewhere and rob a bank."

He looked at her as if she might be serious. She explained about the movie *Bonnie and Clyde*.

The weather had turned hot and humid. Michael drove toward Manchester, but for once shopping was not what Nancy had in mind.

"Let's go down to Bennington," she said.

Michael got on Route 7 and drove south for twenty-five miles. They wound up in downtown Bennington, where North Street becomes South Street and where Main Street goes west. Muggy heat radiated from the dull brick of buildings that housed failing or already failed businesses. They stopped at a red light at the four corners intersection in the charmless center of the town.

"Which way?" Michael asked.

"I don't know. Turn right."

A block and a half later, she said, "Stop! Pull in here. I can't wait another minute to make love!"

The Kirkside Motor Lodge was not exactly a destination resort. It was a blue-collar motel for a blue-collar lover. She went into the office and paid sixty dollars, cash, for the room.

Although Michael was finding her an eager and vigorous lover, he couldn't shake the sense that for Nancy the act was merely prelude to the aftermath, when she begged him to hold her tightly and to protect her and to promise her that he'd always be there.

"Don't worry, baby doll, I'll be here," he told her over and over again.

"Call me 'baby doll.' Call me 'butterfly.' I want to be your baby doll and your butterfly for the rest of my life."

But later in the afternoon at the Kirkside Motor Lodge, with the air-conditioning window unit wheezing and rattling as it battled the heat, he called her Nancy.

She sat bolt upright in the bed.

"Don't call me that when we're in bed! *Don't ever call me by my name when we're in bed together!*"

"Why not?"

"Because *he* calls me that and I hate him! With him, bed means pain and humiliation. He hurts me, Michael."

"Physically?"

She began to cry even harder than she had in the parking lot outside the Riverview Café. Her whole body convulsed with her cries. Finally—Michael clocked it at seventeen minutes—her crying subsided into sobs.

"You touch me so tenderly," she said. "You care about how I feel. You don't know, you don't know how awful it's been." And again she started to cry so hard she wasn't able to speak.

Eventually, she said, "I'm sorry. You're going to think that all I ever do is cry. But you don't know how much you mean to me, Michael. I've been living in hell and now you've come to rescue me."

"What do you mean?"

"When Rob calls me by my name, the way he says it . . . it terrifies me. Because I know what it's going to lead to."

"What?"

"He beats me. He abuses me. He forces me to have sex."

"Baby doll . . ."

"He gets drunk and he snorts coke and he comes after me with his fists. He's broken my ribs. He doesn't care. It's gotten worse and worse and I don't know what to do. I don't have anyone to confide in. I'm so afraid, but I can't leave. We've got this whole life in Hong Kong and everyone says we're the perfect couple and I can't just walk away from everything."

Michael didn't know what to say except that he would always be there for her. He held her gently for a long, long time. Then they drove back to Stratton so she could feed the children dinner. She picked up burgers, fries, shakes, and McNuggets at the McDonald's in Manchester on the way.

During the days and nights that followed, Nancy said no more about being abused. "I don't want to talk about it. Don't ask again" was her reply when Michael brought it up. For the most part, her spirits were high. She loved her tattoo. She took to driving her Corvette instead of the Lincoln Navigator. She told Michael she was desperate to see where he lived, so they spent an afternoon and evening in his Hinsdale, New Hampshire, double-wide.

On days when she couldn't wait until 9:30 p.m. to see him, she'd book a room at a nearby inn or motel and meet him in the late afternoon, leaving Connie to care for Zoe and Ethan. She'd use her credit card to reserve the room, but when she checked in she'd pay cash so the charge would not appear on a monthly statement.

She didn't want to use the same motel twice, so they wound up driving around like researchers for a travel guide. The Londonderry Inn, the Inn on Magic Mountain, the Greenmount Lodge, the Snowdon Motel, Dostal's—they could have written their own book: *The Adulterer's Guide to South-Central Vermont*. This was their idyllic phase, when Nancy could articulate her visions of their future.

"I never want to leave Vermont," she told him. "I've found a peace within me from being here, from being with you. I want to take a drive in the fall when the leaves have changed color. Fall is my favorite season. We'll pull over somewhere and take a walk through the leaves. The air, it's so crisp. Don't you think everything smells so great in the fall? That's why I love wearing suede—because I love the way it smells."

One day, in a motel, Michael wanted them to take a bubble bath together. Nancy couldn't bring herself to do it. "I'm sorry," she said. "It's because of how I feel about my body. When you spend years of someone telling you how horrible your body looks . . . I just can't shake it. I'm not sure I ever will."

They still weren't able to spend whole nights together. Nancy had to get back to the house before the children went to bed because she was afraid that if she didn't, one of them would mention it to Rob. And when they were at the house Michael couldn't stay over because she couldn't risk having the children see him in the morning. Connie was a different story. She was sure that Connie knew by now, but she was also sure that Connie would never say anything, because if she did Nancy would fire her, and if she didn't have a job she couldn't stay in Hong Kong for more than two weeks. She'd have to go back to the Philippines and poverty.

"I love the first snowfall," she told Michael. "It's so clean. Can't you picture us sitting inside, nice and cozy, a fire going, the snow falling outside? It could be a Saturday afternoon and we're just being lazy. We'll bring some more wood in for the fire, we'll be listening to music, maybe I'll draw or paint. I miss painting. You can write. I like to picture you writing . . . a novel maybe, then getting it published. The clothes have finished drying. I'll take them out of the dryer. I love hot clothes, fresh from the dryer . . ."

He kept calling her "baby doll" and "butterfly." He bought two pairs of blue crystal hearts and gave one to her. That way, each of them could hold two hearts together. To show her gratitude, she went to the Movado store in Manchester and bought him a $7,200 Concord Impresario watch.

"You're the only person I've ever felt safe with," she told him. "I'm in love. I've never been in love before."

One day she noticed that Michael wasn't wearing the watch. He was embarrassed to tell her why. Finally, he said he'd told his brother Lance about the affair, but Lance had been born again and told Michael he was immoral. More to the point, he told Michael he was fired. They argued. Finally, Lance said that Michael could keep his job in return for the watch.

"I didn't want to do it," he said, "but I need the job."

"Of course you do."

She went back to the Movado store in Manchester the next day and bought him another $7,200 Concord Impresario.

———————————

It was only a couple of days later, July 18, that Rob had confronted her. In a tearful panic, she told Michael what had happened. "He grabbed me. He grabbed me by the face and then he spun me around and pushed me up against the wall and my head hit a picture hanging there and the picture fell down. I was screaming and crying and I was afraid the kids were going to hear. I've got a terrible pain in my side. He must have broken my ribs."

17.

Rob

ROCCO GATTA RETURNED TO STRATTON ON MONDAY, JULY 21. The house whose driveway he'd used in June was occupied, so he had to find another location along the side of Stone House Road. From his new vantage point he could observe only the entrance to the driveway, but that turned out to be enough. Once again, it was raining hard and winds were gusting when Del Priore's blue van showed up at 9:20 p.m. The van pulled out of the driveway three and a half hours later.

Gatta called Frank Shea at home to report. It was 1:00 a.m. in New York, 1:00 p.m. in Hong Kong. Frank called Rob.

"Listen," Rob said. "The next time it happens, let me know as soon as he arrives. I want to call the house while he's there."

On Tuesday and Wednesday, Rocco Gatta followed while Nancy took Zoe to day camp in the morning and then drove to Manchester to shop. On both days, she stopped at the Jelly Mill—a kitsch maven's delight. She went back to Manchester on Thursday. Manchester was one of the biggest factory outlet centers in the Northeast. Nancy considered it her playground. She could have driven the fifteen-mile stretch of Route 11 between Londonderry and Manchester Depot with her eyes closed. Thursday morning was hot and humid. Showers were forecast for afternoon. Nancy went to the Jelly Mill, to the Levi's outlet store, and to Carter's for Kids. This was how she passed her days. This was what passed for meaning in her life. It didn't have to be Madison Avenue in New York or Pacific Place or the IFC Mall in Hong Kong—any store with lights on and doors unlocked was a potential source of diversion and delight. She spent most of her waking hours trying to buy either or both.

Nancy didn't see her constant shopping as an addiction. How could it be if it was so socially acceptable? Most of the bankers' wives she'd met at Parkview talked primarily about what they owned and what they were planning to buy next, or about which exclusive resort they'd be going to on their next vacation. Because she fit right in, Nancy saw herself as normal. If you had it you had to flaunt it, or else others might suspect you did not have it. Nancy subscribed wholeheartedly to the Parkview notion that a woman was what she possessed. She knew she overdid it sometimes in order to provoke Rob, but he deserved it for being such a controlling, intrusive, hypercritical son of a bitch. It did not occur to her—or to Rob, for psychological insight was not a quality either he or Nancy possessed in abundance—that she might also have become such a compulsive, conspicuous acquirer in reaction to her mother's lack of materialism, which Nancy had experienced as deprivation. In any event, she led Rocco Gatta a merry chase through the streets of Manchester and eventually back to Stratton Mountain.

To Gatta, Thursday night looked like an early one at 702 Stone House Drive. All inside lights were off by 9:20 p.m. He sat in the dark and waited. It was one hell of a way to grow old.

The blue van arrived at 10:40. Del Priore cut his lights before turning down the driveway. By the time he had parked at the bottom, Gatta was speed-dialing Frank Shea.

As it happened, Frank was speaking to Rob in Hong Kong at the time, telling him that another uneventful day and evening had passed at Stratton Mountain.

"Whoops, hold on, Rob. Rocco's calling on my cell right now . . . Rob? Bingo! Del Priore just showed up."

"Thanks, Frank. This is it. I'm going to call her right now."

"Be careful."

"Careful?"

"I know how upset you are, but remember: at this point, you're the one who's been wronged. You don't want to say anything that could come back and bite you."

Rob called the house. No one answered.

He called again. Still no answer.

He called Bryna. "He's there, Bryna! Right now! He just got there and now Nancy won't answer the phone!"

"Rob, take it easy. Try to stay calm."

"Calm? *He's right there*: in my house, with my wife, and she won't answer the phone!"

"She probably turned the ringer off."

"Oh, yeah? So they won't be disturbed?"

"Don't torture yourself, Rob. Whatever is happening is happening. You can deal with it later. There's nothing you can do about it now."

"I'm calling again."

"Rob . . ."

He called again. No answer.

And again. The same.

And once more. Connie picked up.

"Connie, get Nancy, please, and tell her I need to talk to her right now."

"I'm sorry, Mr. Kissel. I think she's upstairs asleep."

"She's not asleep, Connie. Call her. I want to hear you call her up the stairs. Tell her to come down the goddamned stairs and come to the phone."

He heard voices in the background. Connie came back to the phone. "Mrs. Kissel say she call you tomorrow. She not feeling okay."

He hung up. He called Bryna. "I just talked to Connie. Nancy's up in the bedroom with him and she won't come to the phone."

"Rob, even if she does, what good will it do?"

"I'll let you know."

He called back.

Fifteen minutes later, he called Frank Shea.

"I just talked to her."

"Hold the phone, Rob. I've got Rocco calling on the cell . . . Rob? Yeah, I guess you must have talked to her. Rocco tells me Del Priore's van just pulled out of the driveway. Fast."

"No more surveillance, Frank. She's coming home."

"To Hong Kong?"

"Right away. She'll fly out of JFK tomorrow night."

"I guess that's good news."

"We'll see."

Nancy

Rob's phone call changed everything. Nancy panicked when Connie knocked on the bedroom door. She was in an even worse state twenty minutes later when she ran back up the stairs after talking to Rob on his cell phone.

"*You've got to get out of here right now!*" she told Michael. "I don't know where he is. But he knows you're here! He must be spying on us. He could turn up here any minute!"

Nancy couldn't tell where Rob was calling from. He could be as close as the village at the foot of the hill.

"You've got to go, Michael, you've got to go!" She had turned pale and was gasping for breath. "Oh my God, I think I'm having an asthma attack. Hurry, Michael! He can't find you here! Oh my God, I'm fucked. I don't know what he'll do to me. I'll call you as soon as I can."

Michael drove away fast. The next day, Nancy and Zoe and Ethan and Connie drove to JFK and boarded a flight to Hong Kong.

18.

Rob

BEFORE NANCY ARRIVED, ROB MET WITH SHARON SER, A partner at Hampton, Winter and Glynn, which had just been named Hong Kong's Matrimonial Law Firm of the Year. Ser, who had been educated at the London School of Economics, was vice chairman of the Hong Kong Family Law Association, a fellow of the International Academy of Matrimonial Lawyers, and a contributor to the *Credit Suisse Guide to Management of Wealth in Respect of Divorce and Financial Planning.*

Rob explained that his wife had "issues," one of which was "low self-esteem." He said that since the birth of their third child she'd become "distant, depressed, and unhappy." He said he wanted to explore his options, including separation and divorce. His chief concern, he said, was custody of the children. It was a strange, attenuated conversation because Rob couldn't bring himself to say that Nancy was having an affair.

His mood was quite different by the time he e-mailed Bryna on Wednesday, July 30, to tell her about Nancy's return:

> She was a little cold at the beginning, seeing how I would react. I met
> them at the airport. I was very easy going and nice. It was great to see

the kids. I was and am not wearing my wedding ring. I took off the day from work, and spent all day with the kids and a lot with her.

She involved herself in everything we were doing . . . It felt like a family. She has been warmer than she has in over several years. She even went after my hand to hold it when we were in the playroom.

We talked a bit about me having surgery . . . she said she would come. I said it may not be the right thing given the circumstances. She said she was very confused as to why I would have her come back here to HK now, only to be leaving on Sunday or soon . . . She cried. Later, she got over it, but we haven't talked about it again.

I am still waiting to hear from my doctor about details anyway. Meanwhile, I was shocked she wanted to go with me . . . I will not forget though the pain I have felt and the lies that have been told.

If this were how life was, I would be a very happy man. She is really fucking with my head. I love my kids. They told me never to go away again. And I love her, or the way it was 5 years ago, but there is so much shit to get through . . .

He called Bryna the next day to say Nancy was definitely coming with him to New York. "She really wants to be with me for the surgery. She feels I need her there, and she's right."

"Rob, do you really believe that?"

"Believe what?"

"That she want to go to New York just to be with *you*? I mean, I'm sure she cares about your surgery, but I'll bet anything she's thinking she can see Del Priore."

"No, Bryna, that's wrong. If you could have seen how she's been these past few days—"

"Yeah, but Rob, how could you be forgetting that she was in the middle of an affair? She's going to find a way to see that guy while you're in the hospital."

"She couldn't be that cynical, Bryna. This can't be an act."

"I'm sorry, Rob. I think you're making a big mistake."

———————————

It had been a wet and dreary summer in New York, starting with the rainiest June in more than a hundred years. July brought fourteen more rainy days. And it was raining when Rob and Nancy arrived from Hong Kong on the evening of Saturday, August 2. They checked into their suite at the Pierre on Fifth Avenue and Sixty-first Street, overlooking Central Park.

Despite her double jet lag, Nancy went shopping the next day. While she was out, Rob did something extremely out of character: he wrote two pages of notes, in the tiny capital letters that were his trademark, about the state of his heart and mind, and about his perception of the state of his marriage.

I keep my ring in my pocket.

By taking it off I feel that I am emotionally protected against what I know and against how I feel.

The reminders of our marriage are out of sight, yet out of sight reminds me to remember.

To remember what got us here, to where we are today.

To remember never to forget.

Never to forget what we had, and

Never to forget that one cannot just wear a ring.

One has to work at it

The early years are easy and natural—

The love and the fun.

The later years? The kids are beautiful. Time is short.

Time is stretched and something has to give. Do we see it? Do we hear it?
Do we speak of it?

Communication, remembrances of each other, when we are together, what
we love about each other, what we loved about each other, our time
together, exploring each other—That's what gives.

14 years is a long time.

Things get lost.

People change, communication is gone, feelings are hurt, sometimes the
hurt is deep and painful.

People go astray

The hurt is so deep the whole body weeps.

The mind's eye likes to torture—

between images of someone else and images of our love, our beautiful
past.

But the love is stronger, the love is stronger. It felt right being back together. It's time to try and focus.

Can we get it back, can we find a new place? It will be work for us both.

It is work to remember, work to be patient.

Work to change back to the way we started and to find a new place.

We had a love, a love through and through. We need to remember, we need to find.

That's why I keep my ring in my pocket.

It keeps me safe. It brings me love.

———————————

Since the last time he'd operated on Rob, Dr. O'Leary had moved his offices from Park Avenue to Madison. Rob met him there on Monday afternoon. It was pouring, the heaviest rain in two months. They looked again at X-rays and MRI results. Dr. O'Leary reiterated that surgery was the only option. He scheduled the operation for Thursday at 12:30 p.m. at Lenox Hill Hospital.

Back at the Pierre, Rob found an e-mail from Frank Shea asking if he'd arrived safely in New York and inviting him to the Shea home for a meatball dinner. He replied:

Plans changed a bit, and Nancy came with me. She said she wanted to be with me. Things are going very well with us and we are talking about lots of things that are very critical to our survival. There is still a ton of ground to be covered, but at least there is hope.

It's amazing how a man can swallow even the toughest issues when he still cares deeply about his family and his wife. Also, I am focused on getting better. Surgery is scheduled for Thursday. We have been running around to a bunch of doctors and also spending quality time with each other.

Despite the downpour, Nancy had gone out to shop. She liked the Pierre for its five-star elegance, of course, and for its views of Central Park, but mostly because it was within easy walking distance of her favorite boutiques and department stores, particularly Bloomingdale's. If it hadn't been for her mother's break with the Lazarus family years before, Nancy figured, she would have been a part owner of Bloomingdale's.

And despite the downpour, Bill Kissel arrived from Florida. He and Rob had been on nonspeaking terms once again, but because Bill still considered Rob his good son, as opposed to Andrew, he was willing to wipe the slate clean of whatever he'd scrawled across it during his most recent tirade. Bill had never been able to say—to anyone, about anything—that he was sorry, but he hoped Rob would recognize his coming to New York for the surgery as the act of love and concern that it was.

Rob resumed writing in his journal:

Hurt

> *Lies, deception.*
>
> *Can one give up so quickly something that they had a need for?*
>
> *Does she understand the ramifications of her actions?*
>
> *Had to get her back to HK as soon as possible, or all was lost.*

Is she going to contact him?

Will she do it in my time of need?

Every time she walks out, is she going to call him?

I just want to know.

I can deal with the truth—just not lies and deception.

If it is over, if you still need him, just tell me.

Don't let me hang on, working to save it.

We can then both deal with it.

While accepting that she had sex with him, she has not said it—

What do I expect her to say? I don't know.

It's just that all along she denied it.

She made up her "Friend" story and used it to me

To justify e-mails, letters, etc . . .

Should she be made to acknowledge the lies and deceptions in some
way? How?

I need help in answering these questions.

Rob's situation was not without irony. The internationally acclaimed investment banker, unable to manage the most significant investment of his life. The man noted for his ability to make the right
decision no matter how fraught with pressure the situation, now ac-
knowledging—if only to himself—that he needed help.

When Nancy was with him, he told Bryna, he felt a closeness he'd
not experienced for years. But could he trust it? Could he trust her? He
wrote in his journal on August 6:

What a great week. Even though it is terrible circumstances (my opera-
tion) I feel like I am in love again. At Bloomie's, Nancy picked out some
cologne that she liked for me. It was by the pajama section where we were

getting stuff for my hospital visit. I thought that was sweet and nice. 1st time in at least 5 yrs.

I picked the same side of the bed as when we were first married . . . She sleeps facing me rather than turned against the wall. She touches me and holds my hand without me doing it first. She seems to care about anything I am doing versus not caring if I died.

We call the kids together, wake, eat and sleep together. I love being together. I am grateful, surprised, but blissfully happy about her efforts. I hope it carries on because we have a long road and bumpy road ahead of us. . . .

Being together without kids, other distractions, is great. It is as it was 10 years ago. We seem to be enjoying each other's company very much. But my mind wanders back to what I know.

I find it hard to believe that our couple of discussions, while very meaningful and deep, touching on deep feelings and true feelings, were enough to get us where we are right now . . . walking around in respect, love and having fun together.

There must be an element in both of us trying very hard here, because we are not close to over the top in getting our relationship on solid ground. I still don't trust that she is not writing letters or calling her lover when I am tied up with a doctor or other. But what can I do? I can only show my love. . . .

This is like a weird dream.

The real sadness and emptiness is that I love her but may never trust her.

He e-mailed Frank Shea again:

Here we are in NYC having a great time, but I still don't trust her. We have only spent a couple of times apart for more than 10 minutes and I wouldn't be surprised if she made a call to her friend. I wonder if you think it makes sense to put someone on her during the next couple of days while I am in the hospital? We will spend most of the time together, but I would be interested if she leaves to make phone calls outside our room (on a pay phone).

From my perspective, I want to know how hard I should continue here and whether I should give her an ultimatum when I return to Hong Kong. Because without the trust, there is nothing to save. She needs to know that and I need to know what she is really doing.

Frank replied that he didn't think surveillance of Nancy would be worth the cost. If she used a pay phone to make a call it couldn't be traced, whether someone was tailing her or not. Short of documenting a clandestine meeting with Del Priore, there was little that surveillance could accomplish. He added:

It is possible that he may drive to NYC if they are still talking, but given his "country" nature, I'm not sure he would drive all the way here. I agree that once you get back to Hong Kong hard decisions have to be made, but remember that if she tells you that she loves you and wants to make this work, don't throw it away.

As I said many times before, if you need ANYTHING, I will make sure it is done. We have friends at the Pierre and if you need anything there, let me know.

Dr. O'Leary proclaimed the surgery successful. Rob returned to the Pierre on August 10, having been told to allow two weeks for recovery before flying back to Hong Kong.

Frank came to see him on August 14, a week after the operation. It was another day of oppressive heat and stifling humidity, the temperature already in the nineties by the time he walked into the lobby. Rob hobbled slowly and painfully from the elevator to meet him.

"Are you sure you should be doing this?" Frank asked, glancing at Rob's cane.

"Yeah, I'm used to it. My dad made me walk down to Fifty-seventh Street yesterday so he could buy me a pair of shoes he approved of. It took about an hour, but I made it."

They walked slowly into the Rotunda, the Pierre's splashy, self-conscious, and entirely successful attempt to evoke the ambience of the Gilded Age. Taking afternoon tea in the Rotunda had been an obligatory rite of passage for generations of trust-funded New York debutantes. It was only people from New Jersey like Carmela Soprano who met their daughters for tea at the Plaza.

Frank flashed back to his days and nights in the old Seventy-fifth Precinct. He'd come a long way: from the squad room to the tearoom, from a retooled Chevy to the Mercedes 600SL that he'd just left with valet parking.

"So things are okay with Nancy?"

"I think so. I just wish I could feel I could trust her."

"That takes time to rebuild, Rob. You don't just flip a switch to turn it back on."

"I know. But like right now: she's upstairs in the room and for all I know she's calling him collect or she's arranged for him to call her because she knew I'd be down here."

"Even if she calls him collect, a hotel phone charge will turn up on your bill. I can have that checked to see if she was using the phone while you were out. As I said, I've got friends at this hotel. I can also have somebody monitor the times that the room phone's in use for incoming calls."

"I don't know. She'd just make up excuses anyway. The thing is, Frank, I think I've reached the point where I'm going to have to make a decision. Either throw myself back into trying full-time to save the marriage and sticking with it even if I catch her in a lie, or admitting that it just can't work and cutting my losses by getting a divorce as soon as possible."

"Rob, we're talking as friends now, okay? Because I'm no marriage counselor."

"Understood. What do you think I should do?"

"If you want her, go after her with all your heart and soul. But keep your eyes open and watch your back."

"In other words, don't disable the eBlaster."

"Don't disable the eBlaster and don't let her pay the phone bills and credit card bills every month without you putting them under a microscope first."

"That's a hell of a way to have to live."

"Yeah, but maybe it won't be for long. You'll both be back in Hong Kong, you can sit down and have a few more heart-to-hearts, and you can start working with a couples therapist and Del Priore can crawl back into his cave. Nancy will forget all about him and then spend the rest of her life telling you how sorry she is for what she did."

"I hope you're right."

"So do I."

Nancy

During the three days before Rob's surgery, Nancy used calling cards to phone Michael every time she got out of Rob's sight. During the two days he was in the hospital he insisted that she stay with him around the clock, so it was only after he returned to the Pierre that she was able to make plans. Time was short. Rob had booked her a flight that left on Friday, August 15. He said he'd be fine by then and he wanted her back with the kids. Neither of them acknowledged the real reason.

Michael drove down from New Hampshire early on the morning of Thursday, August 14. He reached midtown by 11:00 a.m. and parked his van. Then he walked a few blocks to the fountain in front of the Plaza, where Nancy had said she'd meet him at noon. He was not so "country" that the city fazed him. Down South he'd spent a fair amount of time in Birmingham, and New York seemed the same, only bigger.

As soon as Rob had left the room to go downstairs for lunch with Frank Shea, Nancy took the elevator to the mezzanine level, walked down a flight of stairs, and went out a side door of the hotel. Then she ran across Fifth Avenue to the fountain. The day was hot and muggy, the air greasy and stale, but Nancy was oblivious to the weather. She had eyes only for Michael, and there he was—right where she'd told him to be.

She summoned a horse and carriage and told the driver she wanted the long trip through Central Park. It was seventy-five dollars for the forty-five-minute tour. As soon as she sat back in the carriage, she broke down in tears. She cried all the way. At the end of the ride she told the driver to go around again. This time, she was able to talk.

"I'm so frightened. If he ever finds out you're here I'll be the one in the hospital. I'm not kidding. He's so used to beating me over nothing; I really think he'd try to kill me if he knew. Do you know what I wish? I wish the fucking doctor had slipped with the scalpel and done him in."

"Hey. That's not funny."

"I didn't mean it to be. Michael, you'll never know how bad it's been. Last Christmas, we were on vacation at a ski resort near Vancouver and he threw me against a wall so hard he broke my ribs. Why? Because I said I needed to stay in the hotel room and take care of my sick son instead of skiing."

"Why would that make him mad?"

"Because his father said they'd come there to ski and everybody had to ski, no exceptions. He told me to have the hotel send someone up to stay with Ethan. I said no. He said he'd warned me about defying him and that this was especially bad because I was doing it in front of his father. I told him he could tell his father to kiss my ass and that he could go fuck himself while he was at it. That's when he threw me against the wall."

"And what happened?"

"I left with Ethan that night. I flew straight back to Hong Kong. As soon as he got back, he said he was going to punish me for defying him and he was going to teach me never to disobey him again. Ever since, whenever he wants sex—and he's always drunk, and usually high on coke, too—I refuse, and then he rips my clothes off and forces me."

"Oh, baby doll . . ."

Their second circuit around the park was almost over. They drew closer to the famed midtown hotels: the Ritz-Carlton, the Essex House, the Helmsley Park Lane, and the Plaza on Central Park South; the Trump International and the Mandarin Oriental on Columbus Circle; and on Fifth Avenue, the Sherry-Netherland, and a bit farther on, the Pierre, where Rob was just finishing lunch with Frank Shea. It was a world Nancy had come to know well. It was a world—the five-star world—on which she depended for what little self-esteem she had. It was a world Michael had never known and never would.

Even in the open carriage, the heat and humidity stifled. Sweat poured off both Nancy and Michael and flies buzzed around the neck of the horse that pulled the carriage.

"Why don't you leave him?" Michael asked.

"I can't. He would destroy me in a divorce. I'd lose everything. I wouldn't walk away with a penny. And he'd probably get the children, too."

"I can't believe that. If you got a good lawyer—"

"Michael, you have no idea how powerful he is! And you have no idea what he's capable of. His whole family: their only pleasure in life is grinding other people into dust."

Nancy had booked Michael into a cheap hotel, paying cash in advance, and he stayed in the city overnight. She called him when Rob and Bill went down to the lobby for a drink and he hurried over and she met him at the elevator on her floor and they rushed into the stairwell and made love standing up, to the sound of the echoes of their moans and the smell of musty concrete.

The next day, he rode with Nancy in her taxi to the airport. Two blocks after he'd hopped into the cab she looked out the rear window and shouted: "We're being followed! Driver, go faster!"

"*What?*" Michael said.

"Don't turn around! We can't let them know we've seen them. I've got to lie down on your lap so they won't see me through the window."

"But they already know you're here. It's *your* taxi."

"Don't contradict me, Michael. I can't stand that."

Once her head was in his lap, he turned around. It was mid-afternoon on a midsummer Friday in Manhattan. All he saw was heavy traffic.

"Nobody's following us, baby doll."

"They *are*! I know it!"

She wouldn't sit up. They were creeping along the Van Wyck Expressway when she screamed: "*They're getting closer!* I can feel it!"

"Baby doll, baby doll, there's nobody there."

"Protect me, Michael. You've got to promise you'll always protect me."

"Sure, sure. Always."

From the start he'd known she was high-strung. But it wouldn't be his problem any longer. He'd had the most interesting summer of his life. He'd had a love affair with the classiest, most beautiful, and richest woman he'd ever met, and he was coming out of it with a seven-thousand-dollar wristwatch. Life didn't get better than that.

The day after she got back to Hong Kong, Nancy got an e-mail from Bryna:

hi . . . just thinking about you . . . have you settled back in? are you still double jetlagged? I know this may sound weird but . . . I feel that we haven't really been connecting for awhile . . . I feel that it seems you have a full plate, and that we haven't really been friends as best friends go for sometime . . . I miss you . . . If you think about it, all of our conversations are really short, kinda superficial and we really don't talk much about anything . . . I know this has been a really stressful last 6 months for you, Rob and the kids, but I love you and am here for you if you feel the need . . . I just felt the need to say something . . . please tell me if you feel I'm wrong or out of line . . . this is just my observation

Nancy wrote back right away:

no its not wrong . . . your always right . . . and so fucking perceptive . . .

its mostly been me . . . iv had a pretty shitty summer . . . and dealing with my marriage has been really difficult . . . especially when everyone around you thinks we have the best marriage in the universe . . . that's what iv been hearing for the past 15 years . . .

I agree to a certain extent . . . about the great marriage part . . . but during these past few years . . . with robs continued success . . . its taken it toll . . . we've both acknowledged this for some time . . . and have agreed to see a counselor . . . only the timing has sucked . . . and being seperate since march . . . well . . . you know I felt like I really just wanted to be by myself all summer . . . kinda soul searching stuff . . . I tried to call you one night in new york . . . I was bouncing off the walls . . . needed to really talk . . . but the circuits were all fucked up . . . then you must have been reading my mind . . . cuz you called the next day . . . but I couldn't really talk with rob right there . . .

rob had this 24-7 need and I needed to be there for him hands down

i'm off to school right now . . . Zoe's first day . . . and yes . . . this double jet lag is pretty brutal!!

xo, N

Bryna replied:

as far as us talking about any stuff that's been going on with you or me, I think its great that you would start seeing a therapist, its always good to have another persons take on things . . . so save it all up and tell that person not me . . . Open up your heart and let it all out . . . it's the only way you'll both know where you both stand with each other . . . 15 years . . . a long time . . . history together . . . 3 beautiful children . . . do your best . . . it is worth it . . . WE ALL HAVE TOUGH SPOTS . . . honesty is the only way to get thru . . . love u

Nancy wrote back:

I think I just need to start talking about life in general . . . rob . . . the kids . . . my self . . . asia . . . kind of a tune up so to speak . . . is this mid life crises . . . ????

xo!!!!!

Midlife crisis. An interesting notion. As Joseph Campbell wrote, "Midlife is when you reach the top of the ladder and find that it was against the wrong wall." He also wrote, "We must be willing to get rid of the life we've planned, so as to have the life that is waiting for us."

And then there was Dante.

Midway in our life's journey, I found myself
In dark woods, the right road lost.

———————————

During the ten days between her own arrival in Hong Kong and Rob's return, Nancy conducted Internet searches, using the following terms:

"sleeping pills," "drug overdose," and "medication causing heart attack." On Sunday, August 24, she also made her first call on her new cell phone. She'd set it up so she'd be billed at the Hong Kong International School. She thought of it as her "Michael phone." She would use it only to talk to him. Rob would never see the bills. She'd take cash out of the ATM and open a secret checking account and use that to pay the bills. She was proud of herself for planning everything so well.

The results of her Internet searches fresh in her mind, she talked to Michael for almost four hours. Later, they would both say they couldn't remember talking about anything special. Certainly, they hadn't talked about sleeping pills or drug overdoses or medication causing heart attack.

Autumn

19. LATE AUGUST/SEPTEMBER

ROB COULDN'T DRIVE, BUT HE RODE TO MAINE IN A LIMOU-
sine to pick up Isabel from summer camp. Then the two of them flew
back to Hong Kong. He e-mailed Frank Shea on Tuesday, August 26,
saying his recovery was progressing more slowly than expected. He
added: "The other parts of the equation don't help."

That evening, as was his custom when he was home, Rob poured
himself a few ounces of single-malt scotch from a crystal decanter kept
on a living room sideboard. He thought it tasted slightly peculiar. When
he stood up, he felt so dizzy he almost fell. He was suddenly overwhelm-
ingly sleepy. He assumed he was having a reaction to jet lag combined
with the painkillers he was taking for his back.

The next day, he paid another visit to the offices of Hampton,
Winter and Glynn, this time speaking to a partner named Robin
Egerton. In addition to telling him that his wife was suffering from depression, he acknowledged that she was "committing adultery." He
said she'd been "unfazed" when he'd confronted her about it. He also
said he didn't want to divorce her but was considering separation.
Egerton told him to keep a close eye on the children's passports, lest
Nancy try to go back to the United States and take them with her. Rob
claimed he wasn't worried about that. He said she "enjoyed the expatriate life" too much to leave it behind. Egerton also suggested that he

change his will. Rob told him that was a good idea and he'd get around to it soon.

He made it a point not to take any painkillers during the day. But halfway through his evening scotch he felt the waves of wooziness coming on. This time, he didn't finish the drink. Instead, he went to his home office and booted up eBlaster and Spector Pro to check Nancy's e-mails and to see what Web sites she'd been visiting. He saw the search terms: "sleeping pills," "drug overdose," and "medication causing heart attack."

While Rob was at work the next day, Nancy drove into Central for an appointment with a psychiatrist named Desmond Fung, whose offices were in New Henry House on Ice House Street.

She told Dr. Fung that her husband was abusing her both verbally and physically. She said they'd have terrible fights and that she was so fearful for her safety when she went to bed that she was unable to sleep. He wrote her a prescription for Stilnox, the brand name under which zolpidem was sold in Hong Kong. In the United States, zolpidem was sold as Ambien.

Over the next two nights, Rob felt even woozier from his scotch. On Sunday, August 31, he got up early so he could look through Nancy's pocketbook while she slept. He found the bottle of Stilnox. At that point, he called Frank Shea in New York, where it was Saturday night. He described how he'd been feeling after having a drink and what he'd discovered about Nancy's Internet searches and what he'd found in her handbag. "I don't want to overreact," he said, "but do you think it's possible that she's drugging my drinks?"

"Of course it's possible."

"But why would she do that?"

"Maybe she wants to knock you out so she can sneak out of the apartment and meet lover boy."

"You don't think he's in Hong Kong, do you?"

"Want me to find out?"

"Can you?"

"One phone call, Rob. I can have somebody check his trailer tomorrow. It will be Sunday, so he ought to be home. Call me back in the morning, which will be Sunday night for you."

When Rob called back, Frank confirmed that Del Priore was in New Hampshire.

"Well, that's something to be thankful for."

"I'm not so sure."

"What do you mean?"

"If she's trying to put you out of commission because she's got him stashed at the hotel there, that's understandable. But he's not there, so that's not it."

"And so?"

"I don't know, Rob. But if I were you, I'd stop drinking that single malt."

As it happened, Frank had business in Hong Kong during the second week of September. He and his wife, Denise, would be there for several days, staying at the Harbour Plaza, a four-star hotel on the Kowloon side of Victoria Harbour. Although Rob was no longer a client, Frank remained concerned about him. He also enjoyed his company. When he e-mailed Rob to ask about getting together, Rob replied with an invitation for dinner at the China Club on Tuesday, September 9.

The China Club was private; it would not do for an investment banker as successful as Rob to invite guests to a restaurant that was open to the public. But even among Hong Kong's private dining venues, the China Club was considered unique. David Tang, Hong Kong's highest-profile and most eclectic entrepreneur, had opened it in 1991.

The place became a genuine social phenomenon that brought together political and business leaders of the East and West and encouraged them to mingle in an atmosphere of privilege, leavened with touches of quirky humor. Nowhere else in the world could one have found Princess Diana and the artist Deng Lin, daughter of Deng Xiaoping, sipping cocktails together at the Long March Bar.

In addition to its restaurant—perhaps *the* best in a city acclaimed for its ability to fuse the finest elements of Eastern and Western cuisine—the club contained an art gallery, library, smoking room, and recital hall, where Tang presented lectures, poetry readings, and chamber music concerts. But it was the club's 350 works of art that garnered the most attention. Ranging from Maoist propaganda prototypes to the avant-garde, apolitical abstractions of the newest wave of Chinese iconoclasts, Tang's collection, in the words of the author Orville Schell, "makes the China Club more than just a clever replication of old Shanghai for young, culturally defoliated businessmen in search of ersatz atmosphere" and transforms it into "the beating heart of Hong Kong for this new up-and-coming generation of entrepreneurs."

Many a deal had been broached, many a multimillion-dollar commitment had been secured, many a birthday and anniversary had been celebrated, many a banquet for mainland Chinese dignitaries had been held, many a promise had been made, and many a confidence betrayed at the China Club since its opening twelve years earlier, but it is entirely possible that not until Rob Kissel dined there with Frank Shea and his wife on the night of September 9, 2003, had it been the venue in which a man was told that his wife might be planning to kill him.

Rob was still in pain, walking gingerly and relying heavily on his cane. Nonetheless, throughout the meal he played the role of gracious host. Afterward, he took the Sheas on a tour of the club. When Frank's wife tactfully said she'd like to linger a bit with the artwork, Rob and Frank went to the smoking room, where Rob lit a large Cuban cigar. It should have been a moment of contentment. It was not.

"They're writing to each other," Rob said. "He's sending his letters to the school. I found some in her handbag last week. I was wondering why she was doing so much more volunteer work this year. Now I know."

"These are love letters?" Frank asked. "Not just letters between friends?"

Rob unfolded a piece of paper and read: *"Another day down. Another day closer to seeing you. I am going crazy thinking about you. Whenever a customer comes in the store I want to say, 'Don't bother me. I am thinking about Nancy.' I miss holding you, hearing your voice. I love it when you call my name. It makes me melt."*

"He ain't Shakespeare," Frank said. "But 'another day closer' is not good. Anything funny with your drinks?"

"I took your advice. No scotch at night. But now the coffee in the morning is doing a job. I practically fall asleep at the wheel on my way to the office, and as soon as I get there all I want to do is lie down on my couch and take a nap."

"How much life insurance do you have?"

"About ten million."

"And she's the beneficiary?"

"That's right."

There was a pause. Frank looked deep in concentration. Rob took a long draw on his cigar.

"You might want to change the beneficiary and make sure she knows that you've done it."

"I don't know, Frank. I think that would raise her suspicions."

"*Her* suspicions? About what? That you know the affair is still going on? I think it might be a wake-up call."

"Do you really think I need to worry?"

"Let's review the bidding, Rob. She gets ten million dollars if you die. She's still secretly in touch with her lover. She brings home a bottle of sleeping pills from a doctor you didn't even know she was going to see. And she's on the Web looking for drugs that can kill somebody without leaving a trace. Analyze *that*."

"When you put it that way, it doesn't sound good."

From New York the following week, Frank e-mailed Rob asking him to send hair and urine samples for laboratory analysis. "We will need sample of liquid in glass or rubber vial. Hair closely shaved from underarm or head, 2" long and pencil thick in group. I am getting another opinion on amount tomorrow from another lab we use for hair samples."

Rob replied: "Strange development at home. Nancy has made a 180 degree turn and wants to stay together. A bit of a roller coaster, I have to say. I am going to send the stuff anyway . . ."

When nothing had arrived three days later, Frank got back in touch: "Just following up on my last e-mail about getting the test and forwarding a sample of the liquid."

Rob replied: "I got it. Thanks! Been crazy busy. I am going to send it out today. Kind of in denial, too."

At this point, had this been a movie, the audience would have been shouting to Rob: "Send the samples!" But it wasn't a movie. There wasn't any audience, and Rob never sent the samples. Instead, to take his mind off his troubles, he went out and bought a new Porsche. On September 25, he e-mailed Bryna O'Shea:

Hey . . . I have been crazy busy. Have not gotten home before 11pm for the last couple of nights. We just got approved on a US$100mm deal in korea. First of its kind for Merrill.

Since Nancy came to my office last Tuesday (16th), things have been going along fairly well. We are talking about things and about life, and enjoying each others company, with a little bit of restraint on both sides. I am able to focus on business, and also enjoy the kids. . . . She is taking it slow on the physical side, and that part feels kind of ironic given the circumstances, but I am being patient about this . . .

The car is AWESOME, and I haven't come that close to killing myself.

I am having dinner on Oct. 8th with ex-president Bush in HK . . .

xoxo

Rob

He followed the e-mail with a phone call to Bryna in which he said that he and Nancy had gone to a counseling session on Monday, September 15, and that it had deteriorated when Nancy had jumped up and said, "I want a divorce!" and then had sat down again and had refused to speak further.

But she came to his office the next day, he said—the first time in all the years they'd been in Hong Kong that she'd ever come to his office—and cleared a space on his desk and sat on it and leaned forward and said, "I'm really sorry. I didn't mean what I said in therapy. I don't want a divorce. I really love you."

"So maybe the worst is over," Rob said to Bryna.

"Do you believe that?"

"I don't know. I think she's confused. I don't think she knows what she wants. At least she's with me and not with him. On the other hand, she might be trying to kill me."

"What?"

He told her how he'd had to stop drinking his own scotch and had stopped drinking the coffee Nancy made for him, and about how Frank Shea wanted him to have a lab analyze blood, urine, and hair samples, as well as samples of any drink he thought she'd doctored. He also told her about the Internet searches and the sites to which the results had led Nancy.

"They're dark, creepy, all about drugs and death. Do *you* think she's trying to kill me?"

"Oh, *please*," she said. She knew Nancy well enough to be able to laugh that one off. "Hey, Rob. If you think she is, make sure you remember me in your will."

Rob didn't laugh. Instead, he said, "Promise me that if anything happens you'll make sure my kids are okay."

By the end of September, Rob and Nancy were like intelligence agents operating under deep cover on behalf of warring superpowers. Neither admitted to having a hidden agenda, but each was trying to unearth the other's most closely guarded secrets.

Nancy rifled through the summer's Hong Kong phone bills and found that in June and July Rob had made repeated calls to three different numbers on Long Island. She called Del Priore on her secret cell phone and told him to check the numbers. He called back to say that one of them belonged to an investigation agency named Alpha Group.

"I told you!" she said. "I told you he hired a private detective. I told you he was having me followed, didn't I? Didn't I say he'd stop at nothing? God knows what he's doing now—tapping the phones, bugging my car so he can hear everything I say while I'm driving . . . Michael, he's probably tapping your phone, too. He's probably listening to us talking right now! That fucking son of a bitch. Do you see what I mean? Do you see how he's always in my face? We can't trust him, Michael. There's no telling what he might do."

Meanwhile, Rob was searching obsessively through all of Nancy's drawers and closets, her handbag and her wallet and the pockets of her clothes. He was looking for pills, for love letters, for mysterious receipts. He found nothing. So Rob thought that September had passed without Nancy having spoken to Del Priore. He didn't know that she'd called him forty-eight times.

20. OCTOBER

AS OCTOBER BEGAN, NANCY'S CALLS TO DEL PRIORE BECAME more frequent. Usually, she'd be crying when he answered. Almost always, she'd start by saying that she and Rob had just had a terrible fight and that he'd beaten her and that she was scared.

"I wish I'd never come back," she said. "I wish I'd stayed with you in Vermont. He's having me followed, I *know* he is. And he told me not to bother thinking about taking the kids with me and flying to New York, because he'd locked their passports in a safe."

Del Priore asked her how bad the abuse was. "You don't want to know" was all she'd say. She began to call three or four times a day. She sounded increasingly fearful and more prone to hysteria.

"I don't have any friends here," she said. "I've got no one to talk to. And if I said something now—if I started to talk about how he's beating me, and for how long it's been going on—people would think I was loony for not saying something sooner." She told him that she'd started putting small doses of sleep medication in Rob's drinks, hoping he'd pass out before he tried to force her to have sex. Often, she said, she'd have to lock herself in the bathroom while she waited for the drugs to take effect.

Rob had reached the point where he'd drink nothing but previously un-opened bottles of mineral water at home. He felt tired all the time. The emotional strain of not knowing what to think or how to feel about his wife, combined with the extra stress of trying to make up for all the time he'd lost at work and the lingering aftereffects of spinal surgery, were taking pounds off him that he didn't need to lose and engraving dark circles under his eyes.

He *was* hounding her about Del Priore. He didn't believe her when she insisted that everything between them was over. For one thing, after her seemingly spontaneous visit to his office, she'd gone right back to treating him the way she had ever since he'd come back to Hong Kong. When he was home, she stayed as far from him as possible, clos-ing herself inside her home office for hours at a time, leaving him to care for the children, with Connie's help. He didn't know what else he could say to her so he said nothing, which seemed the better part of valor given the way her face froze into an expression of contempt at the sound of his voice.

At the same time, he felt guilty for not trusting her. He told him-self he was being unfair. He sought to keep matters in perspective. What had the affair been, really? A brief summer fling with a workman dur-ing a period of enforced isolation. It had been an indiscretion, not a true affair. He'd seen Del Priore, he'd talked to the man, he knew for himself that such a trailer-park slug could have nothing of substance to offer Nancy.

As for the insubstantial? There may have been the quick thrill of illicit sex. Distasteful, but hardly uncommon. Expat life was a minefield that few married partners crossed without triggering at least one such explosion. Desires, not all of them licit, could be satisfied with ease while living the imperial life in service to the capitalist raj.

The expat lifestyle was redolent with implicit suggestion: you *can* have it all, you can have it all *now*, and you can have it exactly the way you want it. Moreover, you *should* have it all, because you are a higher form of the species—not tethered to the commonplace, not burdened by the humdrum, not bound by the pedestrian rules that constricted the life of the commoner.

Expat men burned themselves into cinders, working five hundred hours a month to keep the earnings stream flowing—the earnings stream that was the lifeblood of the family. If, on occasion, they enjoyed some of the unspoken fringe benefits of expat life, so be it. As for the women, all that free time and all that free money were overlaid atop a sense of entitlement they wore like Chanel. What was the point of having it all if you couldn't indulge in a bit of white mischief?

It was remarkable, really, how many members of Hong Kong's expat elite who had no time for their own wives managed to find time for the wife of a neighbor or colleague. Less remarkable, perhaps, was how many wives went the way of Nancy: fleshing out their rough-trade fantasies through dalliance with social inferiors, seeking the tingle that had animated Lady Chatterley when she'd heard gamekeeper Mellors say, "Let's live for summat else. Let's not live ter make money."

It could be great fun to play on the other side of the tracks as long as you knew you'd never have to live there. So why wouldn't Nancy glory in her dream? "The least little bit o' money'll really do," Mellors the gamekeeper told Lady Chatterley. "Just make up your mind to it, an' you've got out o' th' mess."

But Nancy was cut from a different cloth than Constance Chatterley. Even as she keened over her lost youth and freedom, she could not help but embrace her chains. "When you come right down to it," she told one Hong Kong acquaintance, "there's really nothing in the world as good as money."

Then Rob took that away from her, or at least took away her ability to spend it freely. In early October, he examined bank charges for September. There were repeated ATM withdrawals of $1,500 and $1,000. Nancy had converted the cash to checks that she sent to Del Priore to compensate him for having lost his job because of her.

"What's this?" he asked Nancy. "Why were you withdrawing that much cash?"

"I don't know. I remember I gave Connie some to buy groceries. And I think I had lunch somewhere that didn't take credit cards. I tipped some of the staff at the Marina Club. *Listen, goddamn it, I can't remember!* Why are you giving me a hard time?"

"You're sending money to Del Priore, aren't you?"

"You're crazy, do you know that? Do you think you can insult me that way?"

She ran at him and tried to punch him. He grabbed her arm and spun her into a wall.

Her face went white. "Oh, boy, you've just made a *big* mistake. I'm not going to let you live *this* down. You'll pay for this, you bastard. And I want my credit cards back."

Rob cut the credit cards up and left the pieces in a pile on her desk. Before leaving for work the next morning, he said, "Here's the way it's going to work: every morning from now on, you're going to tell me exactly what you need for household expenses and I'll give you exactly that much in cash. And at the end of the day I want to see the receipts."

"Fuck you," she said, in front of Connie and the children.

Rob called Bryna to tell her what had happened.

"Be careful, Rob," she said. "Now you've stripped away her dignity. You take away her credit cards, you take away her sense of self. She's not going to accept that lying down."

———————————

The Bank of Taiwan planned to honor former president George H. W. Bush at a banquet on October 8. Rob and Nancy had been invited not only to the banquet, but also to the much more exclusive cocktail reception before the dinner.

Rob had become a Republican almost as soon as he'd become an investment banker—two sides of the same coin was how he viewed it—and he held the entire Bush family in high esteem. The Bushes knew how to make money and they knew how to spend it to buy power, two of the skills he most admired. In addition, Prescott Sheldon Bush, father of George H. W. Bush and grandfather of current president George W. Bush, had been a significant investment banker in his time.

And Rob wasn't the sort of Jew who fretted about the foundation of the Bush fortune. As a director of both Brown Brothers Harriman and the Union Banking Company, whose assets were seized by the United States government in 1942 under a trafficking with the enemy law, Prescott S. Bush had invested both for and in German companies known to be aiding and abetting the Nazi Party.

As the British newspaper *The Guardian* put it, "even after America had entered the war and when there was already significant information about the Nazis' plans and policies, he worked for and profited from companies closely involved with the very German businesses that financed Hitler's rise to power . . . the money he made from these dealings helped to establish the Bush family fortune and set up its political dynasty."

Like politics, investment banking was not work for the morally squeamish.

Nancy's concern was her dress. Obviously, it had to be new. It also had to be both expensive and attention-getting. Paying for it would not be a problem, even without her credit cards. Like all bankers' wives in Hong Kong, she knew dress shops eager to have milady open a personal charge account.

As the big night grew near, Nancy began to glow with excitement. Proximity to a former Republican president of the United States, no matter how brief, would give her massive social cred in tower 17. She followed her sense of adventure in buying her banquet dress.

Other than Nancy, no one but Rob, Connie, and the salesperson who sold it to her ever saw the dress. Later, Connie shied from attempting to describe it. All she would say was that it had permitted Nancy to showcase the new tattoos on her shoulder and that it had triggered a furious fight.

Nancy later claimed Rob had physically torn the dress from her body. Connie didn't see that, but she later told Bryna that the argument had lasted so long that—after Nancy retreated to her closet to put on something less outrageous—they were so late leaving that they missed the reception.

It threatened to be the worst social catastrophe of their stay in

Hong Kong, but Nancy wasn't the sort to let opportunity slip entirely from her hands. In the middle of the banquet, she left the table at which she and Rob were seated and approached the ex-president. In fact, she tapped him on the shoulder as he ate.

"My husband is a great fan of yours," she said. "Would you mind if he talks to you?"

Bush, ever the gentleman, obliged. He excused himself from his table, stood, and walked with Nancy to meet Rob. He even posed for a picture with them both.

———————

The next day Nancy e-mailed Bryna. She made no mention of having had her credit cards taken away or of meeting George Bush or of having any quarrel about a dress. She was thinking about her body. She was thinking about making it look better for Michael. She was thinking about how she could get to the United States to see Michael. She knew Rob would never let her go to New York. But if she had a reason to go to San Francisco... "Things here on the home front are really terrific ... I wanna talk to you on the phone ... these past few mornings for me have been so hectic ... then all of a sudden its 4 in the afternoon ... midnight for you ... I miss u!!!!!"

Two days later, she told Rob, "Guess what. I'm going to San Francisco for a boob job."

"I don't think so."

"It doesn't matter what you think. Bryna and I are going to have boob jobs together. She's already made the appointment."

Rob called Bryna. "I think she's using you as an excuse," he said. "I think she's going to see Del Priore."

"I don't know, Rob. The day after a boob job isn't the best time for a clandestine meeting with your lover."

"Think about it: why else would she have it done in San Francisco? Why not do it right here?"

"A: she doesn't trust Chinese doctors. B: I'm still her best friend and she thinks it'll be fun to have it done together."

"This time, I think *you're* being naïve."

He found the phone bills the next day. He'd been searching obsessively for proof that she was still in touch with Del Priore. One shred of evidence that she was still lying to him and he could stop the charade, put an end to the anguish of uncertainty, call Sharon Ser at Hampton, Winter and Glynn and move ahead with the divorce.

She'd left her handbag lying on a side table in the dining room, right next to the lead statuette. He opened it and there were two months of bills for a cell phone he'd known nothing about, addressed to Nancy care of the Hong Kong International School. They showed more than a dozen calls to Del Priore in late August, forty-eight calls to him in September, and more than thirty calls to him during the first week of October—almost a hundred calls to the man with whom she'd claimed that she was no longer having an affair. Everything she'd said and done since early June had been a lie. He felt sick.

He did not confront her. There was no point. There was no point in anything to do with her anymore. For perhaps the first time in his life, this driven, relentlessly competitive man was forced to admit defeat. He'd lost his true love to the stereo guy. Except for custody of the children, the rest was just arithmetic.

He did not confront her, but when he found the cell phone itself hidden beneath her underwear in a bedroom dresser drawer, he took it. As he drove to work the next day he threw it out his Porsche window.

He told Bryna about it. He said he'd give Nancy anything she wanted except the children. "I won't let her move back to New York or Vermont with the kids. I'll be based in Tokyo, and I'll fly back here and see them on weekends. I'll get my own apartment in Parkview. Connie can live there and work for me. I'm not going to fight her. As far as I'm concerned, she can even bring Del Priore to Hong Kong. All I care about is being able to see my kids."

"Maybe you're not going to fight," Bryna said, "but she is. Think about it. She'll be losing a lot and she's not going to let it go without a battle."

"Losing what? She won't be losing anything except me. And she's not going to consider that a loss."

"Money, Rob. Lifestyle. You say you're not going to fight about money, but whatever she gets in a divorce will have to last her for the rest of her life. You won't be supporting her anymore. And there's quite a difference between being Mrs. Kissel and being Mrs. Del Priore. Her life has revolved around her special status as an expat wife for the past six years, and she'll lose that overnight."

"It's her choice."

"That's not how she'll see it. You'll be taking her lifestyle away from her, Rob. And one thing we both know about Nan: to her, there's not much difference between lifestyle and life."

When Nancy discovered that both her phone and phone bills were missing, she could feel Rob closing in. Her affair with Michael was the one thing in her life that was hers and hers alone, the one thing over which she and she alone had control. And now Rob, who, as she saw it, had taken her individuality, her youth, her looks, her creativity, her spontaneity, and her independence, was going to take her love affair away from her, too.

She panicked. She began to spend all day in Central, calling Michael collect from pay phones. There were days when she would call him every ten minutes, always from a new pay phone in Central, her voice brittle with fear, her words giving way to her sobs. His phone bill for October was more than ten thousand dollars. He later negotiated a settlement with AT&T.

She went to Central because she thought she'd be safer there, in the crowds. She told him she was sure Rob was having her followed. She was afraid he might do more. Suppose he ordered his men to grab her and drive her somewhere and beat her? Suppose he arranged to have her kidnapped? Suppose he used his power and money to have the police arrest her and charge her with some awful crime?

"He's hired people, Michael. I know it. I can feel them watching me wherever I go. Oh, God—I think that's one of them! I've got to get off this phone."

Five minutes later: "They're after me. His people. They've been following me ever since I left the apartment—wait, I've got to go. I can't stay here."

It was worse than the taxi ride to JFK.

"Michael, have *your* phone checked. He's probably having it tapped. I can't take this anymore. I'm not safe anywhere. I don't know what to do."

"Do you want me to fly out there?"

"No, no! You can't do that. There's no telling what his people would do. You have no idea how powerful he is, how high up. You don't know how much he can control. Nobody can stop him. He can do whatever he wants."

Five minutes later: "He's on such a warpath I don't know what to do. The hammer has come down. I'm fucked. Oh, I'm so, so fucked."

Michael wondered what passersby in Hong Kong must have thought: an American lady, surely well dressed, clutching a pay phone, looking around frantically, crying loudly enough to be heard over traffic.

She told Michael she'd sent him a love letter via Federal Express and that a few days later Rob had angrily quoted back to her some of the exact language she'd used in the letter.

"Do you see what I mean, Michael? He's so powerful he's able to bribe FedEx."

Yet she was active and appeared energetic and untroubled to acquaintances as she took photographs at the Hong Kong International School to get ready for a fund drive. In e-mails to Bryna she seemed upbeat and chipper, eager to get to San Francisco. Her ability to step in and out of a state of tormented agitation, seemingly at will, was remarkable.

As for Rob, even as he readied himself to tell Nancy that he was going to seek a divorce, even in the midst of detailed analysis of the billions of dollars of distressed debt that the Bank of China would be auctioning on November 4—by a considerable margin the largest debt portfolio he'd ever had the chance to acquire—he tried to keep things in perspective. At 10:21 a.m. on October 22 he was in the middle of a high-level meeting about the Bank of China bid. It was 10:21 p.m. in Florida and Rob, a lifelong Yankees fan, knew the third game of the Yankees-Marlins World Series was on. He texted Frank Shea: "What's the score?"

Frank replied: "1-1 Top 6th Jeter on 1st 0 outs Giambi up."

Rob: "Keep me up on the score if you can! In an all day meeting . . . what a hassle . . ."

Frank: "Top of 7th very tough Miami 6th for Yanks but still 1-1."

The Yankees scored in the top of eighth inning and added four runs in the ninth to win the game.

―――――――――――

On Thursday, October 23, Nancy saw her internist, Dr. Annabelle Dytham, one of the first expat women she'd met in Hong Kong and someone she considered not only her doctor but her friend. It had been a year since her last appointment and Dr. Dytham greeted her by saying, "Well, you're certainly looking good."

That wasn't what Nancy wanted to hear. She immediately let fly a torrent of complaints about how bad she was feeling and why. She said her husband had been beating her regularly since an incident that had occurred during a ski vacation the previous Christmas. She said he was constantly demanding sex and would hit her when she refused. "Alleged assault and subsequent violations," Dr. Dytham wrote, then jotted, "low libido."

The doctor found no visible signs of physical abuse, but Nancy said her husband's violence had her living in a state of constant terror. She said that despite taking the Stilnox that Dr. Fung had prescribed, she wasn't able to sleep. She said she needed something stronger—perhaps Rohypnol, which she had learned about in her Internet research.

Rohypnol, a.k.a. Mexican Valium a.k.a. roofies, was often referred to as the date-rape drug. Besides being ten times stronger than Valium, it had the unique effect of causing anterograde amnesia, meaning that events that occur after ingestion of the drug do not reach long-term memory. The practical effect was that a woman who was raped after having been rendered unconscious, or nearly so, by Rohypnol would be unable to recall the event. Its sale was banned in the United States, where it was classified as a Schedule IV substance under the Controlled Substances Act. Possession or distribution of Rohypnol carried the same penalties for possession or distribution as Schedule I drugs such as heroin. But throughout Europe and South America, as well as in Hong Kong, Rohypnol could be prescribed and sold legally. Nancy persuaded Dr. Dytham that nothing less potent would enable her to escape to the arms of Morpheus.

Rob was confident he'd be well represented in his divorce action by Hampton, Winter and Glynn. But there were a lot of capable lawyers doing lucrative matrimonial work in Hong Kong because there were a lot of expat marriages falling apart. What if Nancy found a lawyer who was even better than his?

Rob knew he was the wronged party and therefore should be able to dictate the terms of the divorce. But he also knew the law didn't necessarily favor the righteous—it rewarded whoever knew how to play the system best. It was a competition, just like investment banking. Right and wrong had nothing to do with it, and you had to do whatever was necessary to win. He recalled an episode of *The Sopranos* in which Tony had contacted all the best divorce lawyers in New Jersey to make certain that if Carmela tried to hire one they'd have to say no, that representing her would be a conflict of interest because they'd already had a discussion with her husband. The tactic had worked well for Tony.

On the morning of Friday, October 24, Rob called the corporate headhunter who'd recruited him for Merrill Lynch to ask if he could provide a list of the most prominent divorce lawyers in Hong Kong. The headhunter said he could and that he'd fax the names to Rob early the following week.

Over the weekend, the Florida Marlins beat the Yankees to win the World Series. On Sunday, October 26, Rob e-mailed Frank Shea: "Frank—I am in tears after that game . . . On to the next . . . Go Knicks!"

In his office for the next three days, Rob paid more attention than usual to incoming faxes. When the list of divorce lawyers had not arrived by Wednesday, October 29, he called the headhunter.

"I faxed it Monday afternoon," the headhunter said. "Hold on, let me check . . . yeah, I sent it to . . ." He read the number to which he'd faxed the list.

"Oh, shit!" Rob said. "That's my home number, not the office."

Ruefully, he described the mix-up to his Merrill Lynch colleague and friend, David Noh, the only person besides Bryna in whom he'd been confiding about Nancy.

"I'm going to have to talk to her," Rob told Noh. "She's seen the list."

The next day, Thursday, October 30, he gave Noh an update: "It wasn't so bad. She said she didn't want to talk about it until next week because she didn't want to spoil Halloween for the kids."

On Tuesday, October 28, Nancy had gone to a walk-in clinic, complaining of back pain. She was given a prescription for twenty tablets of dextropropoxythene, a drug that, according to an English National Health Service report available on the Internet, "can cause rapid death."

On Thursday, she went back to Dr. Fung and told him that the Stilnox had not improved her insomnia. Noting that she had a "very tenacious sleep problem," he gave her prescriptions for three additional medications: lorazepam (Lorivan), Axotal, and amitriptyline. Lorivan was a benzodiazepine and central nervous system depressant whose most common side effect was drowsiness. Axotal contained a barbiturate that caused drowsiness, an effect markedly increased if taken in conjunction with a central nervous system depressant such as Lorivan. Amitriptyline was a tricyclic antidepressant that frequently caused drowsiness.

By the time she took her children trick-or-treating in Parkview on Friday night, October 31, Nancy had in her possession Stilnox (a.k.a. Ambien), Rohypnol, dextropropoxythene, Lorivan, Axotal, and amitriptyline: four drugs that caused drowsiness, one that caused outright unconsciousness, and one that could cause sudden death.

That night, she e-mailed Bryna O'Shea: "I got a better deal at the Fairmont . . . $US.205 per night . . . the Ritz is $US.230 . . . im pretty excited about all of this . . . mostly to see you!!!! I miss you terribly . . ."

Rob had met with Robin Egerton at Hampton, Winter and Glynn that afternoon. Egerton found him to be "pragmatic and analytical" during their discussion about divorce. Rob mentioned that he'd raised the subject with Nancy earlier in the week but that she'd wanted to defer a serious talk about it until after Halloween. He said he planned to have that talk with her on Sunday.

21. NOVEMBER

ON SATURDAY MORNING, NOVEMBER 1, NANCY WAS A BUN-
dle of energy. Bringing Isabel and Zoe with her, she photographed the
children of her Parkview friend Samantha Kriegel. Nancy had been
taking a lot of pictures at Parkview, at HKIS, and at the United Jewish
Congregation. She told acquaintances that she wanted to open her own
photo studio but that her husband wouldn't let her because he considered it "a waste of time."

When she finished taking the Kriegel pictures, she put Isabel into
the Mercedes and took her to HKIS for her dance lesson. Connie took
Zoe to a playdate. Rob remained upstairs in the apartment with Ethan.
When Connie came back from dropping Zoe at the playdate, she saw
Rob sitting cross-legged on the playroom floor, head in hands.

He looked up at her and said, "I have no idea what's going on." She
didn't know if he meant about the day's schedule or about what was
happening to his marriage and his life. She did not think it appropriate
to ask.

Sunday, November 2, brought unusually thick haze to Hong Kong.
Visibility at the airport fell to three thousand feet, the lowest ever re-

corded due solely to haze. You couldn't even see across the harbor. Cars passed with headlights on, and the air carried the metallic taste of smog.

Rob and Nancy had an early-morning argument. He got tired of waiting for her to perfect her appearance before going to the Sunday-morning discussion group at the United Jewish Congregation. He put the children in his new Porsche and drove them to Sunday school at the UJC on Robinson Road in Mid-Levels. Nancy left in her Mercedes a few minutes later.

As she drove past the Parkview Hotel, she noticed a father and daughter walking toward the taxi stand. The girl was carrying a UJC school bag.

"If you're on your way to UJC, I can give you a ride," Nancy said.

Andrew Tanzer, Hong Kong bureau chief for *Forbes* magazine and a resident of tower 3, was glad to accept. He and his daughter, Leah, got into the Mercedes. He made a remark about the foul air.

"Isn't it awful?" Nancy said. "My husband is with Merrill Lynch. We've been here since ninety-seven and it gets worse every year. At this rate, we'll have to leave, just for the sake of the children's lungs." The poor visibility didn't slow Nancy's driving. She sped along the winding two-lane road that led to the Aberdeen Tunnel, chattering cheerfully all the way.

The Sunday school program lasted until 12:30 p.m., which gave parents ample time to socialize after the adult gathering. The morning's discussion, led by UJC rabbi Lee Diamond, had focused on Malaysian prime minister Mahathir Mohamad's recent statement that "Jews rule this world by proxy. They get others to fight and die for them." Unsurprisingly, UJC sentiment ran strongly against Mr. Mohamad's point of view. Rob participated actively.

He was still energized afterward, as he stood in the cafeteria lobby among a group of the fellow bankers and lawyers who made up a large part of the UJC's membership. The group included Jonathan Zonis of the law firm Clifford Chance, Ian Ingram-Johnson of the law firm Allen and Overy, and Jonathan Ross, a Bank of China lawyer (formerly with Skadden, Arps) who had the distinction of being the bank's only *gweilo* executive. They were discussing the Bank of China's unprecedented distressed-debt auction, scheduled for Tuesday.

With sealed bids due in forty-eight hours, the time seemed ripe for circumspection. To the surprise of the others, however, Rob began to outline details of the Merrill Lynch offer. He also had a few pointed words for Jonathan Ross, complaining about a lack of documentation in some of the information the Bank of China had supplied.

Nancy interrupted to say she was leaving in order to take Isabel to a party at the Aberdeen Marina Club. Rob brought Zoe and Ethan into the cafeteria for lunch. Zoe and Leah Tanzer were in the same Sunday school class. Zoe asked if she could have Leah over for an afternoon playdate. Because it was Connie's day off, Rob called Nancy for approval.

Once arrangements were made, Rob got up to leave. He told Tanzer, whom he'd not met before, to bring Leah over as soon as he could.

"Daddy, I want to ride with Zoe," Leah said.

Rob smiled but shook his head. "Sorry," he said to Andrew Tanzer. "I'm in my new Porsche. There's not enough room."

They said good-bye and Tanzer and his daughter started walking across the parking lot to the taxi stand. Halfway there, he saw Rob zip past in his silver Porsche, top down and lights on in the smog. The front passenger seat was empty. At first, Tanzer thought it odd that Rob had turned down Leah's request for a ride, but he concluded that he must be such a conscientious parent that he wouldn't let a child ride in the front seat.

Zoe had given Leah the door code to tower 17, so Tanzer and his daughter were able to take the elevator to the twenty-second floor without calling first from below. Tanzer rang the bell and Rob answered. As Leah ran in to join Zoe, Rob invited Tanzer to step inside. It was 2:30 p.m.

The two men walked into the living room and gazed out the windows at the miasma of smog, which showed no signs of dissipating. Rob smiled cordially but did not ask Tanzer to sit. The *Forbes* man, who was about Rob's age, made small talk about working in Hong Kong. He could hear his daughter and Zoe laughing happily as Ethan ran into the playroom to join them. He saw no sign of Nancy.

"You've got an excellent Bordeaux there," Tanzer said, pointing at a bottle of wine that stood next to the decanter of single-malt scotch on the sideboard. The level of single malt had not dropped in weeks.

"Yes, I find there are still some good buys here, if you know where to look."

Their conversation sputtered along. Rob seemed in no hurry to show Tanzer the door, but neither did he offer his visitor either a seat or a drink. After half an hour, Tanzer asked for a glass of water. Rob went to the kitchen and returned with one for each of them. As he finished his, Tanzer said he'd better be going and asked Rob to call when he wanted someone to come back for Leah.

The two men walked toward the door.

"Don't go, Daddy!" Leah shouted, running in from the kitchen. "We're making milk shakes with Zoe's mommy."

Zoe ran in from the kitchen, too. "Wait 'til you taste these!" she said, jumping with excitement.

Rob shrugged at Tanzer and smiled. Tanzer was by now more

than a little impatient to leave but realized it would be rude to decline the children's offer.

A moment later, Zoe and Leah reappeared. Each girl was holding a tall glass filled with thick pink liquid.

"Here it is, Daddy!" Zoe said. "Special for you!" At the same time, Leah handed a glass to her father.

"Drink it, Daddy," Zoe said to Rob. "It's yummy."

Tanzer took a sip. "What's in it?" he asked.

"Lots of good stuff," his daughter said. "There's bananas and crunched-up cookies and lots and lots of other things."

"How's yours, Daddy?" Zoe asked.

"Mmmm," said Rob, a pink milk mustache on his upper lip.

"Okay, here goes," Tanzer said, draining his glass in one gulp.

Rob did the same. "You're right, sweetie," he said to Zoe. "That was delicious."

Tanzer smiled gamely. He'd found the shake appallingly sweet and with a consistency reminiscent of Metamucil. It also left an unpleasant aftertaste. He thanked Rob again and said he'd be back later for Leah.

As he was walking out the door, Nancy popped out of the kitchen. "Hi and good-bye," she said. "The girls are having a great time."

"Thanks again," Tanzer said. "By the way, what was in that milk shake?"

"Oh, I can't tell you *that*. It's a secret recipe."

An hour later, Andrew Tanzer passed out on his living room couch. His wife couldn't wake him. This was so out of character that she bent down to see if she could smell alcohol on his breath.

At about the same time, Rob brought Ethan down to the Parkview playground. He thought Zoe and Leah deserved some playtime by themselves. The main item on his agenda for the rest of the day was a 7:30 p.m. conference call with his distressed-debt team—a final dot the *i*'s and cross the *t*'s session in advance of Tuesday's Bank of China auction.

Even at Parkview, the late afternoon air was scarcely breathable. Rob brought Ethan to the indoor section of the playground. He sat on a lawn chair to watch his son play. For a few minutes, he chatted with a Parkview neighbor named David Friedland. Then David Noh called. Noh wanted to straighten out a few details in advance of the seven-thirty conference call.

Less than a minute into the conversation, Noh realized something was amiss. He'd asked a question about the anticipated growth rate of the value of certain parcels of Hong Kong real estate that the Bank of China was including in the auction.

"It's the export growth," Rob said. "We gotta pay attention to import-export."

"Rob? No, no, I'm talking about the property value estimates."

"Do you know what's happening with exports? What we really need is better Internet connections with the mainland."

"Rob? Are you feeling all right?"

"Import-export, David. That's the name of the game." He laughed. His voice was slurred. "It's all about the balance of trade. The balance of trade. But what about the balance of traders? Nobody's looking at that."

"Rob, you're not making much sense. Are you sure you're all right?"

"You can't have an import without an export. That's what everybody forgets."

"Listen, Rob. I'm going to give you a couple of hours to clear your head. I'll have the conference call ready to go at seven thirty."

Noh hung up, worried. He knew that this was the day when Rob intended to tell Nancy he was going to divorce her. Perhaps Rob had taken a few drinks to get his courage up. But it wasn't like Rob to drink in advance of a crucial conference call. Perhaps he'd already told her, and her reaction had driven him to drink. That scenario didn't make sense either. None of it made sense to David Noh, but he was sure Rob would explain it in the morning.

Connie was still out at a Sunday afternoon concert, but Min had come back to the apartment.

"I know it's your day off, Min, but I have to ask you to do me a favor," Nancy said. "Zoe and her friend are playing, and I don't want to leave them alone, but Ethan is supposed to be at a picnic by six o'clock. Would you take him, please? He's down in the playground with Mr. Kissel. Mr. Kissel will tell you where the picnic is. He can't stay long. I want him back here by seven. And tell Mr. Kissel that I need *him* up here right away."

As soon as Min left, Nancy called the Tanzer apartment to say that Leah was welcome to stay for supper.

"Thank you," her mother said, "but not tonight. She still has homework and a piano lesson."

"That's too bad," Nancy said. "Then I guess Mr. Tanzer will stop by soon to pick her up?"

"I'll have to send our maid," Mrs. Tanzer said. "As soon as my husband got back here this afternoon, he passed out on the couch. I've never seen anything like it. He's breathing, but I still can't wake him. I'm actually starting to worry."

"Oh, don't worry," Nancy said, "I'm sure he'll be fine. When will you be sending your maid?"

"Would seven o'clock be too late? I'm just starting to make supper."

"Not at all. The girls are having a great time. Seven it is."

———

At the playground, Min told Rob that Nancy needed him upstairs right away. She asked if she could borrow his watch in order to be sure she got Ethan home on time.

"Take good care of it," Rob said, handing Min his $15,000 gold Cartier.

He sounded sleepy. He also seemed unsteady on his feet.

Parkview's closed circuit television cameras showed him entering the tower 17 elevator at 6:06 p.m.

———

The Tanzers' maid arrived at the Kissel apartment precisely at 7:00 p.m. to pick up Leah. Isabel was just returning from the party at the Aberdeen Marina Club. Min showed up with Ethan at the same time, adding to the commotion.

"Shush, shush, shhhhhh!" Nancy said, waving a finger. "Keep your voices down."

She gestured down the hallway toward the closed bedroom door.

"Daddy is sleeping."

PART THREE
THE HOUR OF LEAD

After great pain, a formal feeling comes—
The Nerves sit ceremonious, like Tombs—

· ·

This is the Hour of Lead—
Remembered, if outlived,
As Freezing persons, recollect the Snow—
First—Chill—then Stupor—then the letting go—

—EMILY DICKINSON

Missing Person

22.

Changes which occur within the first 2 hours after death are referred to as early postmortem changes. These alterations are caused by lack of effective cardiac pumping of oxygenated blood resulting in a loss of the usual skin color. This "pallor" is first noticed in very light-skinned people as early as 15 to 30 minutes after death . . . At the same time, the skeletal muscles of the body, including the sphincters, relax. It is during this period that fecal soiling may occur . . .

Rigor mortis, algor mortis and livor mortis are referred to as late postmortem changes because they are first observed beginning at about 2 to 4 hours after death.

Rigor mortis, or the postmortem stiffening of the muscles, is a reversible chemical change of the muscles. It begins in all skeletal muscles shortly after death, but is first noticeable in the facial muscles as tightening of the jaw at 2 to 3 hours postmortem . . . After 24 hours, the entire body will be rigid . . .

Algor mortis is the normal cooling of a body which takes place as the body equilibrates with the environment after death. The normal metabolic processes of the body which maintain a core temperature of 98.6°F during life cease at death and the body temperature will tend to approach the ambient temperature. In most circumstances, this means that bodies cool after death at an approximate rate of 1.5°F per hour . . .

Livor mortis (also called livor or lividity) refers to the gravitational pooling of blood in dependent parts which occurs after death. In other words, the blood pools on the down side of the body because it is no longer being circulated by the heart. Livor can be first recognized as soon as 15 minutes after death by trained observers, but it is ordinarily first evident at about 2 hours postmortem . . .

—*Forensic Taphonomy: The Postmortem Fate of Human Remains,* edited by William D. Haglund and Marcella H. Sorg

WHEN NANCY CAME INTO THE KITCHEN MONDAY MORNING to supervise Connie's serving of breakfast to the children, Connie noticed a bandage between the thumb and forefinger of her right hand.

"It's nothing," Nancy said. "I burned it on the toaster."

One of the children asked where Daddy was.

"He's at work. He had to leave early today."

Connie looked at the counter next to the breakfast table where Min had left Rob's Cartier watch the night before. Connie could never remember him having gone to work without it.

Nancy called Min into the kitchen. "You won't need to clean the bedroom this morning," she said. "I don't want you to go in there today. Do you understand?" Min said she did.

Connie took Isabel and Zoe down to wait for the school bus at seven thirty. Then she walked Ethan to his preschool, the Parkview International Pre-School, called PIPS. Nancy went back to the bedroom and closed the door. She called Michael Del Priore in New Hampshire, where it was just after 7:30 on Sunday night. They spoke for twenty-four minutes.

She hung up. Then she wrote an e-mail to Scotty the Clown. She had booked Scotty and his partner Lulu for a show at the Hong Kong International School. She was supposed to meet Scotty for lunch on Tuesday, but she canceled. She wrote: "My husband is not well and I need to take care of some things. Sorry. I will be in touch soon."

When Connie returned to the apartment after having taken Ethan to PIPS, Nancy told her to run down to the Parkview PARKnSHOP Superstore.

"I need some bleach powder," Nancy said.

As soon as Connie left, Nancy went back to the bedroom and closed the door. She called Links Relocations on Des Voeux Road in Central, a leading mover of expats and their goods between Hong Kong, Shanghai, Beijing, and anywhere else in the world. She said she wanted twenty packing cartons delivered that afternoon. No, she didn't yet want to discuss details of any impending move, for now she just wanted the cartons.

She also called the Parkview property manager. "We have a storeroom in the basement of tower fifteen," she said, "but I'd like to rent another one right away." He told her that none were available. She expressed considerable annoyance and hung up.

Then she went out to shop.

The weather had changed dramatically overnight. High pressure had wiped the sky clear of haze, the sun was shining brilliantly, and the relative humidity had dropped to a year's low of 30 percent. With the temperature climbing toward the mid-eighties, the weather was as close to perfect as Hong Kong weather got.

Nancy drove to the twenty-thousand-square-foot Tequila Kola Designer Warehouse in the thirty-story Horizon Plaza shopping mega-mall on Ap Lei Chau Island in Aberdeen. Tequila Kola, promising "Seduction of the Senses," was a home furnishings store that catered almost entirely to expats who didn't have to count the zeroes before the decimal point. Nancy knew it well. She breezed in at about 10:00 a.m. on Monday, talking loud and fast and keeping her sunglasses on. "I love that Spanish chandelier," she called out to the first salesperson she saw, Suzara Serquina. "It's *awesome!*" Then she beckoned. "Get over here. There's a lot I need and I don't have much time."

Over the next hour she bought sheets, pillows, pillowcases, cushions, a bedspread, a small rug, and a chaise longue. She insisted on Tuesday-morning delivery. She said she'd be back Tuesday afternoon to look at carpets. Ms. Serquina noted that she signed the charge slips without even looking at the total.

When she got back to the apartment she told Min to stop housecleaning because there was more shopping to be done. She gave her a list:

rope

packing tape

polyethylene sheeting (large sheets)

When Min left, Nancy went into the bedroom and closed the door. Between 11:30 a.m. and 5:00 p.m. she emerged only long enough to get the bleach powder that Connie had bought and the various items purchased by Min and bring them back to the bedroom.

Connie picked Ethan up at PIPS, brought him home, fed him lunch, put him down for his nap, got him up again, and took him to his

3:00 p.m. swimming lesson. Isabel and Zoe were occupied by after-school activities and did not return home until almost 5:00 p.m.

As Connie microwaved dinner, she asked Isabel if she knew whether her father would be home to join them.

"No," Isabel said. "Mommy said he went to New York."

Rob's Cartier wristwatch still lay on the kitchen counter. Connie looked at it and exchanged a glance with Min.

Nancy emerged from the bedroom only briefly. "Just feed the children," she said. "I don't feel like eating dinner." Then she returned to the bed-room and closed the door.

Shortly before 7:00 p.m. she went online to look at the missing persons Web site maintained by the Hong Kong Police Force. Then she called her father in Chicago to tell him about the terrible fight she'd had with Rob and about how Rob had left and had not yet come back. As soon as she'd finished talking to her father, she called Bryna O'Shea. It was 8:30 p.m. in Hong Kong, 5:30 a.m. in San Francisco. The ringing half-awakened Bryna, but she did not answer the phone.

When she did wake up at 8:00 a.m. she listened to the message Nancy had left.

"You've got to call me. It's very important. I just called my dad and he's flying down here. Rob and I had a fight; he chased me around the room. He wanted to have sex. He beat me up. Call me. Please."

Bryna called immediately.

"Rob beat the shit out of me last night," Nancy said. "He was chas-ing me around the bedroom, demanding sex. It was terrible. He was drunk. I tried to fight him off, but he kept punching me and kicking me.

He wouldn't stop beating me. I've got two broken ribs. I'm going to the doctor. I'm going to get this documented."

"Nan, wait a minute. Where is Rob now?"

"I don't know. He just ran out of the apartment. He probably flew to New York."

To Bryna, that did not sound entirely plausible. She had shared too much of Rob's recent sorrow, she was too aware of the resignation—not anger—she'd been hearing in his voice. And she knew that Rob had been planning to tell Nancy that he was going to file for divorce. The scene, as Nancy described it, would not come into focus.

"This was in your bedroom? Were you dressed?"

"Yes, yes. Well, he was getting undressed and then he started trying to tear my clothes off. He was trying to force me onto the bed."

"And you were screaming, fighting him off?"

"Yes. I guess so. I don't know. I didn't want the kids to hear."

"So . . . how did you make him stop?"

"I don't know. I guess he realized how much he'd hurt me. All of a sudden he was running out of the bedroom and down the hall. Then he was gone. God, my ribs hurt. Listen, I can't talk anymore right now. I just wanted you to know first."

Bryna hung up feeling that things at Parkview had gone badly amiss, but not necessarily in the way Nancy had just described. "She wasn't believable," Bryna would say later. "The whole story of the fight in the bedroom: it didn't sound right. It sounded made up."

Nancy emerged briefly to say good night to the children as Connie put them to bed. Then she told Connie and Min to go to their room and to stay there. Then she went back into the bedroom and closed the door.

23.

Decomposition, or putrefaction, is a combination of two processes:
autolysis and bacterial action. Autolysis is the breakdown of cells
and organs through an aseptic chemical process caused by intracel-
lular enzymes . . . Bacterial action results in the conversion of soft
tissues in the body to liquids and gases . . . Putrefaction begins
immediately upon death and usually becomes noticeable within 24
hours. As soon as death occurs, the bacteria or microorganisms
within the intestinal tract escape from the bowel into the other
tissues of the body. As they grow, they begin to produce gases and
other properties that distort and discolor the tissues of the body.

The discoloration is a dark greenish combination of colors and
is generally pronounced within 36 hours. As a result, the body
begins to swell from the putrefactive gases, emitting an extremely
repugnant odor.

—*Practical Homicide Investigation: Tactics, Procedures, and
Forensic Techniques* (fourth edition), Vernon J. Geberth

THE FIRST THING NANCY DID TUESDAY MORNING WAS TO
send Min to the PARKnSAVE to buy peppermint oil. "It should be in
their herbal section, or maybe pharmacy. It comes in small bottles. Get

at least six. No, get twelve. If they don't sell it, find someplace that does," she said.

Next, Nancy called Dr. Dytham to say she needed an immediate appointment because her husband had beaten her up and had hurt her. Dr. Dytham told Nancy to come in right away.

The morning was even cooler than Monday had been. The humidity was slowly building, there were still just a few clouds in the sky. Nancy drove her Mercedes to Dr. Dytham's office, which was located next to the Immigration Tower on Gloucester Road in the tony Wan Chai district. She arrived just before 9:00 a.m.

She made a strong first impression. For one thing, she was dressed plainly, in a white top and dark slacks. It was the first time Dytham had seen Nancy when she had not been dressed to impress. Even her sunglasses were less flashy than usual. Second, she seemed barely able to walk. She was hunched over almost double and crept slowly across the waiting room as if each step caused her great pain. As soon as she entered the examining room she sat down and started to cry.

Between sobs, she managed to say that her husband had tried to force her to have sex on Sunday night and that he'd grabbed her and punched her and kicked her when she'd refused. She said she was in pain all over her body and that she was sure her ribs were broken. Dytham noted "slow to move, total body pain."

Then the doctor began an examination, searching for the sources of the pain. She observed a puncture wound between the thumb and forefinger of Nancy's right hand. This was the injury that Nancy had told Connie was a burn from the toaster. She told Dr. Dytham that she had tried to defend herself against her husband with a fork that she'd held upside down and that the tines of the fork must have punctured her hand as Rob was hitting her.

No matter where the doctor touched, Nancy flinched and gasped in pain. Dytham found this puzzling, because there were very few visible bruises. Nancy's right hand was swollen, her lips were dry and cracked, there were rug burns on both knees and a bruise about six inches long and three inches wide on her right shin. There were also lighter bruises that appeared to be finger marks on her upper right arm. Nancy said her collarbone, sternum, ribs, and spine were hurting badly. She said she couldn't bend over and could barely move her upper right leg. She was sure her ribs were broken, she said again.

The examination was interrupted briefly when Nancy received a phone call from Michael del Priore. "I'm with Annabelle at the moment," she said. "I'll call you back." After clicking off, she said, "That was a good friend from the U.S. He's been giving me a lot of support."

When the X-rays came back negative, Dytham began to think that Nancy was exaggerating her injuries in an attempt to bolster any assault and battery claim she might later file against her husband. The only thing about which Dytham could be certain was that there was a significant discrepancy between the severity of the "total body pain" that Nancy complained of and the presence of any visible injuries that could have caused it.

On her way home from the doctor, Nancy stopped at Tequila Kola again to buy two more carpets. Nancy said she'd take them with her. She didn't care what they cost. A Tequila Kola employee managed to fit them in the Mercedes. When she got to Parkview, Nancy took them out and carried them, one at a time, to the lobby elevator and up to the apartment herself.

"Min! Where's the peppermint oil?"

Min pointed to six one-ounce bottles on the kitchen counter.

"I want you to go down to the storage room and make more space. There are some things I'll be sending down there soon and right now there's not enough room."

That afternoon Connie noticed the smell of incense coming from behind the closed bedroom door. That struck her as peculiar; she'd never known Nancy to burn incense in the bedroom before. She also noticed a white spot on the carpet just outside the bedroom door. It looked as if Nancy had used the new bleach powder to clean up a stain. That, too, seemed odd. Nancy was definitely *not* the sort of person who cleaned up her own stains.

Isabel and Zoe stayed at HKIS for after-class activities again. As soon as Ethan awoke from his nap at 3:00 p.m., Nancy told Connie to take him to the Aberdeen Marina Club and to keep him there until dinnertime at 7:00 p.m. She said she needed some time alone.

When Connie returned with Ethan, she noticed that several of the newly arrived packing cartons that had been stacked in the dining room were no longer there. She also was surprised to see a brand-new rug in the living room.

Nancy emerged from the bedroom at dinnertime only to say, as she had the night before, that she would not be eating with the children. "I'm going to take a shower," she said. An hour later, in fresh clothes, she came into the kitchen and made herself some bacon and eggs. But she barely picked at the food.

"Connie, I have to talk to you," she said. "Get the girls into their rooms. Tell them they can read in bed. Ethan can stay in the playroom. He'll keep himself busy. We can go into his room to talk."

Nancy sat on Ethan's bed. Connie stood at its foot.

"Rob and I had a terrible fight on Sunday night," Nancy said. "That's why I've been upset. He grabbed me and he hit me. He just kept on hitting me. He knocked me down and then he started kicking me. He really hurt me. Connie, look, he broke my ribs."

She lifted her top and pointed to the right side of her rib cage. "Can you believe that? *He broke my ribs!*"

Connie looked but saw no sign of any injury.

Nancy pulled up the right leg of her slacks. "And look: here's where he kicked me."

Connie saw a bruise on the shin.

"And you've already seen this," Nancy said and held out her right hand, bandaged between forefinger and thumb. She'd told Connie she'd burnt it on the toaster. She'd told Dr. Dytham she'd suffered puncture wounds from holding a fork the wrong way.

"It's worse than I thought. My wrist may be broken. He was really drunk. Totally out of control. You and Min were in your room so you wouldn't have heard anything. And the children, thank goodness, stayed asleep. Besides, I was too scared to scream. I was afraid he'd kill me if I screamed."

"Mrs. Kissel, how long has this been going on?"

"About a year. It's been getting worse. He's just—the stress of his work—he became a different person. His whole life—it got to be all about power and money."

Connie was shocked. Never in the six years she'd worked for Rob and Nancy had she seen any sign that he'd abused her. She'd seen him irritated, snappish, annoyed on occasion, but in general he was pleasant, thoughtful, caring, and calm, and always full of love for his children. He'd seemed a man in complete control of himself and his impulses. Nancy, not Rob, was the one with the temper.

And Rob in a drunken rage? The only time Connie could recall having seen Rob even a bit tipsy—it had been at the end of August, as he'd celebrated his return from the surgery in New York—he'd been giggly, not angry, and the evening had wound up with everyone laughing themselves silly.

"Have you been to a doctor?" Connie asked.

"Yes, I got a checkup this morning. They took X-rays—my ribs and my wrist—but we don't have results yet."

"Where is Mr. Kissel now?"

"I don't know. But I don't think he's ever coming back."

————————

Bryna had been expecting to hear from Rob. He'd said he'd call or e-mail to tell her how Nancy had handled the news that he'd be divorcing her. Instead, Nancy had called to describe the terrible fight. Bryna called him on his cell phone several times on Monday morning and left messages. He didn't call back. Just before noon, she sent an e-mail: "Now I'm getting worried . . ." She did not receive a reply. She kept calling until late Monday night. Early Tuesday morning she sent another e-mail: "I couldn't sleep . . . will you please call?"

On Tuesday afternoon (the middle of the night in Hong Kong) Bryna remembered something else. She e-mailed Nancy: "Do you want me to cancel your surgery date?"

She kept calling Rob's cell phone. He had apparently turned it off. That night (Wednesday morning in Hong Kong), she called Nancy again. The more she'd thought about what Nancy had told her about the fight, the more skeptical she grew. For one thing, the night you tell your wife you've decided to file for divorce would not likely be a night when you'd chase her around the bedroom demanding sex. For another, Nancy's distress had sounded forced. And she hadn't cried. Bryna had seen Nancy cry when a store clerk told her a particular item was out of stock. But as she'd described the beating she'd suffered at Rob's hands there had been no hint of tears in her voice.

This time, she sounded aggravated when she picked up the phone. "That fucking Rob. I'm sitting here trying to deal with our bills, but he's got all our money tied up at Merrill Lynch. I can't even write a check to pay the school tuition."

"Have you heard from him?" Bryna asked. "Do you know where he is?"

"He probably flew to New York."

"Why would he have flown to New York?"

"I don't know. Where else would he go?"

"Nan, think back to Sunday night. When he left, did he take his wallet?"

"No, he just ran out."

"Did he take his keys?"

"What difference does that make? No. No, they're still here."

"How about his shoes, Nan? Did he put on his shoes before he left?"

"I already told you: he just ran out."

"Without his shoes."

"Yeah, without his shoes."

"So he was beating you and trying to throw you onto the bed to force you to have sex and then he just stopped and ran out of the apartment without his wallet, his keys, or his shoes? Come on, Nan. That doesn't make sense. He couldn't have gone to New York."

"Well, maybe he didn't. He's a grown-up. He can take care of himself. And I'm fine, Bryna. You don't need to worry about me."

"But I guess I'd better cancel your boob job."

"No, don't do that. I'll be there."

As soon as Nancy hung up, Bryna started calling Hong Kong's five-star hotels, asking if a Robert Kissel was registered. He wasn't at the Mandarin Oriental. He wasn't at the Ritz-Carlton. He wasn't at the Grand Hyatt. He wasn't at the Langham. He wasn't at either the Peninsula or the Shangri-La in Kowloon. He wasn't at the InterContinental. He wasn't at the Excelsior in Causeway Bay.

She called Merrill Lynch, was told Mr. Kissel was not available, and eventually was put through to David Noh.

"Please bear with me for a minute," Bryna said. "This is going to sound weird, but I'm a very close friend of Rob and Nancy's from San Francisco."

"Bryna O'Shea," Noh said. "Rob talks about you a lot."

"Well, I've been trying to reach him, but I can't. He hasn't returned calls or answered e-mails since Sunday. I've talked to Nancy a couple of times and she says she doesn't know where he is. I thought he might be staying in a hotel, so I've been calling around, but—"

"So have I," Noh said.

"Excuse me?"

"Let's save ourselves some time, Bryna. Rob has told me how he's been confiding in you."

"And he's told me he's been confiding in *you*."

"So we can be frank. I'm worried. In fact, we've just had a meeting here about Rob. You and I both know that he was going to tell Nancy on Sunday night that he'd decided to file for divorce."

"And he was worried about how she'd react. But now she's saying he attacked her Sunday night and beat the shit out of her and ran out of the apartment. She says she thinks he went to New York."

"Is that what she's telling you? Well, he didn't go to New York. His passport is still in his desk drawer. Bryna, I talked to him at five-thirty Sunday afternoon and he sounded completely out of it. Like he was drugged or something—not like a man about to tell his wife the marriage was over. Then he missed a conference call on Sunday night—a really, *really* important call. Everybody was stunned that he'd blown it. Then he didn't show up for work on Monday. I called Nancy and she told me he was busy 'resolving family issues.' That's what she said, 'resolving family issues.' I had no idea what she meant."

"Maybe she was talking about the divorce."

"When he didn't show up for work yesterday or today either, I called Nancy again. This time she told me he was dealing with 'health issues' and might not be coming to work for a while. That's when I called the meeting here. We're not people quick to panic, but we've decided that if no one hears from him overnight we'll contact the police in the morning."

Bryna took a deep breath. "David, do you think—please pardon the cliché—that Nancy 'knows more than she's telling'?"

"Trust me: right now, you don't want to know what I think."

Bryna stayed up through the night, sending Rob e-mail after e-mail: "I can't be of any help if you don't respond!!!" "YOUR FAMILY IS RE-

ALLY CONCERNED ABOUT YOU . . . CALL ME." "Rob . . . Please call me . . . Please . . . I know something is happening and I'm really worried . . . Please let me know you are okay." "Rob, this isn't funny . . . Please call me . . . Nan's okay. PLEASE." "Rob . . . Please Please . . . call me. I'm all alone and want to talk to you . . . it's very important . . ." "Rob, we have a very strong friendship . . . please call." "ROB . . . YOU HAVE TO CALL ME NOW!!!!! IT'S VERY IMPORTANT . . . Please."

Rob did not reply.

24.

In temperate climates, early decomposition becomes manifest
within twenty-four to thirty hours with greenish discoloration of
the abdomen . . . followed by gaseous bloating, dark greenish to
purple discoloration of the face and *purging* of bloody decomposition fluids from the nose and mouth. The tongue swells and
progressively protrudes from the mouth, and the eyes bulge
because of accumulating retrobulbar decomposition gases.

As decomposition progresses, the skin becomes slippery with
vesicles and slippage of the epidermis, and generally after three
days the entire body becomes markedly bloated. Swelling is
particularly dramatic in areas of loose skin (eyelids, scrotum and
penis). The skin of the hands often sheds, together with nails, in
"glove" like fashion and the skin of the legs in a "stocking" like
pattern.

—*Spitz and Fisher's Medicolegal Investigation of Death: Guide-
lines for the Application of Pathology to Crime Investigation*, edited
by Werner U. Spitz.

NANCY WAS SITTING AT THE KITCHEN TABLE ON WEDNES-
day morning when Connie came in at 7:00 a.m. to make breakfast for
the children.

"I've got a list for you," Nancy said. "After you take Ethan to PIPS, I want you to go down to Stanley and buy a new bedspread. I've written down the size. It's for the bed in my bedroom."

"The spread you have is very nice," Connie said.

"I know, but I have to put a new one on. The old one reminds me too much of Mr. Kissel. It makes me sad. It makes me feel very lonely."

Then Nancy told Min to go to Adventist Hospital on Stubbs Road in Happy Valley to buy a Velcro strap that she could use to support the ribs she kept saying were broken.

"Everybody move fast," she said. "We've got a lot to do today. Grandpa Ira will be getting here tonight. Oh, Connie, while you're down in Stanley pick up some more peppermint oil. Oh, and Min, stop at the hardware store in Stanley on your way back and buy some more rope. I want nylon-coated rope. Do you understand that? Nylon-coated."

The morning was cloudy, with rising humidity. It was going to be a sticky afternoon. Min got back to the apartment first. As she walked into the living room with the Velcro strap and the nylon-coated rope she smelled something awful, like rotting fish.

"Put those things down, Min. I need you to do something else right away. Go down to the storeroom and start clearing out those boxes you rearranged. There's still not enough room. Bring them up and stack them in the hallway."

Trying not to breathe deeply, Min glanced around the living room. Nancy was standing on the new carpet from Tequila Kola. The old carpet had been rolled up and dragged behind the living room couch. Its bulkiness suggested that something had been rolled up inside it. It seemed to be the source of the stench.

"Why big?" Min asked, pointing toward the old carpet.

"Oh, I stuffed some old sheets and pillows inside it. I'm having it moved down to the storeroom this afternoon. Now you get down to the storeroom and start clearing out those boxes."

Min did not go directly to the storeroom. She called Connie. She explained about the rolled-up carpet and the smell. She asked Connie how soon she'd be back. In ten or fifteen minutes, Connie said.

———————

It was just after 11:30 a.m. when Connie carried the new bedspread and the peppermint oil into the apartment. The smell hit her as soon as she stepped into the living room. She looked at the new carpet on the floor. Then she looked at the old carpet rolled up behind the couch. The old carpet had to be the source of the odor. It was also so large in circumference that Connie knew it contained something more than old sheets and pillows.

Connie and Min went into their tiny room behind the kitchen to confer.

"I think Mrs. Kissel has done wrong," Min said.

"Yes," Connie said.

"Do you think—the carpet—the bad smell—"

"Yes," Connie said. "Mr. Kissel."

The two women hugged each other and cried.

———————

When she regained her composure, Connie e-mailed Bryna O'Shea, whom she had come to consider a friend. The tone of the e-mail did not suggest an emergency, but the very fact of receiving an e-mail from Connie would alert Bryna that something out of the ordinary had occurred.

> Hi Bryna,
>
> Just want to talk to you if you have time. Can you please e-mail me your phone number or you can call me @ this number.
>
> Home: 852-281-2274 Mobile: 852-9348-3902
>
> Thanks,
>
> Connie

————————————

Chow Yiu-kwong rang the doorbell of the Kissel apartment at 2:00 p.m. Wednesday. He and a three-man Parkview maintenance crew had come to move the carpet to the storeroom. Min answered the door. Having dragged several tightly sealed moving cartons into the living room and pushed them next to the carpet, Nancy had gone into the bedroom to nap. The carpet was eight feet long. Chow could see that it had been rolled around a bulky object about six feet long. He and his crew could also smell the carpet. One of the men retched. Chow told two men to roll in the luggage trolley. Grunting loudly while trying not to inhale, the four men lifted the stinking, untidy heap onto the wheeled platform. They stacked the cartons next to it.

Ethan had been napping, but the noise from the living room woke

him up. He ran out from his bedroom just as the workmen were starting to push the heavy trolley toward the door. To be helpful, Ethan ran
ahead and opened the door.

As they passed, he shouted, "Yuck! Bad smell!" Min took him by
the arm and pulled him away from the carpet. She gagged.

Chow came back from the storeroom at about 2:45 p.m. to return
the keys. This time, Nancy answered the door.

"Is everything all right?" she asked as Chow handed her the keys.

"No, miss," he said. "Very bad smell in the carpet. Something
wrong. Very bad smell."

"Oh, that's nothing," Nancy said. "Forget about it."

Connie's cell phone rang just after 10:00 p.m. It was 6:00 a.m. in San
Francisco. Bryna had just woken up and had seen Connie's e-mail.
"What's going on, Connie?" she asked.

The words poured out of Connie in a torrent: Mrs. Kissel had not
let anyone in the bedroom since Monday morning, Mr. Kissel had disappeared, there was a new carpet in the living room and workmen had
just taken the old one down to storage and it was rolled up as if there
was something inside it and whatever was inside it smelled horrible.

"Connie, I'm worried about Mr. Kissel, too, but if you're saying
what I think you're saying—no, that's impossible."

"You did not smell the carpet."

"Connie, do you think Mr. Kissel is in the rug?"

"I don't know!"

"You've got to go down to the storeroom and look!"

"No, no! No, I can't do that. I'm afraid!"

Bryna called David Noh, but she wasn't able to reach him until 5:00 p.m. by which time it was almost 9:00 a.m. Thursday in Hong Kong.

Noh didn't have to be asked twice to call Connie. As soon as Connie told him about the bulky, heavy carpet that smelled like death, his last doubts about Rob's fate disappeared. He left the Merrill Lynch office right away and went to the nearest police district headquarters—Western Division on Des Voeux Road—to not only file a missing persons report, but to explain that he had a pretty good idea of where the missing person could be found.

He gave a statement to officer Ng Yuk-ying. When he got to the part about Connie telling him that "a large, stinky carpet" had been moved from the Kissel apartment to a storeroom the day before, she excused herself. She came back within minutes, accompanied by Detective Senior Inspector See Kwong-tak, the officer in charge of Western District Crime Squad 2.

In plainclothes, nearing retirement, his face weathered if not quite wizened, Inspector See was a steadying presence. He listened attentively, writing down names, dates, phone numbers, and addresses. Noh's account was so clear and complete and his delivery of it so polished that Inspector See asked very few questions.

"What happens now?" Noh asked.

"Now, I am sorry to say, we will find your missing person."

Inspector See didn't even have to go to Parkview to confirm that what David Noh had told him was true. On the phone the supervisor of the maintenance division told him that the foul-smelling carpet had been a major topic of conversation all day.

See pondered his next move. These were *gweilos*. Very wealthy *gweilos*. Merrill Lynch was a significant corporate force in Hong Kong. If indeed a *gweilo* Merrill Lynch multimillionaire investment banker had been killed, and especially if it turned out that he'd been killed by his wife, the case would cause a sensation in the expatriate community. Overnight, it would acquire a profile higher than any case on which See had worked during his nearly thirty years with the Hong Kong Police Force.

He cautioned himself to proceed with care. Wealthy expats didn't have quite the influence at the highest levels that they'd had before the handover, but there were so many more of them, especially Americans, that they remained a constituency requiring delicate handling. The merest hint of police heavy-handedness could provoke an international incident, with *gweilos* yelping all over the newspapers and television about Chinese insensitivity to human rights.

From See's perspective, there was more to be lost than won here. No great glory would attach to making an arrest in the case because—if David Noh's suspicions were confirmed—there would be precious little detective work required. Yet the echoes of any blunder would pursue him through the rest of his years.

See obtained a search warrant that would permit entry into the store-room even over the objections of Nancy Kissel. Accompanied by an officer named Chan Ping-kong, he arrived at Parkview at 7:00 p.m. He went to the property management office, where he'd arranged to take statements from the men who had moved the carpet the day before. He sent Chan to the storeroom in tower 15. He told Chan to "inspect" the storeroom but under no circumstances to try to enter it.

"Sir, I am not sure what you mean by 'inspect,' " Chan said.

"I was trying to be discreet," See replied. "I mean smell it."

Chan returned in twenty minutes. "Inspector," he said, "I smelled it. I think we will need to go inside, sir."

"First, we will speak to Mrs. Kissel."

Nancy was back from Isabel's dance lesson in time to take a call from Bryna at 9:30 p.m.

"No word from Rob?" Bryna asked.

"No. You know, Bryna, I've always worried about Rob's safety."

"You have? You've never said that before. Why?"

"So many things can happen. But I'm telling myself not to worry. Right now, it's all about staying calm."

Under Arrest

25.

AS HE RUSHED DOWN THE HALLWAY TEN MINUTES AFTER
having been awakened by the 11:00 p.m. call from Nancy, Ira saw three
policemen in plainclothes standing outside the apartment door. He
nodded, they stepped aside, and he went in. Nancy was sitting at the
dining room table, surrounded by police officers, some in plainclothes,
some in uniform. She was silent, trembling, and staring off toward nowhere.

"Nancy! Are you all right?"

She stared at him as if she'd never seen him before. She didn't
speak. She was shaking.

A slender, middle-aged man dressed in polo shirt and chinos rose
from the table and introduced himself to Ira.

"You are Mr. Keeshin?" he said. "I am Senior Inspector See." He
gestured toward the living room. "Perhaps if we may speak a word in
private?"

Ira walked into the living room but did not sit. See looked as
fresh and lively as if he'd just stepped out of the shower to start his
day. Ira had the bizarre thought that the inspector would be heading
for a golf course as soon as the sun rose. What drove that notion
from Ira's mind was the expression on Inspector See's face. Like most
Westerners, Ira found it difficult to read Chinese faces. But Inspec-

tor See's expression was all too scrutable: it signified profound sadness.

"Sir, we know where your son-in-law is," he said.

"Where?"

"In a storeroom in the basement of tower fifteen. We are quite certain."

Ira gazed at the inspector, trying to process.

"We would like to ask your daughter for a key to the storeroom. In any case, we have a search warrant that permits us to enter it."

"But why—"

"Mr. Keeshin, we are quite sure the body of your son-in-law is in the storeroom, wrapped inside a carpet that Mrs. Kissel had some men move from this apartment yesterday."

Ira suffered the onset of comprehension.

"Oh, my God!"

See, who was almost exactly the same height as Ira, stepped forward and placed an arm gently around his shoulders. "I understand," he said. "I am a father, too."

"Oh, my God! Oh, my God, I can't believe it! Oh, my God, it can't be!"

Ira spun as if the inspector had just slapped him. He put his hands to his face. *"Oh, my God! Oh, my God, no!"* He reeled back toward the dining room, his cheeks already slick with tears.

See followed. "We have asked your daughter for the key to the storeroom but she tells us she has lost it."

Ira turned to face Nancy, who continued to stare into space.

"Give them the goddamned key!"

Shaking hard, she whispered, "Kitchen drawer."

A uniformed officer returned with the key a moment later. Ira could hear Ethan crying in his bedroom. Nancy seemed locked into a catatonic state. Connie, awakened by the sound of Ethan's cries on her intercom, hurried through the kitchen and into the living room.

"Connie," Ira said, "please stay in the kitchen until I call you."

She pointed toward Ethan's room.

"He must be wet," Ira said. "I'll change him."

Nancy was shaking so hard her chair rattled on the dining room floor.

"We are going to the storeroom now," Inspector See said softly to Ira. "If you wish, you may come with us."

"No, no," Ira said. "I need to make a phone call. And my daughter— look at her, she needs to get to a hospital. I want you to call an ambulance for my daughter."

"One is already on its way."

Two constables, a man and a woman, stayed in the dining room with Nancy. The rest of the police followed See to the storeroom. Ira changed Ethan's diaper. He made sure Isabel and Zoe were still asleep. He called his wife in Winnetka to tell her to call her son-in-law at Skadden, Arps in Chicago and ask him to find the best lawyer in Hong Kong right away.

The doorbell rang. It was two ambulance attendants with a wheelchair. As they helped Nancy up from her dining room chair, Ira stepped into the kitchen and spoke to Connie. He told her he would reserve a suite at the Parkview Hotel for the children. When they woke up she was to tell them that Mommy and Daddy were busy and that instead of going to school they were going to the hotel, where they could play all day long.

"Keep them there," Ira said. "Keep them busy. Don't let them watch TV by themselves. I'm sure this will be on the news."

Connie was crying her sweet *amah*'s heart out. She looked up at Ira and nodded. "I will take care of them, Mr. Keeshin," she said.

––––––––––––

The stench assaulted the policemen as soon as they opened the storeroom door. It was the smell emitted by a decomposing and putrefying human body approximately ninety-six hours after death. The grotesquely swollen carpet lay on the floor. Nancy had fitted black plastic garbage bags over each end and had secured them with adhesive tape. She had then wrapped the entire carpet in polyethylene sheeting. After taping that shut, she'd tied four cushions to the outside of it, using blue nylon rope.

Scientific Officer Mak Chung-hung got down on one knee and slit open the black plastic bag at one end. He stuck a gloved hand inside. He felt a human head. He looked up at Inspector See and nodded. It was 2:15 a.m., Friday, November 7.

––––––––––––

Connie called Bryna in San Francisco, where it was late Thursday morning.

"The police came. They took Mrs. Kissel away. They said Mr. Kissel is in the storeroom. There were so many police here. So many." She shut her cell phone when she started to cry too hard to say anything more.

Bryna realized that no one in the Kissel family even knew that

1

**SEASON'S GREETINGS
FROM
THE KISSELS**

RIGHT: *Rob and Nancy's 1990 holiday card.*

BELOW: *Nancy showing off her new wedding ring to friend Bryna O'Shea, September 10, 1989.*

2

ABOVE: *Rob and Nancy, circa 2000.*

RIGHT: *Rob and Nancy at dinner with President George H. W. Bush in Hong Kong, October 8, 2003.*

BELOW: *Rob and Nancy.*

6

RIGHT: *Andrew with friends in Key West, April 2005.*

7

ABOVE: *Andrew's yacht,* Special K's.

RIGHT: *Andrew on his yacht, May 2005.*

8

RIGHT: *Michael Del Priore.*

BELOW: *Parkview Estates, Rob and Nancy's Hong Kong residence in the Tai Tam district, on the south side of Hong Kong island.*

Andrew's body being removed from his home in Greenwich,
April 3, 2006.

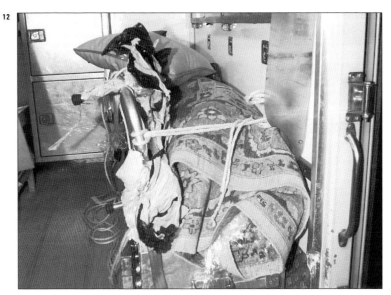

The carpet in the storage room.

Nancy at her hearing.

Nancy in Hong Kong,
January 24, 1994.

Nancy's half brother and father,
Brooks and Ira Keeshin,
at Nancy's trial.

Nancy in the van on her way to prison.

RIGHT: *Hayley Kissel in September 2005, leaving the New York Surrogate's Court after a custody hearing for Rob and Nancy's children.*

17

18

LEFT: Bill Kissel at Nancy's hearing.

BELOW: *Jane, Rob's sister, leaving Nancy's hearing.*

19

Andrew entertaining friends in his limousine in Miami,
May 2005.

Andrew's funeral, April 7, 2006.

Rob had been missing. She thought it would be better if she told some-one instead of waiting for the Hong Kong police to make the call. She didn't want to call Bill because the news might kill him. She didn't want to call Jane because she couldn't bear to be the one to give the news to Rob's adoring little sister. Eventually, she called Andrew in Greenwich, where it was early evening.

Hayley answered. She said Andrew was busy talking to a contractor.

"I have to talk to him. It's really important."

"Can't I take a message?"

"No, it's too important for a message."

Andrew came to the phone impatiently. "What is it, Bryna?"

"Andrew, I think you'd better sit down."

"For Christ's sake, Bryna, what do you want?"

"It's Rob. He's . . . gone."

"I know he's gone. He told me he was going to tell Nancy last week-end that he wanted a divorce. He's left her. So?"

"He didn't leave her. She killed him."

"Bryna, are you out of your mind?"

"She killed him, Andrew. The Hong Kong police have just ar-rested her. She wrapped his body in a carpet and tried to hide it in a storeroom."

Bryna heard the phone drop. She heard Andrew scream. Hayley picked up the phone.

"What's going on?"

"Nancy killed Rob. She's been arrested."

Andrew was screaming so loudly in the background that Bryna couldn't hear Hayley's reply. Then she heard the children start to cry.

"I'm sorry," Bryna said, and hung up.

A week earlier, Andrew had paid $4.7 million in restitution to the board of 200 East Seventy-fourth Street in return for assurance that no criminal charges would be filed against him. To raise the money, he'd liquidated Hanrock's $25 million portfolio of New Jersey real estate. Investors, including Rob, should have received $15 million from the sales. Instead of paying them, however, Andrew covered up the fact that he'd sold the New Jersey properties. He used the $20 million he retained after settling with the co-op board to finance a plunge into Connecticut real estate. Using forged documents and a stolen notary public stamp, he was able to defraud banks into issuing huge mortgages on properties he'd already mortgaged elsewhere. He was convinced that as long as he stayed current on interest payments, no one would be the wiser. Meanwhile, he used the illegally obtained proceeds to make down payments on new properties, on which he then obtained even larger mortgage loans from unsuspecting banks.

It was a scam that required both a clear head and a firm hand on the tiller, neither of which Andrew possessed in the best of times. The shock of learning that Nancy had killed Rob was not one he was well equipped to absorb.

As soon as the ambulance pulled out of the Parkview driveway, Ira looked out the back window and was astonished by what he saw. They were being followed by dozens of cars and trucks, some with flashing lights, some with television broadcasting equipment mounted on top.

"Jesus Christ," Ira said out loud. "What did the police do, tip off the entire fucking Asian press corps?"

Nancy lay under a blanket, still shaking, apparently still not able to speak.

Ruttonjee Hospital, the closest to Parkview, was on Queen's Road East in Wan Chai, not far from the offices of Dr. Dytham, whom Nancy had visited on Tuesday morning. As they turned off Queen's Road into the hospital driveway, the ambulance slowed to a standstill. Still more television station news crew trucks were double-parked on both sides. A swarm of cameramen and photographers had gathered by the emergency room door.

The ambulance stopped and the attendants got out to unfold the wheelchair and to open the swinging doors to the back. Cameramen and photographers, shouting and shoving, surged forward. Strobe units and television lights turned the driveway as bright as a beach in the midday sun. Nancy swayed back and forth, her eyes shut, shivering spasmodically, her arms clasped tightly around her chest.

Ira climbed out of the back of the ambulance and pushed shouting cameramen out of the way. As soon as the attendants placed Nancy in the wheelchair, Ira put a blanket over her head to shield her from the pulsing and flashing of the lights.

In the emergency room, Nancy was examined by a female physician named Li Wei-sum. Emerging briefly from her trancelike state, Nancy told the doctor that her ribs were hurting badly and were undoubtedly broken. Dr. Li, however, could detect no sign of injury to the ribs. She did note "abrasions of lip, chest, knees and feet," as well as "bruising on upper and lower forearms, shoulders and backs of hands." Judging from the color of the bruises, Dr. Li noted, they were unlikely to have been more than two days old.

Inspector See, who had just arrived at the hospital, waited for Li to finish her examination. Then he stepped forward and told Nancy that she was under arrest, charged with the murder of her husband. She gazed at him as if she hadn't understood a word he'd said. Her shaking approached the level of spastic paralysis.

Shortly before 4:00 a.m., she was brought to an upstairs ward. Ira gazed in and couldn't believe it: there must have been fifty women lying on cots.

"What is this?" he said. "You can't put her in there!" Then he realized that they could. She was under arrest now, charged with murder. They could put her wherever they wanted.

When Nancy saw the ward she emerged from her apparent catatonia in a hurry. She began screaming. She screamed louder than Ira had ever heard anyone scream. *I'm not staying here! You can't do this to me! Let me go, let me go! I've got to get out!*

Ira and two nurses helped her to a bed as she screamed. It was a single bed in a long row of single beds, all the others occupied by Chinese women of the sort that for six years Nancy had forsaken public transportation in order to avoid.

She finally screamed herself into exhaustion. Ira stood by her, stroking her head, waiting for the sedative she'd been given to take effect. By 5:00 a.m. she'd fallen asleep and the ward was quiet, except for the static coming from the radios of the two uniformed policemen who stood guard at the foot of Nancy's bed.

"Can you turn down those radios, please?" Ira asked. "Down? You know, down?" He gestured the turning of a dial. The policemen understood him. With slight bows of apology they lowered the volume of the static. Ira asked them when someone in authority would arrive. He wanted to know what was going to happen next. Their lack of English made communication difficult, but they eventually conveyed to Ira that a ranking officer would be there by 9:00 a.m. Ira looked at his wrist-watch and allowed himself to feel how stupefyingly exhausted he was. He went back to the Parkview Hotel to try to sleep for an hour or two.

———————

The pathologist found that Rob had been killed by five blows to the right side of his head from a blunt object. The blows had been so hard that much of the right side of his skull had been crushed in upon his brain, resulting in the extrusion of significant amounts of brain matter. The consistency of the wounds' severity and their grouping in such close proximity to one another led the pathologist to conclude that all five blows had been struck with the victim in a stationary, quite likely prone position.

It was not hard to reconstruct what she had done with his body after she'd killed him.

She had slid a black plastic garbage bag over his head and had tied the bag shut with blue nylon cord. She had covered the body with tow-els. She had put the towel-covered body into a children's sleeping bag later identified as having come from her daughters' room. She had wrapped the bag in sheets of polyethylene and had sealed the sheets with adhesive tape.

She had brought a rug into the bedroom from the living room and had rolled her husband's body up inside it. She had covered each end of the carpet with black plastic garbage bags and secured the ends with adhesive tape. She had sealed the entire roll with more adhesive tape. She had wrapped more polyethylene sheeting around it and had taped that shut. She had tied four cushions to the outside of the carpet.

On the third day, she had dragged it into the living room. And then she had called the workmen to take it away.

Investigators who opened the packing cartons that had been sent to the storeroom with the body found them filled with blood-soaked sheets and towels and other bloody debris. At the bottom of one, they found a broken lead statuette. A thick coating of dried blood covered its base. Alongside were the broken figurines of two little girls. Bent metal screws that had attached the figurines to the base indicated that they'd been broken from it forcefully, as would have occurred if Nancy had used the figurines as a handle while she'd swung the statuette down at the head of her immobile husband, shattering his skull five times with the heavy lead base.

When he returned to Ruttonjee at 9:00 a.m., Ira spoke to a police officer who said that Nancy would shortly be transferred to Queen Elizabeth Hospital in Kowloon, which had a "custodial facility." He found both a representative of the United States consulate and a young lawyer from the Hong Kong firm of Mallesons Stephen Jaques standing at the end of Nancy's bed.

The woman from the consulate said she would be available to answer any questions that might arise but that U.S. officials would have no direct involvement in the case. The lawyer told Ira that Mallesons had been contacted by Skadden, Arps and that a Mallesons partner named

Simon Clarke was prepared to act as Nancy's solicitor and would meet them at Queen Elizabeth Hospital.

Nancy herself was not speaking. She remained flat on her back, her eyes wide open, her face devoid of expression. Ira said good morning. She did not respond. He reached for her hand and squeezed it. She squeezed back.

As they left the ward for the trip to Queen Elizabeth at noon, Ira was almost swept off his feet by a clamoring horde of cameramen and photographers. The crush of press was even worse than it had been outside the emergency room. The attendant pushing Nancy's wheelchair followed a phalanx of uniformed police to the elevator as Ira scrambled to stay close behind.

———————

All day Friday, Hong Kong police evidence technicians combed through the bedroom in which Rob had died. They found bloodstains on walls, heavier bloodstains on the bed, bloodstains on the headboard of the bed, and more bloodstains on various pieces of furniture and spattered across the screen of the television set. The heaviest staining was on a section of carpet at the foot of the bed. It appeared that someone had attempted to conceal this by covering it with a new rug.

The police also noted that the portion of bedspread that had hung down from the footboard of the bed had been sheared off and was not in the bedroom. Given its proximity to the heavy staining on the carpet, police concluded that when they found that portion of the bedspread they'd find that it, too, was heavily stained.

There were no smears of blood on the walls, as there would have been if a bleeding man had been standing up and moving as he fought for his life. No blood spatters were found more than four feet above the floor, indicating the victim had been lying down when he was struck. There were no spatters of blood on the ceiling, indicating that the assailant had used not a long weapon such as a golf club, but a short, heavy weapon, such as a lead statuette.

———————————

The Sydney-based law firm of Mallesons Stephen Jaques was growing rapidly into one of the largest and most respected in Hong Kong. As a full partner, Simon Clarke had just cause to believe himself to be among the more sought-after of the territory's five thousand solicitors. He was a chipper, cordial thirty-nine-year-old Australian who'd been in Hong Kong since 1994, first with Jewkes Chan and then Kwok & Yih before Mallesons. He specialized in representing multinational corporations seeking to assure themselves and others that none of their business practices, no matter how unfavorably construed, would be seen as having drifted across the fine line that separated innocent avarice from white-collar crime.

Because he had no experience with homicide, Clarke quickly obtained the services of someone who did. In the British legal system, which by and large remained in force in Hong Kong, the client hired a solicitor, who could do everything except try a case, and the solicitor hired a barrister, who represented the client at trial. Even before meeting Nancy, Clarke had contacted Alexander King, a highly regarded forty-eight-year-old barrister who'd worked as a criminal defense lawyer in England, a Crown prosecutor in New Zealand, and who'd been doing criminal trial and appeal work in Hong Kong since 1986.

The two attorneys were waiting in a conference room off the lobby of Queen Elizabeth Hospital when Ira returned to see Nancy early Friday evening. Ira wrote a check for twenty thousand dollars to get the ball rolling. It was the first of many such checks to Mallesons, none of them for a smaller amount.

Nancy was wheeled into the room. Except for her tremors, she seemed frozen into the chair. Her gaze was blank. She did not speak. Ira explained about her emotional condition. Clarke stood and stepped toward her.

"Are you able to understand me?" he said. "Blink if you can."

Nancy blinked.

He explained who he and Alexander King were and why they were there. Then he asked, "Do I have your full attention?"

Nancy blinked.

"All right: listen very carefully and remember this. Don't talk to anybody. I repeat: do—not—talk—to—*anybody*. Don't talk to the police. Don't talk to any doctors or nurses. Don't talk to any psychiatrists or psychologists. From this moment forward I do not want you to talk to anyone in the world—including your father—unless I personally give you permission. Don't forget that. Nothing could be more important. Blink if you understand."

Nancy blinked.

Simon Clarke turned to Ira. "Do *not* ask her what happened," he said. "Do *not* ask her what she did. She has already told you what she's told you. Leave it at that. And tell everyone you talk to the same thing: do not ask Nancy any questions. From now on, only I ask the questions."

Ira went upstairs with Nancy to her room, which was really a cell. There were bars on three sides. A police matron sat at a desk just outside the door. Among her tasks was to accompany Nancy to the bathroom when necessary. A small metal nightstand and a narrow cot with a mattress no thicker than Ira's thumb were the only pieces of furniture in the room. Now Ira knew what "custodial facility" meant.

Nancy lay rigid, trembling and staring into space. Ira sat at the edge of her bed.

"I don't know if you can understand me, sweetie," he said. "But please don't kill yourself. That would make everything worse. Remember how much the children need you. We're all doing everything we can to help you. So please don't do anything to harm yourself."

She squeezed Ira's hand when he said that. But she said nothing, not a word.

Connie realized that she hadn't packed enough clothes for Isabel and Zoe. She walked to the apartment from the hotel on Friday evening, prepared to ask the police officer guarding the door if she could be permitted inside—under supervision—to gather some clothing.

But there was no police officer guarding the door. Connie used her key to open it. There were no police inside the apartment and no tape or signs or other indications that any of the rooms were off-limits. Connie went into the girls' bedroom and opened the clothes closet.

The stench hit her hard. It forced her backward, hands covering her mouth and nose. She flipped the light switch outside the closet door. She saw two black plastic garbage bags on a shelf. Those bags had never been there before. And whatever was inside them was producing the stench.

She ran back to the hotel and called the police. Two officers arrived within the hour. They took the two garbage bags out of the closet. One of the officers opened a bag to look inside. He immediately dropped it and raced to the bathroom to vomit.

The bags were filled with blood-soaked towels, pillows, and other matter, possibly organic.

Ira woke up worried at 6:00 a.m. on Saturday. He knew, of course, that he'd be worried—or worse—for the rest of his life. But he'd been awakened by a specific, immediate worry that was now flitting about just below the level of his consciousness.

He went into the bathroom and splashed cold water on his face. Then he remembered: *the newspaper.* Parkview hung the new day's edition of the *South China Morning Post* on the doorknob of every occupied room in the hotel. Given Friday's press frenzies, Ira was sure there would be a front-page headline and story about Rob's death and Nancy's arrest. He didn't want the children to see that story. He walked down the hall to take the newspaper off the doorknob outside their suite.

He'd been right:

TOP US BANKER BLUDGEONED TO DEATH

The wife of Merrill Lynch executive Robert Kissel is arrested after his body is found at the luxury Parkview apartments

A prominent American investment banker has been found blud-

geoned to death and dumped in a storeroom at the luxury Parkview residential complex in Tai Tam.

The body of 40-year-old Robert Kissel, Asia-Pacific managing director of global principal products for Merrill Lynch, was found wrapped in plastic sheets and rolled in a carpet in the room under block 15 of the estate.

He had been dead for three to four days and sources said it was suspected he had been beaten with a golf club.

His wife, Nancy, 39, also an American, has been arrested for murder and last night was under police guard in the custodial wing of Queen Elizabeth Hospital.

She went to Western police station on Thursday morning, alleging she had been assaulted by her husband on Sunday afternoon.

She was taken to Queen Mary Hospital for examination but disappeared soon after.

A colleague of Mr. Kissel's contacted police later that afternoon to report he had not been seen since Sunday.

Officers of the Western Division Crime Squad led by Detective Chief Inspector See Kwong-tak visited the couple's flat in block 17 late on Thursday night and questioned Mrs. Kissel.

While questioning her, police found a key to the couple's rented storeroom.

At about 11.45 pm, the officers opened the storeroom and discovered Kissel's body.

A post-mortem examination revealed that he died from severe head injuries, which sources indicate may have been caused by a golf club. It is believed the couple have three children, although it could not be established whether they live in Hong Kong.

Sources claim the pair argued last Sunday.

The post-mortem results led police to classify the case as a homicide.

Detectives were searching the Kissels' flat and the storeroom for further evidence and the murder weapon last night.

Police are investigating whether accomplices might have helped move the body.

The storeroom is located 100 metres uphill from the estate's block 17.

In 2000, Kissel joined Merrill Lynch from Goldman Sachs, where he co-headed the bank's Asian special situations group.

A spokesman for Merrill Lynch said the firm's head office in New York had been informed of Kissel's death, and that he had been a well-liked figure around the office.

"He was very well respected, both in the firm and in the industry," said R. G. Rosso, Merrill Lynch's head of marketing communications for the Asia-Pacific region.

"He will be missed."

26.

IRA KNEW THE TIME HAD COME TO TELL THE CHILDREN. He brought Isabel, the oldest, to his room after breakfast. He'd spent a lot of time on the phone with his second wife, whose psychological insights he valued. She'd given him what she called a "script" containing precise language for him to use when breaking the news. His son, Ryan, the medical student, would be arriving at midday. He and Ira had agreed that given Ryan's training in child psychology it would be better for him to tell Zoe, six, and Ethan, four. He could stay with them after he told them to gauge their reactions and he could offer further solace and reassurance when needed. But nine-year-old Isabel was all too likely to overhear a stray phrase or to stumble inadvertently upon television news coverage, no matter how assiduous Connie was in shielding the children from all media. And Isabel would start asking questions. The answers, carelessly worded, could worsen the unavoidable trauma.

"I need to tell you something, Isabel," Ira began. "Your mommy and daddy had an argument—a fight, the way people sometimes have fights—and Daddy did not survive."

Did not survive. That was the key phrase, Ira's second wife had told him.

"Your daddy did not survive, and Mommy is very sick. She's in the hospital to get better and you won't be able to see her for a very long time. But you're safe. Nothing will happen to you or Zoe or Ethan. All the people in the family who love you are going to take very, very good care of you. You'll always be safe."

"Is Daddy dead?" Isabel asked.

"Yes, he is," Ira answered.

Her eyes filled with tears and she was silent for a moment.

"Uncle Ryan will be here soon and he'll tell Zoe and Ethan all about this, so you don't have to worry about them. You have no responsibility for telling them. Do you understand that?"

"Yes. Can I go back to my room now?"

Zoe and Ethan were jumping on the beds when they got there. Isabel ran in and joined them, giggling and shouting. To judge from outward appearances, it was as if Ira had said nothing at all.

———————

Despite his arduous journey from Cincinnati, Ryan went straight to the Parkview Hotel on Saturday afternoon and plunged into childcare alongside Connie. At what seemed the proper moment, he sat down with Zoe and Ethan and carefully and lovingly told them what they needed to know, emphasizing, as Ira had, that they were safe and loved and would always be safe and surrounded by people who would love them and take care of them.

———————

As a hard rain fell, the rest of the Kissel family arrived in Hong Kong on Saturday afternoon. Bill, Andrew and Hayley, and Jane and Richard had all flown to Tokyo from their different points of origin. After gathering there, they'd flown to Hong Kong together. Bill was heavily sedated, and Andrew was even edgier than usual, perhaps suffering from abrupt cocaine withdrawal. Bill had booked rooms for them all at the five-star JW Marriott in Pacific Place, in the Admiralty section of Central. But as soon as they'd dropped off their luggage and freshened up after the four-and-a-half-hour flight, they took taxis to the Parkview Hotel to see the children. In keeping with family custom, they brought plenty of presents.

They'd all been talking about the children. What should they do with the children? Clearly, they'd have to bring them back to the United States. But where should the children live? Who should have custody? Bill had strong feelings about the matter and, as usual, he was determined to get his way. Upon their arrival, he booked a conference room at the Marriott for a meeting the next day at which the Kissels and the Keeshins would discuss the question of the children. Or—as Bill saw it— a meeting at which he would explain to Ira and his son the way things were going to be.

Chaos ensued upon the Kissels' arrival at the Parkview Hotel. The children tore the wrapping paper off their presents. Bill began roughhousing with Ethan on the floor. The girls resumed jumping on the beds. Andrew took one, then the other, and twirled them around at top speed, laughing as they screamed. Bill produced even more presents. The children shrieked louder. "Let's make this a special time!" Andrew shouted, clapping his hands. "Let's have a celebration!"

Ryan was dumbfounded. What was the message this kind of behavior was sending these poor kids? *Daddy's dead so we get lots of new presents, hurray!*

———————

On Sunday morning, Ryan paid his first visit to Nancy. She was lying on a cot pushed against the back wall of the cell. Her hair was a mess, something Ryan had never thought he'd see. When she realized he was there, she rose slowly from the cot. She moved feebly toward him, hunched in apparent pain. Her breathing was shallow. Her hospital-issue slippers scraped across the concrete floor. They didn't say much. Ryan followed the instruction to not ask her what happened. And Nancy didn't seem to want to talk. She did ask about the children. Ryan told her they were fine.

Later, he would recall the ten minutes spent with Nancy as the most awkward of his life. "There was nothing to say. Nothing."

As he was leaving, Nancy suddenly remarked, "Someone in Vermont is going to be very worried about me."

———————

Rain was still falling at midday Sunday when Ira and Ryan arrived at the Marriott to meet with the Kissels. They were wearing whatever clean clothes they'd been able to find: jeans and T-shirt for Ryan, polo shirt and wrinkled slacks for Ira. The Kissels walked into the conference room dressed as if for a Goldman Sachs board meeting. They also brought a lawyer with them.

Ira walked up to Bill, put his arms around him and hugged him. Bill stood stiffly, his face reddening. He was not a huggable man in the best of times, and he clearly wanted no part of an embrace from the father of the woman who'd killed his son.

As the lawyer began to introduce himself, Ira held up a hand. "We've all had a great loss," he said. "And I think this is a family matter. With all respect, we don't need lawyers here. I'm sure we can work this out ourselves."

Bill and Andrew huddled with the lawyer. "All right," Andrew said. "We'll try it your way." The lawyer left.

The meeting lasted for an hour and a half and was conducted in businesslike fashion. So much so that it seemed to Ryan as if they were discussing a corporate takeover, not the lives of Isabel, Zoe, and Ethan, three shell-shocked children who didn't know why they'd lost their father and didn't know when they'd see their mother and who didn't know what continent they'd be on by the end of the week.

The continent was about the only thing they agreed on. Nancy had written a note to Simon Clarke saying that she wanted Ira to have custody of the children. Clarke had passed the note on to Ira. Producing it, Ira said he thought that the mother's wishes should be respected, despite the extraordinary circumstances. Bill's face grew so red and veins pulsed so hard in his temples that more than one person at the table feared that he was about to suffer either a heart attack or a stroke.

Ira said he was prepared to move the children into the house he and his wife shared in Winnetka and get them into local schools as soon as possible. He said they could be ready to leave within a week. Bill reacted as if Ira had said he was planning to sell the children into white slavery.

Bill wanted the children to go to Andrew and Hayley. As Rob's brother, Bill said, Andrew had a stronger claim on the children than did the father of the evil woman who had killed him. In addition, Bill said, Andrew and Hayley were themselves wealthy enough so that the children would not suffer any loss of lifestyle. Although Ira was certainly well off, he was not in the multi-multimillionaire league of Andrew, whose real estate empire now stretched from Jersey City to New Haven.

Andrew and Hayley lived in Greenwich, not in some suburb of Chicago. Bill conceded that Winnetka did seem to have adequate schools and a per capita income he approved of, but it was still a part of the wasteland that he considered the Midwest to be, and he was goddamned if he was going to have his grandchildren raised in a wasteland. With Andrew and Hayley, the children would be closer to Stratton Mountain. And Andrew and Hayley had two daughters of their own who were about the same ages as Isabel and Zoe.

What Bill did not say, but what was by far the most important item on his unspoken agenda, was that Andrew and Hayley would protect the children from any attempt by Ira to portray their mother as anything other than a crazed and vicious murderess.

Likewise, Ira's strongest argument was one he couldn't make: he truly loved the children, while Andrew, he strongly suspected, was an alcoholic cokehead who loved no one but himself.

Meanwhile, Andrew had his own reasons for wanting custody: the children came with a $20 million trust fund attached. Assuming Nancy was convicted of Rob's murder—and it seemed obvious to Andrew that she would be—the children would be beneficiaries of Rob's estate. In the meantime, whoever had custody could bill the estate for all expenses involved in caring for them. This struck Andrew as an extraordinary opportunity.

The meeting ended disagreeably, with no resolution. First thing Monday morning, Bill went to Rob's Merrill Lynch office, where he was permitted to take the children's passports from Rob's desk drawer. Without their passports, Ira couldn't take them anywhere.

———————

The same morning, Simon Clarke and Ryan went to the Parkview apartment to gather items Nancy said she wanted. Most important, she said, were her laptop and her jewelry. Clarke was amazed that the police were not controlling access to the apartment. Anyone with a key could get inside. One of Nancy's Parkview friends had a key and had brought several other Parkview wives for a tour of the crime scene the day before. He was even more amazed that the police had not seized Nancy's laptop. Didn't they care what she'd been saying in her e-mails? Didn't they care who she'd been e-mailing? How about Web sites she'd visited? What about searches? Suppose she'd been keeping a diary on her laptop. Even if it contained nothing incriminating, it would have offered insight into her state of mind in the days and weeks leading up to the killing. Now the police would never know. He sensed they didn't care. No doubt they considered the case open and shut.

As soon as Ryan opened the door to the apartment, he wished he hadn't. A stink of rot still filled the air. Even five days after Rob's body had been moved, the stench lingered. Nonetheless, the two of them walked from room to room, gathering as many of the items on Nancy's list as they could find. They saved the bedroom—where the smell was strongest—for last.

Three dressers stood against a wall on the left side of the bedroom. Two tall ones at either end were separated by a wide, shorter dresser in the middle. Clarke spotted a baseball bat on the floor behind the wide dresser. He got down on his hands and knees and reached under the dresser to retrieve it.

"I'm surprised the police didn't take this," he said. He put it, handle end up, in a shopping bag filled with other items from Nancy's list.

Nancy was scheduled to appear in Eastern Magistrates' Court on Monday, November 10, to offer a plea in response to the charge of murder. But she began to shake and she fell mute and she was too weak even to get into her wheelchair in the hospital, so Alexander King informed the magistrate that she was "medically unfit" and unable to appear. Her arraignment was rescheduled for Friday.

The police searched Rob's office and his Porsche. In the car, they found life insurance policies with a value of $6.75 million, naming Nancy as beneficiary. In his office, they found the surveillance reports and videos that Frank Shea had sent. They also found several love letters to Nancy from Michael Del Priore in a drawer.

Inspector See began to consider the question of motive.

Police also viewed pictures from the Parkview security department's closed-circuit television cameras. One set showed Nancy Kissel getting out of her Mercedes in the parking lot the previous Wednesday and hoisting a six-foot-long green carpet on her shoulder and carrying it with no apparent difficulty into the lobby of tower 17. It appeared to be the same rug that had been laid over the massively bloodstained section of carpet the police had found at the foot of the bed. It was the second rug she had carried into the apartment in two days. See began to consider the question of how badly hurt Nancy had really been by the ferocious beating she'd said she'd suffered at the hands of her husband.

The police also did a further search of the apartment. On Wednesday, November 12, they found a handbag of Nancy's tucked away behind a cushion. Inside were bottles of five different prescription medications. They took the bottles to their laboratory for analysis. When the results came back, See compared them to the toxicology report he'd just received that disclosed the presence of five different hypnotic and sedative drugs in Robert Kissel's stomach. The results matched. The drugs in Rob's stomach were the same as those contained in five of the six prescription bottles obtained by Nancy in the weeks leading up to Rob's death.

See began to consider the question of means. He'd been puzzled by Rob's lack of resistance to Nancy's attack. Now he saw a possible answer: only hours before he was killed, Rob had ingested five different prescription drugs, any one of which, in sufficient dose, could have rendered him unconscious. But why would he do that? Why would he have taken the five sedatives that his wife had obtained by prescription? Inspector See didn't know, but he was confident that he'd find out. All in the fullness of time.

Late on the afternoon of Wednesday, November 12, the police said they had completed their work at the apartment. Connie and Min spent the day cleaning it. The next day, the children returned. The only rule was that they were not allowed to go into the master bedroom. That door stayed closed. None of the children asked why.

In Nancy's absence, Ryan and Connie acted as surrogate parents. Connie, of course, had served in that role for several years, especially with Ethan. It was new to Ryan, but he took to it instinctively. He didn't think it was yet time for long, searching talks with the children about their feelings. His goal was to get them out of Hong Kong without subjecting them to further trauma. He was one future physician who'd managed not to leave his compassion behind in medical school.

When they were not in school, he kept them as physically active as possible and let them watch television with their meals. Television had been used to numb them all their lives. Ryan didn't approve of that, but he found himself grateful for the effects of it now. For the moment, the less time they spent thinking and wondering, the better.

The police changed visitation procedures at Queen Elizabeth Hospital. No longer could visitors sit in Nancy's cell, or just outside it, and talk to her. All visits—supervised by the matron—were to take place in a conference room.

Ryan went to see Nancy almost every day, but he often found Parkview neighbors with her when he arrived. A small clique of expat wives, drawn by her sudden notoriety, had suddenly become Nancy's best friends. During his first few visits, Nancy asked about the children. She said how much she missed them. Any reference to them made her cry. But after a few days, she stopped asking. Ryan didn't know why. It almost seemed to him that she'd decided she had more important things—such as her own fate—to worry about.

Ira and Bill were still squabbling about custody, but they were running out of time. The children would have to be out of Hong Kong by November 21 because that was the day Connie's work visa expired. Domestic helpers were not permitted to remain in the territory for more than two weeks after their employment had been terminated. The clock had started ticking for both Connie and Min at the moment of Nancy's arrest. Min would no longer be needed, but neither Ira nor Andrew and Hayley could contemplate raising the children without Connie.

On the afternoon of Thursday, November 13, as part of the packing process, Min was cleaning out Ethan's bedroom closet. Suddenly, she screamed. Ryan ran in from the living room. Min was frantically pointing at the closet. Min's English was imperfect even when she hadn't had a shock, but Ryan soon understood that she'd found a black plastic garbage bag in the back of Ethan's closet that didn't belong there.

Ryan called Simon Clarke. The solicitor called the police. They came to collect yet another bag of potential evidence that they had overlooked. When the bag was opened at Western Division headquarters it was found to contain wads of bloodstained tissues and a bloody glove, as well as the blood-soaked bottom piece that had been sheared from the bedspread before the police had first arrived at the scene.

The implication was clear: whatever detritus Nancy had not disposed of in the packing cartons, she'd tried to hide inside her children's closets.

On Friday, November 14, Alexander King appeared again in Eastern Magistrates' Court to say that Nancy remained "medically unfit" and could not be present. The magistrate continued the case until the following Friday, November 21.

Nancy's level of fitness, both physical and psychological, seemed remarkably dependent on circumstance. In the first days following November 2, she'd not only been able to buy a carpet and tote it home from the store, but to roll up a 165-pound body inside it and then drag it from one room of her apartment to another. Yet since her arrest she'd seemed scarcely able to walk. Doctors found no physical reason for this disability.

She had seemed unable to speak one moment, yet had been able to scream an hour later, such as when she'd seen the ward she was being taken to at Ruttonjee Hospital. She had to blink to communicate with her solicitor, yet she could tell her half-brother that someone in Vermont must be worried about her. She could converse freely with Parkview friends, and with her lawyer, but she couldn't appear in court to offer a plea.

There was no indication that she'd ever read up on the psychological condition that Freud termed "secondary gain"—an advantage derived from an illness or injury, such as release from responsibility or avoidance of a difficult situation—but she seemed to know instinctively how to achieve it. Secondary gain was often associated with hysteria.

From the moment the police found the key to the storeroom, Nancy had seemed hysterical, perhaps gripped by conversion hysteria.

Conversion hysteria, is described by the U.S. National Institutes of Health as "a psychiatric condition in which emotional distress or unconscious conflict are expressed through physical symptoms." For example: the sudden onset of an inability to walk or talk, or violent, uncontrollable shaking.

The secondary gain associated with Nancy's symptoms was to postpone the moment when she would have to confront the consequences of her actions in a court of law. The custodial ward of Queen Elizabeth Hospital must have seemed far less threatening to her than a public appearance in Eastern District Magistrates' Court, or anything else that was waiting down the line.

———————————

The question of where the children would go was not resolved until November 15, the day before Ira flew out of Hong Kong. Bill continued to insist—to demand—that the children go to Greenwich to live with Andrew and Hayley. But he'd never sought Hayley's opinion.

Eventually, she gave it anyway. She said she thought the children would be better off with Ira. "I like him. The kids obviously love him and he loves them. They have a great relationship. I like his wife. They have a lot of extended family in Chicago. Ira's got the energy to handle this. They've got a big house in Winnetka where the schools are great." Besides, Hayley had two children of her own to occupy her time and energy, and her relationship with Andrew was—to put it mildly—strained. In Greenwich, there would be no guarantee of either tranquillity or stability.

For the moment, Bill was too grief-stricken to fight. He met Ira in the lobby of the Marriott on the evening of November 15 and signed a document that granted Ira temporary custody. Ira flew out of Hong Kong the next day. The children flew to Chicago with Ryan and Connie on November 19. Their father's body had already been shipped to New York for burial in the Kissel family plot in New Jersey.

Only Nancy stayed behind.

PART FOUR

THE CONSEQUENCES OF TRUTH

Pretrial

27. THE CHILDREN

AS FOR THE CHILDREN: HAVING HAD THE ONLY LIFE THEY'D ever known yanked violently out from under them, in late November they were tossed head over heels halfway around the world to land on Grandpa Ira's doorstep in Winnetka, Illinois. Two weeks later, they were shuffled off to a Holiday Inn in Cincinnati.

From the day they arrived in Winnetka, Ira knew he and his wife wouldn't be able to raise them, not even with Connie's help. His love for the children was abundant, but he was sixty-one years old and traumatized. He'd been under such stress in Hong Kong that he simply hadn't thought the matter through. He'd also failed to anticipate his wife's reaction. Sickened by what Nancy had done, Ira's wife wanted no part of her children, and she'd made that emphatically clear to Ira while he was still in Hong Kong. He'd hoped her reaction would prove temporary. It did not.

Even so, Ira was not about to hand the children over to the Kissels. He knew the Kissels would poison the children's minds against their mother. Ryan, who was now twenty-four, volunteered to raise them in Cincinnati. He said he'd take a leave of absence from medical school. With the help of both Connie and his mother—Ira's second wife, Joyce—he was confident that he could provide them with a safe and stable environment.

Fearing that Bill Kissel would seek a court order to keep the children in Illinois until a full-scale custody battle could be launched, Ira took them to Cincinnati, where, as he made arrangements for their future, he stayed with them and Connie in the Holiday Inn. On the spot, he also bought a house that he felt would make a suitable home. It was a middle-class house in a middle-class neighborhood. While it was being refurbished—a matter of weeks—the children and Connie moved into the basement of Ryan's apartment. On December 7, Ira wrote the Kissels a letter:

I feel we have a clear vision of the best scenario for the children long term. We all agree that they need to be in an ongoing loving environment and that [my wife] and I cannot physically and mentally meet the demands of being the care providers for three young children . . .

It is remarkable how well Isabel, Zoe and Ethan have adjusted to the situation. Because of the continuity of Connie and the care of Ryan, the children are doing Great . . .

Ryan has shown over the past month that he is certainly, with the aid of Connie, able to manage the children's every day needs (school, doctors, playmates, homework, bedtime stories to Ethan, getting up at night with Ethan, etc. . . . .

Some life events require sound judgments, some require emotion, some experience, some love, and some merely faith. And some life experiences are so extraordinary that they require all of the above and much more.

We have thought long and hard using our heads and our hearts concerning this matter, and although we feel this plan is lacking in some experience and requires a whole lot of faith, we feel as though being with

Ryan has thus far been very successful for the children and should
continue in Cincinnati.

There is no question that these three little children have an incredible
guardian angel that has thus far kept them safe and enabled them to
preserve their childhood throughout this whole life-changing ordeal.

Cincinnati will ensure that the works of the angels will not be in vain,
but instead continue as these three remarkable children mature and grow
in their understanding of the world, their family, and themselves.

It is our hope that this decision will in no way be a source of conflict
between the Kissel and the Keeshin families. Now more than ever this is
the time for support, love, and committing ourselves to the very best for
Isabel, Zoe and Ethan . . .

GOD BLESS US ALL

IRA

Bill Kissel didn't see any evidence of "the works of the angels" in Ira's
plan.

He rallied Andrew and Hayley and led a Christmas assault on
Cincinnati. Bill didn't like having to rely on Andrew, but he recognized
that Andrew and Hayley and their wealth and opulent Greenwich lifestyle represented the alternative most likely to be persuasive to a court
should the dispute reach the point of litigation. He was also determined
that the children should suffer no drop in their standard of living. In
that respect, Greenwich trumped Cincinnati.

Andrew's agenda was different, but his goal was the same. Hayley
had stopped working at Merrill Lynch when they'd hightailed it out of

200 East Seventy-fourth Street in the spring. She and Connie should be
able to raise five children in Greenwich effortlessly. And Andrew han-
kered after the $20 million trust fund.

Greenwich was a dangerous place for a man like Andrew to
live. Essentially, it was only Parkview with more acreage and a water-
front. The general principles were the same: having tens of millions
meant nothing if you didn't flaunt them shamelessly, and there was no
such thing as enough. Just as Nancy had with Parkview, Andrew wore
Greenwich like a glove. He also shared Nancy's defining characteristic:
the compulsion to acquire and display.

Andrew had started collecting luxury cars. Even as a child, his favorite toys had been cars. It was no different now, except the toys were
bigger and more expensive. He was especially fond of Ferraris. But different models appealed in different ways. Andrew couldn't decide. So he
bought four. Then he learned that in Greenwich luxury cars meant
nothing. In Greenwich, a man was measured by the size of his yacht.
For $2.85 million, Andrew bought a seventy-five-foot Hatteras. He con-
sidered it his starter yacht.

Bill, Andrew and Hayley, and Jane and Richard installed themselves in
a Marriott near the airport and summoned Ira and Ryan to a meeting
on the afternoon of Christmas Day. Before the meeting, Bill and Andrew visited Ryan's apartment. Bill termed it "nothing but a basement
firetrap." Andrew brought a legal pad and walked around looking at
plumbing and wiring, shaking his head and muttering, as if making
note of code violations. Ryan thought he was heavily under the influence of cocaine.

The meeting took place in the living room of Bill's suite at the Marriott, as the children, under Connie's supervision, played with their many new presents next door. Bill began by announcing that Andrew and Hayley would be bringing the children and Connie to Connecticut with them when they left. "Don't fight me on this," he warned Ira. "You can't out-money me. I'll bankrupt you. I'll never, ever, *ever* let this go."

"I don't think it's right," Ira said, "but if—"

Ryan interrupted. "No, we're not giving in." He pointed at Andrew, who was sniffling and rubbing his nose. "Do you really think *he* can raise these children?"

"You'd better watch yourself," Andrew said, suddenly attentive. "I've got plenty of money to hire lawyers of my own."

"Look, Andrew, we all know your family has the most money. But it's not like the kids are for sale. This shouldn't be an auction, where the high bid wins. Sure, you can sue us and eventually win because we won't have enough money to keep fighting. But can't you see that this isn't about winning? This is about what's best for the kids."

"Stop being such a Boy Scout," Bill said. "The grown-ups are having a meeting."

Ryan turned toward him. "I'm going to say something here that I know you won't want to hear. Even my dad is afraid to bring this up. But I think it's important. The children should stay in an environment where their mother is spoken about fondly, so that in the event of . . . of . . . *reunification*, they'll want to be with her again."

Bill's face turned Christmas-ribbon red.

"I know that's an awkward subject," Ryan said, "but the presumption of innocence is still part of the law, even if it doesn't exist in this room. We can't know yet what's going to happen in the Hong Kong courts. As long as there's any chance that my sister will have her children back someday, I don't think they should be taught to hate her."

"Let's go for a walk, sonny boy," Bill said. "You and I need to have a little talk in private."

Bill and Ryan took the elevator down to the lobby. Except for a massive, brightly lit tree, the lobby was empty on Christmas afternoon. Even so, Bill walked to the farthest corner before finding a spot he deemed suitable. He sat on a couch and gestured for Ryan to sit next to him.

He leaned in so close that Ryan could smell his breath. "The children will not be staying here," he said. "Your father knows that. You can see he's going to cave in. And you're a son. You've got to listen to your father." He leaned even closer. "That's what sons do."

"No. Even if you bully him, you're not going to bully me."

"Why, aren't you the brave little idealist. I've already told you I'll bankrupt your father. I'll ruin your mother, too. And—now listen carefully—I will make sure that you never practice medicine in this country."

"What kind of threat is that supposed to be?"

Bill began to shake his finger at Ryan. "And if you think your girlfriend is going to stick around after I destroy you, you're wrong."

"I don't know what you're talking about, Mr. Kissel."

Bill smiled. "Look at it this way," he said. "Why would a twenty-year-old kid—"

"I'm twenty-four."

"Don't interrupt me. Why would a twenty-year-old kid—twenty-four, I don't care—want to raise three young children by himself, the girls ten and seven, the boy four? And then the next year the oldest girl eleven? And the year after that, the oldest girl twelve?"

Again, he leaned in so close that Ryan could both smell and feel his breath.

"I can think of only one reason: to molest them."

Ryan was too stunned to reply.

"And I'll make sure people know what you're doing. Your medical school first. Then your girlfriend. Then the newspapers. I'll put it all over the country. There won't be anywhere you can go. Think about it: *child molester*. There won't be anything you can do."

Bill pointed his finger directly at Ryan's face. His voice was barely a whisper. "Don't think for a minute I don't mean it." Then he stood and walked back to the elevator, leaving Ryan alone with the Christmas tree in the lobby.

Even Andrew apologized that night. "My father," he said to Ira and Ryan, "I can't explain—he's been like this his whole life."

28. SIU LAM

NANCY WAS TRANSFERRED TO THE SIU LAM PSYCHIATRIC
Centre in the western New Territories in late November. Her expat status may not have been the only factor in the decision to incarcerate her
there instead of in the notoriously overcrowded maximum security Tai
Lam Centre for Women, but it did not work to her disadvantage.

Not even Human Rights Watch could find much wrong with Siu
Lam. A 1997 report noted that "the facility is quite pleasant: its rooms
and corridors are spacious, airy, and painted in soothing colors. It also
possesses attractive gardens with flowers, fish, and birds, tended by
some of the inmates. As the facility is located on the side of a hill, inmates held there enjoy rather dramatic views of the surrounding
area."

On the day of her admission, Nancy was evaluated by psychiatrist
Henry Yuen, who was chief of service at Siu Lam's Department of Forensic Science. Yuen summarized his impressions in a report he wrote
the next day: "consciousness level: alert; mood: neutral; attitude: cooperative; speech: relevant and coherent; suicidal idea: deny." At no time
did any doctor who examined her at Siu Lam detect any sign of mental
illness.

Nancy was soon adopted by a small coterie of Parkview wives who
believed that turning her into a cause might bring meaning to their

lives. They made into an article of faith the proposition that Nancy had been a battered wife who'd finally put an end to years of abuse by the only means available to her.

Siu Lam's liberal visitation policy (hours were from 9:00 a.m. to 5:00 p.m. seven days a week, except Mondays and Wednesdays, when the hours were 9:00 a.m. to 1:00 p.m.) allowed these women to spend half their waking hours in Nancy's presence. The closer to her they claimed to be, the greater Parkview cachet they acquired.

Nancy decided she also needed her mother. She asked her new friends to tell Jean that she would welcome a visit. Offered a reprieve from the shunning that she'd expected to last for the rest of her life, Jean flew to Hong Kong immediately. In their first moment together in almost five years, Jean said, "We just kind of melted into each other." From that day forward, Nancy and her mother were inseparable. They never discussed the past. To both of them, only the future mattered.

In July 2004—more than seven months after she'd arrived at Siu Lam—Nancy contacted her children for the first time. They'd been in Andrew and Hayley's custody all year. Ira would have fought Bill in court until he was bankrupt, but he would not let Bill harm his son. Because he had no doubt that Bill would carry out every threat he'd made against Ryan, Ira allowed Andrew and Hayley to bring the children back to Greenwich. Andrew used the private Marquis jet in which he owned a time-share. He billed the seven-thousand-dollar cost to the estate. Andrew and Hayley's expansive house—newspapers described it as a mansion—on two and a half acres in the exclusive backcountry section of Greenwich became the children's fourth home in eight weeks, not counting hotels.

On July 4, Nancy wrote to Zoe and Ethan in Greenwich, and to Isabel at summer camp in Maine. To Zoe and Ethan she wrote: "Hello!!

What's new and exciting today? Enjoying your summer activities? I'll bet you both do about 100 things each day . . . There are so many fun things to do all summer long . . ."

To Isabel she wrote: "Is it really hot at camp right now? . . . I'll bet you are making some really nice things in Arts and Crafts . . . How is the camp food this year? . . . I remember at Parent Weekend, sneaking back through the back door to grab more potato chips!! I'll bet your drinking tons of Coke . . . My favorite too . . . Keep having lots of fun!!"

She didn't say anything in either about where she was, or why, or when (or if) she might ever see them again.

In August, she sent Zoe and Ethan drawings of strawberries. She asked, "Can you count all the times you ate ice cream? I'll bet you both have had at least 100 ice cream cones this summer!! I love strawberry and chocolate ice cream ymmmmm . . . I miss you . . . I'm feeling a little better but still need some rest . . ."

She also drew strawberries on her letter to Isabel at camp. She wrote: "I went to camp at age 9 for 8 weeks—a girls camp in Indiana called Camp Pokegan (Poe-kay-gen) . . . I always ate a bacon, lettuce and tomato sandwich with extra bacon!!"

Ira drove to Maine to pick up Isabel at camp and bring her back to his house for a visit. Nancy wrote to her there: "How is Chicago . . . remember when Zoe took our picture in the car park? I was hugging you and I was wearing my jeans with the Red Dragon on the front . . . I'm sure Grandpa Ira has plenty of macaroni and cheese & waffles. Make sure he takes you out for pizza!! . . . I'm feeling much better but still need to rest a bit longer . . ."

She wrote to Isabel again in early September: "How was camp? I'll bet this summer was better than last summer . . . Did your horse remember you? . . . Was the food the same? Did they still have that giant bowl of potato chips? I can't believe you've been to camp 2 summers in a row!! It will be really fun to have Zoe go with you one of these summers . . . she'll have a blast!!"

She wrote to all three children a week later: "Are you all ready for school to start? New school supplies—Zoe—2nd grade! Isabel 5th grade! WOW!! And Ethany-Boy kindergarden! Wow you are all getting so old—so grown up . . ."

Nancy drew hearts and flowers on the pages of her letters and closed each one with "I love you . . . I hug you . . . I kiss you . . . I squeeeeeze you," followed by a heart with "Love Mommy" inside.

———

Not all intra-Kissel communications that summer were so affectionate. The teacher-student bond that Hayley and Jane formed on the Stratton Mountain ski slopes had strengthened over the years to the point where Jane sometimes described Hayley as "the sister I never had." In June, Hayley turned to Jane in order to vent about Andrew in much the same way as Rob had turned to Bryna to vent about Nancy the year before.

In one phone call, Hayley told Jane that she was going to leave Andrew. She'd learned that he was having an affair with a Greenwich woman he'd hired as a public relations agent as he tried to raise his business and social profiles. "I am busting my ass taking care of five kids, while he's off having dinner with her in nice restaurants," Hayley wrote in an e-mail. "It amazes me that I've let him treat me like that. I'm a smart person. I can't believe I've stayed in the relationship this long. But this is the ultimate humiliation and I can't take it."

Andrew seemed unbothered by Hayley's pique. He traded in his $2.85 million, seventy-five-foot yacht for a $3.6 million ninety-three-footer. He'd named the first yacht *The Five Keys* after himself, Rob, Jane, Hayley, and Nancy. He was more selective the second time. He called the new yacht *Special K's* and he liked to point out, "That's singular."

Cushioned by the $20 million trust fund, he also began to diversify his business holdings. One of his daughters liked horseback riding, so he bought the stable. He grew annoyed one night at having to wait for a table in a Greenwich waterfront restaurant, so he bought a controlling interest in it the next day. He was drinking more, so he bought a liquor store. Most colorfully, he acquired partners in Sicily and began to import olive oil.

Hayley told Jane she suspected that not all of Andrew's business dealings were legal. She said she was getting worried, for the children's sake and for her own. "I don't want to have to explain to the kids why he's in jail," she said.

Shortly before Halloween, Nancy wrote the children another letter: "Zoe's first Halloween we dressed her up as a baby pumpkin—she couldn't walk yet and just rolled around on the floor. Isabel—your first Halloween you were Tinkerbell . . . we took you trick or treating at Uncle Andy's apartment . . . Ethan was only two days old for his first Halloween so no trick or treating for him!!"

Then Nancy was released on bail. No one awaiting trial on murder charges in Hong Kong had ever before been freed on bail. And no one would ever know why Nancy was. On November 1, 2004—almost exactly one year after she'd killed her husband—a secret hearing was held in the chambers of Mr. Justice Michael Burrell of the Court of First Instance, the court in which Nancy would be tried. For reasons never disclosed, Mr. Justice Burrell voided Nancy's no-bail status and set bail at US $1 million, a sum quickly produced by the members of Nancy's Parkview coterie.

Burrell's ruling was unprecedented. There is little doubt that it would have stirred controversy in the press. Under Hong Kong law, however, the judge could not only seal the transcript of the hearing but could order the press not to report the result. Thus, when Nancy was set free on the afternoon of November 4, 2004, no one in Hong Kong outside her closest circle knew anything about it.

29. OUT ON BAIL

FROM SIU LAM, NANCY WAS TAKEN DIRECTLY TO A NINTH-floor apartment in a nondescript housing unit located just below the intersection of Bonham Road and Pok Fu Lam Road, near the University of Hong Kong. Her Parkview coterie had rented the apartment for her.

Paying the rent might not have been a problem for Nancy, but paying her legal fees was. Ira had continued to write checks to Mallesons Stephen Jaques in amounts sufficient to keep Simon Clarke's batteries charged, but with trial not scheduled to begin until May 2005, the major legal expenses still lay ahead.

Having exhausted his own life savings of $800,000, Ira raised another $225,000 by auctioning a Bridget Riley op art painting that had been in his family since 1975. But Clarke estimated that he'd need at least another million dollars.

At this point Nancy's fortunes received a boost from an unexpected source. And quite a boost it was. A Goldman Sachs partner—a former colleague of Rob's in the Hong Kong office—let it be known discreetly that as long as his anonymity was guaranteed he would underwrite the cost of Nancy's defense. Excitedly, she wrote to Michael Del Priore to tell him that the colleague had just written a check for $1 million, with more to come.

She also wrote to her children: "Its almost Thanksgiving! Turkey Day gobble-gobble!! . . . Is it getting cold outside? All the leaves start turning colors—my favorite time of year. I like stepping on the leaves and hearing them CRUNCH! . . ."

Simon Clarke flew to New York in December to take a statement from Michael Del Priore. Clarke knew the affair could not be kept secret. He also knew that the existence of a lover could be used to explain Nancy's motivation for killing Rob. When he learned that telephone records documented more than three thousand minutes of talk between Nancy and Del Priore in the month leading up to the killing, and more than a dozen conversations in the days between the killing and Nancy's arrest, Clarke realized he'd better meet the man. In addition, Nancy would not stop talking about him.

Clarke and his barrister, Alexander "Sandy" King, had seen from the start how unlikely it would seem that in fifty hours of conversation the two lovers had never discussed getting the wealthy and purportedly abusive husband out of the way. And who would believe that after the fact she hadn't told her lover she had done it and asked for his help in regard to disposing of the body and incriminating evidence?

But unless Nancy were to implicate him—which she could not do without admitting her own guilt—there was no basis for filing charges against Del Priore or even for requiring him to give a statement under oath. Yes, there would be innuendo. But innuendo was not enough for extradition.

Clarke spent two days with him in New York City, explaining that he could have no contact with Nancy until after the trial. The prosecutor would certainly ask her when she'd last been in touch with her lover. Clarke spelled out for Del Priore how vital it was that Nancy be able to deny truthfully that there had been any communication between the two of them since her arrest. By the time of her trial, Del Priore had to be portrayed as just an indiscretion, a regrettable part of Nancy's distant past.

In Clarke's absence—growing in confidence daily and urged on by her Parkview supporters—Nancy installed herself in his office at Mallesons. Upon his return, she told him she was taking charge of her own defense. She—not Clarke and not King—would map out the strategy, just as she would determine tactics during the trial. She arrived at Mallesons every morning and soon tyrannized paralegals and clerical help. She spoke to Clarke as if he were a houseboy and, more than once, when irked by his disagreement with a position she took, she threw a coffee mug or paperweight at his head. Clarke found himself facing the double-edged sword familiar to criminal defense attorneys on all continents: money from heaven, client from hell.

She wasn't much fun to live with, either. Her mother had moved in with her. Ira and Ryan visited. "There was so much tension," Ira said. "I was walking on pins and needles the whole time," Ryan said. "The only thing I ever asked her was, 'What do you want for dinner?' "

On occasion, she would call Ryan into the kitchen and tell him to sit. Chain-smoking, she'd start to talk. Her major topic was how Rob had forced her to have sex. She could talk about that for hours as Ryan choked on the smoke.

He couldn't quite manage empathy, but intermittently he felt stirrings of compassion for this baffling half sister toward whom—as he'd grown up almost fifteen years younger and a thousand miles away—he'd felt a younger brother's admiration and affection. He didn't know how she intended to testify at trial and he was grateful that it was none of his business. His role was to listen when she found herself wanting to talk, not to try to draw her out toward ground that could suddenly give way beneath the weight of her overwrought psyche.

His psychiatric training enabled him to listen to her in ways that others could not. "There was a great separation between what she said and how she said it," he later remarked. "She'd talk on and on about how Rob raped her and beat her, but her demeanor wasn't congruent with her subject. Professionally, I suppose you could call it blunted affect. There was never a lot of feeling in her voice. There was something almost ritualistic about the way she'd describe all that stuff."

It was different with her mother. "She couldn't talk about any of that," Jean later said. "She could only talk about the present. If the conversation ever got close to anything to do with that night she would get into a hysterical state. She wouldn't be able to walk or even stand up. It was clear to me that she was having flashbacks. One day we took the train to a flower market in Kowloon. It turned out to be more than she could handle. She was overcome with panic and we had to take a taxi back to the flat. In the taxi she suddenly said, 'You know he raped me. A lot. For five or six years. I couldn't say anything.' Then she completely broke down, screaming and crying. When we got back she went straight to her room and closed the door and didn't come out for hours. We never talked about it again."

Simon Clarke explained to Nancy that Hong Kong's legal system, by and large, remained based on English law. This would enable her to offer a defense of "provocation." If the jury found that she had been "provoked (whether by things done or by things said or by both together) to lose [her] self-control," they could convict her not of murder, but manslaughter. The difference was between a mandatory sentence of life imprisonment and a discretionary sentence imposed by the judge—perhaps ten years or less.

She said she wouldn't do it. The only defense that could lead to acquittal was self-defense. She said she was going to plead self-defense. Clarke tried to explain why she shouldn't. To acquit on self-defense, the jury would have to find that the amount of force Nancy had used was "reasonable in the circumstances." Five skull-shattering blows with an eight-pound lead ornament—any one of them fatal in itself—could hardly be construed as reasonable, even if Rob had been punching and kicking her and chasing her around the bedroom demanding sex.

As the English Privy Council ruled in the 1971 case of *Palmer v. The Queen*: "If there is some relatively minor attack it would not be common sense to permit some action of retaliation which was wholly out of proportion to the necessities of the situation."

But what if the attack had not been relatively minor? Nancy asked. What if she'd been fighting for her life? Suppose Rob had come at her with a weapon, intending to kill her? What if Rob had attacked her not with his bare hands, but with a potentially lethal club?

The police had not found a club in the bedroom, but Clarke had. He'd found the baseball bat on the bedroom floor. Suppose Rob had used *that* as a weapon? Suppose he'd charged at her swinging the bat, shouting, "I'm going to kill you, you bitch!"? In that case, she would have been justified in defending herself with the statuette. Why had she hit him five times? She didn't know, she couldn't remember. Suppose the trauma of the attack had triggered a state of dissociative amnesia?

The Cleveland Clinic Web site—easily available to an experienced searcher such as Nancy—explains, "Dissociative amnesia occurs when a person blocks out certain information, usually associated with a stressful or traumatic event, leaving him or her unable to remember important personal information. With this disorder, the degree of memory loss goes beyond normal forgetfulness and includes gaps in memory for long periods of time or of memories involving the traumatic event."

If Nancy had experienced dissociative amnesia, she wouldn't be able to recall anything between Rob's attack and, say, the arrival of the police at the apartment. Why had she kept the body in the bedroom for two and a half days? Why had she rolled it up in a carpet? Why hadn't she simply called the police as soon as she realized Rob was dead to tell them that her husband had just tried to kill her but that she'd apparently killed him in self-defense?

Simple: she couldn't remember anything that had happened. She'd been in a state of dissociative amnesia.

Once she was free on bail, Nancy could have had her children flown to Hong Kong at any time. She'd chosen not to. She'd said it would have been too much of an emotional strain for her. She had not written to them since November, and she had never talked to them by phone. Now, as her trial approached, she shut them completely out of her life.

She told her mother she did not want to receive any more letters from the children, nor photographs of them, nor news about them. She was sure they'd be fine with Andrew and Hayley. She had herself to worry about.

How fine the children actually were as Andrew and Hayley's troubled marriage staggered toward dissolution was unclear. Hayley, who had filed for divorce in February, said they were thriving, despite the worsening domestic chaos. Jane wasn't so sure, particularly after a phone call in which Hayley said (according to notes Jane made at the time of the call), "I hate to say it, but every time I see Rob's kids now, I see Andrew in them. I hate to take it out on them, but I can't help it."

Hayley's filing seemed to have driven Andrew past some personal point of no return. He would bring a bottle of scotch into his Hanrock office in Stamford and spend hours forging and falsely notarizing the documents needed to obtain fraudulent loans. Then he would decide it was party time and nobody would see him for days.

He'd invested in an off-Broadway show called *Pieces (of Ass)*. It consisted of "a series of original monologues from a rotating cast of beautiful women," a press release said. "These pieces aim to go beneath the beautiful façade and examine the concept of 'hot chick angst.' " Andrew developed a personal interest in the subject, and in a number of the actresses from the show.

On Friday, May 20, he used the private jet to fly a group of actresses and business associates to Miami, where they boarded the *Special K's*. Although he was already shopping for a bigger yacht, Andrew made the most of the $3.6 million ninety-three-footer—"kicking off his drinking binges at 11 a.m. and cavorting with a bevy of actresses," as the *New York Post* reported.

The party ended Sunday night when Hayley, at the end of a long day with the five children, called the yacht. Andrew had assured her that only male business associates were aboard—ostensibly to analyze opportunities in Florida real estate—but a woman answered. She wasn't sober. Hayley wasn't pleased. She hung up and sent Jane an e-mail that said: "GOD, I HATE YOUR BROTHER!!!!!!!!!!!!!!! Sorry, just had to vent."

Jane replied the next morning, asking Hayley if she was all right. Hayley replied:

I am okay. He is just such an awful pathetic person. I just fucking hate him, his I am the King attitude, his value system (or lack thereof), his anger, his meanness. I JUST HATE HIM!!!!!!!!!!!!!!!! HE WILL NEVER BE A GOOD, RESPONSIBLE PERSON. I just can't believe how he can so readily shirk his responsibility to his family . . . HE IS HORRIBLE, JUST HORRIBLE AND I HATE HIS FUCKING GUTS. Do you know last night in bed I could actually see myself pummeling him to death and just enjoying the sensation of each and every shot and then this morning as I pulled out of the garage to go to spin class all I wanted to do was crash into his Ferraris. He put this stupid pole in the garage so that I would know where to stop my car when I pulled into the garage because you know how incompetent I am that I can't even park my car. Do you know I intentionally bang into the thing every time I park as an act of defiance . . . I HAAAAAAAAAAAAAAAATTTTTTTTTTTTTEEEEEEEEEE HHHHHIIIIIMMMMM!!!!!!!!!!!!!!!!!"

That was enough for Jane. She wasn't going to leave Rob's children in a madhouse. She told Andrew she wanted custody of the children. He said she couldn't have it. They accused each other of caring more about the trust fund than the children. Jane said she'd sue for custody if she had to. Andrew said, "I can't believe you're doing this to me. I'll fight you." Then Hayley chimed in. She told Jane that Andrew was essentially bankrupt and that she'd be left with nothing after the divorce. But the trust fund could help her maintain her standard of living. "If I keep the kids," she said, "it may not be the best thing for them, but at least I won't be on the street. I'm not going to let the Kissels take anything more from me. I've given enough. I'm going to do what's best for myself." Bill called from Florida to tell Hayley she was "a money-grubbing bitch."

It was just the Kissels being Kissels.

The Trial

30. JUNE 7–JULY 30

THE TRIAL BEGAN ON TUESDAY, JUNE 7, 2005, IN THE COURT of First Instance in room 33 of the High Court Building on Queensway in Central. The presiding judge was Mr. Justice Michael Lunn, Q.C., a Cambridge-educated fifty-five-year-old Zimbabwean. He'd been in private practice in Hong Kong for more than twenty years before being appointed to the bench in 2003. Lunn was highly regarded, known in particular for his courtesy and personal warmth. "Old school, first class, a gentleman," a Hong Kong journalist said. The prosecutor was the experienced Peter Chapman. He was a large man who exuded self-confidence without arrogance. Juries liked him, and so did Mr. Justice Lunn.

Alexander King had proven himself to be one of Hong Kong's most skillful barristers, but as do many highly successful, wealthy defense attorneys, he had attracted his share of criticism. One observer called him a "mountebank." His style was to dazzle, even if, on occasion, it risked a loss of dignity. If Nancy was determined to pursue a strategy of self-defense, King had a better chance than most of selling it.

"Chapman versus King: it's a battle of heavyweight champions," a Hong Kong barrister said. "And only one of them will be standing at the end."

The courtroom was so small that spectators in the sixty public seats would almost be able to hear lawyers, witnesses, and even Mr. Justice Lunn breathe between sentences. The inadequacy of the air-conditioning assured that the breaths would be hot. The first week of June had been exceedingly steamy even by Hong Kong standards. Thunderstorms rolled across the island with regularity. Daytime temperatures reached the mid-nineties, with humidity near 100 percent. There was little cooling at night.

Even with pretrial publicity prohibited in Hong Kong, the expat community was in a tizzy. "We have a female who is accused of murdering her husband, a leading member of Hong Kong's financial community," University of Hong Kong professor of criminal law Simon Young Ngai-man told Barclay Crawford of the *South China Morning Post.* "They are members of the elite, upper crust of the expat society and we are getting a glimpse inside their private world, finding out intimate details of their lives."

One spectator, requesting anonymity, told the *Post,* "There has never been a trial like this in Hong Kong. It's like it has been scripted for a movie, but the story is one you wouldn't believe." Another newspaper article said, "For Hong Kong expatriates, the Kissel murder trial [is] the OJ Simpson murder trial and the Michael Jackson child abuse drama rolled into one . . . a lurid drama . . . a wild American soap opera transplanted to Asia."

Bill Kissel was among the spectators. He had come to bear witness. He intended to stay to the end. Nancy's mother Jean also attended. She and Nancy continued to live in the apartment in Pok Fu Lam. The prosecution had tried and failed to have Nancy's bail revoked before the start of the trial. Jean and Bill did not speak to each other and avoided eye contact. Just as at Rob and Nancy's wedding sixteen years earlier, they sat on opposite sides of the aisle.

The jury-selection process was brief. After Mr. Justice Lunn said the trial would last two to three months, a number of prospective jurors sought to be excused, citing employment commitments, inadequate English, and, in one case, anti-Semitism. Nonetheless, a jury of five men and two women—all Chinese—was impaneled within a day.

One of Hong Kong's highest-profile barristers, expat Kevin "The Ego" Egan, did not expect them to be sympathetic to Nancy. "Juries here are stone-faced, pragmatic, and with their feet on the ground," he said. "To win this case, you'd need a bunch of cuckoos from Connecticut and neurotics from New York."

Peter Chapman's opening statement was focused, not flamboyant. He said Nancy had rendered Rob unconscious by "lacing a milk-shake with a cocktail of sedative drugs" and had then struck "a series of powerful and fatal blows" with the lead statuette. By grasping the figurines of the two little girls, Chapman said, Nancy had been able to use the ornament "like a hammerhead," causing "massive spillage of brain substance."

The "five types of hypnotic and sedative drugs" that were found in Rob's stomach and liver matched five of the six drugs Nancy had obtained by prescription in the weeks leading up to the murder. "Insignificantly low" amounts of alcohol had been found, contradicting Nancy's story that Rob had attacked her while drunk, while the absence of any defensive injuries indicated he'd been unable even to try to protect himself.

Chapman described how Nancy had attempted to dispose of Rob's body. He pointed out that she'd also tried to hide the broken and bloodied ornament by placing it at the bottom of one of the sealed packing cartons that she'd sent to the storeroom with the body. Then she'd concocted a story about Rob vanishing into the night after having beaten her up. Her motive was simple, Chapman said: to cash in on Rob's $18 million to $20 million estate—the total varied depending on the method used to value assets—before he was able to divorce her. She'd hoped to use the money to fund a new life with "the man in her life," Michael Del Priore.

Alexander King chose not to make an opening statement. He didn't want to commit to a position before seeing how the prosecution developed its case. Chapman began to present evidence. The first week's witnesses included Rob's sister Jane ("Nancy argued a lot, I was very careful when I was with her"), Scotty the Clown ("She was a very caring parent, very easy to deal with . . . She got things done"), and Rocco Gatta, who described his surveillance in Vermont.

An unexpected witness was Dr. Daniel Wu of Adventist Hospital, who told the court he had treated Rob for a "boxer's fracture" of his right little finger in September 1999. Rob said he'd broken the finger punching a wall. Chapman knew the defense would try to portray Rob as uncontrollably violent, and he wanted to deal with the broken finger early on.

Details of Rob's will were revealed. In March 1998, he had directed that if he predeceased her, all his assets should go to Nancy.

Weekend press coverage was predictably breathless. In *The Sunday Telegraph* of London, Simon Parry wrote of "a trial that has captivated the former British colony and horrified its wealthy expatriates." He wrote that "Hong Kong is enthralled by the saga of 'White Mischief' in the expatriate compounds where wealthy foreigners are pampered by Filipina maids and Chinese staff." And he quoted a Chinese reporter as saying, "For us, this case is a throwback to the colonial era. It has all the ingredients our readers are most interested in: sex, murder, *gwei-los*—and lots and lots of money."

South Africa's News24 struck the same theme, citing the trial's "heady brew of sex, power, greed, betrayal, jealousy and, above all in this cash-obsessed town, money . . . [that] has shone a tantalizing light into the usually closed world of Hong Kong's wealthy expats."

Chinese papers emphasized love letters from Del Priore that investigators found hidden in Nancy's bureau after the murder.

Min was on the stand for two and a half days during the second week. She said Nancy "could not forgive" and "if you made a mistake, she would hate you." On cross-examination, she said she'd often seen a baseball bat in the bedroom while cleaning. Andrew Tanzer and his wife talked about the effects of the milk shake. Frank Shea meticulously described his every contact with Rob, and Robin Egerton told the jury of Rob's decision to file for divorce.

The third week brought two days of testimony from Connie, with details added by everyone from the sales clerk at Tequila Kola to the supervisor of the work crew that moved the carpet to the storeroom.

David Noh described his surreal phone conversation with Rob as the drugs from the milk shake began to take hold.

"After that," one observer said, "it was Chinese New Year." Between June 25 and July 29—as waves of violent thunderstorms punctuated weeks of stifling heat—the jury heard testimony from police officers, forensic scientists, toxicologists, lab technicians, and computer experts Yuen Shing-kit, See Kwong-tak, Ng Yuk-ying, Cheung Tseung-sin, Chong Yam-hoi, Mak Chung-hung, Tam Chi-chung, Chan Ping-kong, Lun Tze-shan, Chan Kin-wah, Wong Koon-hung, Pang Chi-ming, Li Wai-sum, Cheung Chun-kit, Cheng Kok-choi, Yeung Hok-keung, and Lau Ming-fai.

Predictably, King tried to show that nobody had done anything right. The police had tricked Nancy into talking, they'd failed to secure the crime scene, they hadn't taken notes, the lab technicians had been sloppy, the toxicology was suspect, the blood spatter analysis flawed, and so on.

In the O. J. Simpson case, Johnnie Cochran and Barry Scheck had shown how effective such a scorched-earth defense could be, but this was not the O. J. Simpson case, where black jurors mistrusted white police. This was Hong Kong, where Chinese jurors respected authority and were not likely to respond favorably to a *gweilo* lawyer's attempt to denigrate the professionalism of their fellow citizens.

Although Nancy sat mute, hunched, and trembling during testimony, occasionally giving way to sobs, her demeanor was quite different during breaks. She was often seen inside a glass-walled conference room gesticulating and shouting at her legal team, leaving no doubt about who was in charge.

By mid-July, the defense strategy was clear: to make the jury find Rob so loathsome that in the end they'd give her a medal for having killed him. King used cross-examination to insinuate. Wasn't it true that Rob had been violent? Wasn't it true that he was prone to drunken rages? Hadn't he physically abused his children? Wasn't he addicted to cocaine? It may not have been true—and no witnesses offered confirmation—but that wasn't the point. The idea was to plant seeds of doubt about Rob's character and personality in the hope that flowers of revulsion might later bloom.

The technique was similar to that employed in a Spanish bullfight. First the picadores and banderilleros weaken the animal, then the matador finishes him off in a geyser of blood and gore. Nancy had already done it literally—she was sure she could do it metaphorically, too.

———————

Her most promising breakthrough came with the appearance of prosecution computer expert Cheung Chun-kit. Chapman called him to testify about Nancy's Internet searches for drugs that killed without leaving a trace. Cheung said he'd found evidence of the searches both on Nancy's Sony VAIO laptop where they had originated and on Rob's IBM ThinkPad, to which the spyware had sent them.

On cross-examination, however, King pointed out that the Kissels had also had two Dell desktop computers in the apartment: one for general use and one for the children. Cheung said he'd been told to focus on the laptops and that he "did not spend much time" examining the contents of the hard drives of the Dells.

That was unfortunate, King said. If he had, he might have found evidence of searches conducted on one of the Dell desktops between April 3 and April 5, 2003, when Nancy was already in Vermont with the children and when—presumably—only Rob would have had access to it.

As Rob was preparing for a three-day trip to Taiwan on April 8, the Dell hard drive recorded searches for "Mpeg sex," "sex in Taiwan," "hot male sex," "anal," "cocks," "gay anal sex," "bisexual," "male ass," "Taiwan escorts," "Taiwan companions," "gay sex or anal sex in Taiwan," "hardcore gay bondage sex," "free black gay porn," "black gay male pictures," "gay black men," "black males," "ebony men," "married and lonely in Hong Kong," "wife is a bitch," and "used Porsches."

That was on the Dell desktop. Then there was the ThinkPad. Although Cheung had found approximately seven thousand of Nancy's e-mails transferred to the IBM ThinkPad by the eBlaster spyware, he had not located indications of searches conducted during May and June of 2003 for "twinks," "actresses for hire in Taiwan," "escorts in Taiwan," "Paris girls for hire," "Paris gay massage," "Paris x-rated escorts," "gay sex," and "anal sex."

It was explained to the jury that "twink" was a gay slang term used to denote an attractive, boyish-looking gay man between the ages of eighteen and twenty-two, slender and with little or no body hair, often blond, often but not necessarily Caucasian.

———————

Bill stormed out of court at the first mention of deviant sex. But there was nowhere to hide from bad news. The day after Cheung finished testifying about Rob's computer searches, the FBI arrested Andrew in Vermont. He was charged with falsifying mortgage documents in order to defraud banks in New York, New Jersey, and Connecticut of at least $25 million and perhaps as much as $50 million. Federal prosecutors said he faced a prison sentence of twenty-five years. After posting a million dollars in bail, he was ordered confined to his house in Greenwich and made to wear an electronic surveillance device on his ankle. His lawyer, Philip Russell, called him "a sick man" and said he was "in extremis." In Hong Kong, Bill told the press he'd seen it coming for years.

Sandy King introduced the baseball bat into evidence on July 28. He recalled Min to the stand to ask her if she recognized the bat as being the same one she'd often seen in the bedroom when she cleaned.

"I can't be sure," she answered in her native Ilokano language.

It didn't matter. After having been secreted in Simon Clarke's office for more than a year and a half, the baseball bat was now in evidence.

Sandy King had set the stage perfectly for Nancy.

31. NANCY'S TESTIMONY

NANCY TOOK THE STAND ON THE MORNING OF MONDAY, August 1. She wore black, as she had from the start. Trembling, stooped, and tearful, her hair a dull brown, her dark eyes glazed behind schoolmarm's glasses, she was the farthest possible cry from the grinning, effervescent blonde who'd posed for a photograph with George H. W. Bush less than two years before.

She'd had eight weeks to try to win the jury's sympathy on appearance and demeanor. Now she could add words and tears. In the front row of the spectators' gallery, Bill Kissel and Jane Chandler Kissel were sitting almost close enough to touch her. Her mother was not much farther away. The room was hot. The air was still. Nancy's fate hung in the balance.

Alexander King's questioning was gentle, deferential, and limned with regret as he coaxed his first answers from his client.

"I don't know how to talk about these things," she said.

She told the jury she'd gained forty pounds during her first pregnancy—her weight rising to 150 pounds—and when she didn't lose it all as soon as Isabel was born, Rob told her she was no longer attractive to him and he couldn't stand to look at her while making love. He'd begun to insist on anal sex, and when she refused he forced her. That had been the start of years of violent sodomy, she said.

She quivered and gasped and fixed her gaze on the floor. Not in all the years of her marriage, nor even after she'd killed Rob—in fact, not until her lawyers had discovered Rob's Internet searches for sites related to anal sex—had Nancy so much as hinted to anyone that her husband had been sodomizing her against her will.

Of course, a terrified battered woman would *not* have spoken about such abuse—wasn't that part of the syndrome? Nancy's friends from Parkview and from the Hong Kong International School understood that, so surely the seven jurors would as well.

"Our marriage changed when we got to Hong Kong," she said. "There was so much stress working for Goldman Sachs. He thrived on it. It's what made him tick: the power of it all, succeeding. But the hours began to take their toll. It was literally twenty-four hours of having to be awake. When the Hong Kong market closed, the New York market opened. They were at opposite ends of the globe. He'd always used cocaine to get through the hours, but now it got to be a lot more. And he would drink. Sometimes he'd stay up drinking all night. He was also taking painkillers for his back. He became a different person. He got rougher."

She said the first time he hit her was in 1999, when she was seven months pregnant with Ethan. He'd wanted her to induce labor so he could be present for the birth before he left on a trip to South Korea.

"To induce labor was nothing to him. When I said no, he said I was disrespecting him and how hard he worked. He punched at me, but he hit the wall because I dodged. He came home with a cast on his hand the next day."

King reminded her that Dr. Wu of Adventist Hospital had testified about treating Rob for a "boxer's fracture" of the finger. "It was that night," Nancy said. "And it happened again—the same argument the following week. The second time, he hit me in the face."

After Ethan was born, she said, Rob became even more disgusted with her body. "From then on, it was predominantly oral sex for him, and anal sex. He'd be sitting at the end of the bed with the TV on and he wouldn't let me walk past him. He'd start this game, toying with me, and he would say things to me, like he could do anything he wanted."

"Were you agreeable to that, Mrs. Kissel?" King asked.

"No," she said. Then she began crying so hard she couldn't talk. Jane stood up and walked out of the courtroom.

Following a short recess, Nancy said, "After Ethan was born, Rob's personality changed so much. It was a routine of him coming home, drinking, and sex. It made me feel nonexistent." She said he would trap her between his legs and pull her hair. "He was just so angry. He wouldn't even look at my face. Then he would throw me on the bed to finish. It would always be a struggle, because he'd try to make me lie on my stomach. Once, he tried flipping me over. I didn't want it. He grabbed me by the hips, just twisting. I felt something pop."

That was the first time he'd broken her ribs, she said. She'd gone to Adventist Hospital and bought a Velcro brace to protect them. "A couple of weeks later, he ripped the brace off and I ended up going to the hospital again. After that, I gave in more and more." She said she often bled from the anus after being sodomized and had to throw out the sheets because she was ashamed to let Min see them.

"Why didn't you tell anyone, Mrs. Kissel?"

"You just don't. You just don't. It's humiliating."

Her tears brought the day to a close.

By Tuesday, it was apparent that Nancy would remain tearful and trembling throughout her testimony. She continued her account of Rob's alleged violence. She described an incident at Whistler Mountain during the Christmas vacation of 2002. Rob was already angry with her for staying in the hotel room with Ethan instead of skiing. He said her conduct "embarrassed" him. On Christmas Eve, he wanted sex. She was wrapping presents and decorating a tree she had ordered for their split-level suite.

"He thought I was fussing too long," she said. "So he grabbed me and pulled me upstairs, because he wanted what he wanted. And I let him. And then I went back downstairs and finished with the presents. That got him even angrier because he had told me not to waste any more time doing that. He said, 'You're not fucking listening to me! I told you not to fucking touch the tree and you did.' " Then, she said, he slammed her against a wall.

They also fought on the day after Christmas, she said. Rob again accused her of not listening to him. She told him to shut up and she waved her finger in his face. "So he hit me. And I fell down the flight of steps and hit my head on the bottom."

She said things got so bad in the spring of 2003 that she came close to killing herself the night before Rob arrived in Vermont in May.

"After Connie and the children were asleep, I went into the garage and turned on the car engine. I don't know how long I was in the car. I cried a lot. Then I got scared of leaving my children. So I turned off the engine and went back into the house."

Rob's visit created friction. "Everything bothered him. The way the children were sitting at the table, Isabel not eating her vegetables.

He grabbed her and started shaking her and she said, 'Daddy, you're hurting me!' but he wouldn't let go. Finally, he went to the computer and printed out some photos of malnourished people and made her look at them, which she hated."

There was another pause while Nancy cried.

As for Michael Del Priore, he'd been scarcely more than a shoulder to cry on. Being with him, she said, "was very easy, very comfortable. I could cry. I cried a lot. There were no questions, no 'do this, do that.' It was basically just letting me talk. It was the first time anybody ever stepped forward for me. In our little expatriate world, people look at you and see change, but they don't really want to know. They're more interested in what you're wearing and how big your diamond ring is and your car."

"Had you formed an intention to leave your husband?"

"No. I never thought about it. I was determined to work through things however they played out. There was no question in my mind that I was Mrs. Kissel. I had been for fifteen years. I was a banker's wife. Vermont, of which Michael was part, was only an escape from my real world."

Suicidal impulses returned. That was why she'd gone on the Internet to search for drugs that could kill without leaving a trace. They hadn't been intended for Rob, but for herself.

From the gallery, Bill Kissel shook his head and muttered, as if scarcely able to believe her perfidy.

"I typed this information about 'sleeping pills' and 'overdose' for myself," Nancy said. "I was pretty desperate, with everything that had happened, and not wanting to face what was going on in my marriage. So the 'causing heart attack' was something I thought about. If I was

going to do something like this—taking pills—I wouldn't want my children to be affected. I wouldn't want them going through the knowledge
of their mother committing suicide. I wouldn't want them to ever know
about it. To feel the loss of their mother caused by a heart attack was
something I wanted to do for their protection. It was an out for me from
being humiliated."

She began to weep and Mr. Justice Lunn called a recess until the
next day.

———————————

All seats in the courtroom had been taken since the first minute of
Nancy's testimony. By Wednesday, long lines stretched down the hallway. Filipina maids vied for places with lawyers, students, and bejew-
eled Parkview wives who, as one newspaper observed, "had come to see
the downfall of one of their own." Court officers were stationed in the
hallway to keep order.

Nancy had laid the groundwork. She'd portrayed Rob as both a
psychological and physical abuser—a drunken, vicious, coke-fueled sod-
omite, to be specific. Now she would have to explain how she had happened to kill him.

"Beginning to tremble," "trembling uncontrollably," "her voice
trembling and barely audible," "often tearful," "shaking as she spoke,"
"still shaking," "speaking almost in a whisper," "weeping"—as the
English-language press described her the next day—Nancy continued
her testimony.

She said their two marriage counseling sessions had triggered
Rob's worst behavior yet. After the first, he'd accused her of wasting his

time and money by not listening to him when he spoke. He'd said he was going to teach her to "show more respect" and he'd sodomized her twice in especially violent fashion.

During the second counseling session, she had said, "I'm done. I want a divorce." Rob had stormed out of the room and she hadn't seen him again until he charged drunkenly into their bedroom at 2:00 a.m.

"He started yelling at me. He said, 'Who do you think you are, asking for a divorce like that? You'll never divorce me. If anyone's doing the divorcing around here, it'll be me!' He wanted to make sure I was listening properly: he made the money, he called the shots. Not me. He wanted to make that understood." Then, she said, he anally raped her, "over and over again, saying how I needed to show respect and that he was in control."

Nancy also wanted it clear that there had been nothing untoward about her hundreds of phone conversations with Del Priore in the weeks leading up to Rob's death. "He gave me comfort on a daily basis," she said, and that was that—at least until cross-examination.

As for the milk shake, nothing could have been more innocent. "Zoe and Leah wanted to have some ice cream. We all went to the kitchen. There were six or seven containers in the freezer, but there was just a little bit left in each, not enough to give them all an equal portion. So we dumped them in the blender to make milk shakes."

She said that she and the two girls peeled and cut bananas, while Ethan crumbled cookies to make crumbs. Zoe wanted to make the shakes look "Halloweeny" so they added red food coloring. When the shakes were made, Zoe and Leah carried them into the living room to their fathers. After Andrew Tanzer and his daughter left, she said, Rob and Ethan came into the kitchen and drank what was left in the blender.

"It was a milk shake that I made for my children and for someone else's child," she said. "I wouldn't harm my own children. I wouldn't harm someone else's child. I made the milk shake for my children in the afternoon. That's all I remember."

Even when she wasn't weeping, Nancy was hard to hear because she spoke in such a soft voice. Repeatedly, both King and Mr. Justice Lunn asked her to talk louder. She would shake her head, sob, and tremble in reply.

"Later that afternoon, I was cleaning the kitchen," she said. "He started yelling at me, asking if I was listening. Then he said, 'I've filed for divorce and I'm taking the kids. It's a done deal. I've talked to the lawyers.' I said, 'What do you mean?' He said, 'If you had listened, you would have heard what I said. I have filed for divorce and I am taking the kids. It's a done deal.' He said I wasn't fit to take care of the kids, that I was sick."

Then, she said, Rob had walked down the hall to the bedroom. She saw him in the doorway, holding a baseball bat in one hand, tapping the barrel against his other palm.

"What's that for?" she said.

"Protection. In case you get violent."

She went into the dining room and picked up the lead statuette. Then she walked down the hallway to confront him.

"What do you mean you've filed and you're taking the kids? And you've told people I'm sick?"

She started waving her finger at him, knowing how much he hated that. He slapped it away once, twice, but the third time he grabbed her hand. "He wouldn't let go, so I spat in his face. He hit me across the mouth. Then he pulled me into the room, threw me onto the bed, and started to have sex with me. I started to struggle with him. He wouldn't let go. I started kicking him and he wouldn't let up. We ended up on the floor.

"I started to crawl away, but he grabbed my ankles and pulled me and wouldn't let go. I knew what he was trying to do. He said, 'I'm not finished with you yet.' He kicked me in the stomach and he wouldn't stop. *He wouldn't stop! I just wanted him to stop!*"

She trembled and sobbed. "I was on the floor and I reached for the statue and I swung it back. I didn't even look. I felt that I hit something, and he let go. I turned around and I looked at him. He was sitting by the closet and I saw that he was bleeding. I tried to help him up and he wouldn't let me. He pulled himself up on the bed and just sat there and I just . . . I just kept looking at him. He touched his head with his hand and saw that it was bleeding."

Her shaking grew more pronounced. "He picked up the bat and started swinging. He said, 'You want to kill me. Bitch! You want to kill me!'

"Then he said, 'I'm going to kill you. I am going to kill you, you bitch.' He repeated several times, 'I'm going to fucking kill you!' He grabbed the bat and came at me. He hit me on the leg, on my knee, and I was swinging back with the statue.

"I ended up on the floor next to the bed and he moved on top with the bat . . . in his hand . . . He came down on me as I was holding the statue in front of my face . . ."

She stopped. For a full minute she sat, silent and trembling, with every eye in the courtroom trained on her face.

"Can you tell us anything more about this fight?" King asked.

She sat shaking for another half minute. Then she said, "I just wanted him to stop swinging the bat." Her stooped shoulders were heaving as she sobbed.

"What was your last recollection of what happened between your husband and yourself in the bedroom that day?"

Trembling and shaking her head, she sobbed, "Just being on the floor next to the bed."

"You know your husband had five injuries on his head, any of which could have been fatal. Can you tell us anything about how they got there?"

Nancy sat shaking and did not answer. Then she broke down completely and the judge called another recess.

King resumed his questioning ten minutes later. "The master bedroom was cleaned up. What recollections do you have of doing that?"

"I don't remember."

"CCTV photos show you in the car park starting from the early morning of Monday, November 3, 2003. Photos also show you carrying a rug on your shoulder."

"I don't remember Monday. I just remember being in my car. I got in my car and I drove down the hill. I don't know where I went."

"Can you explain why your fingerprints were found on the sticky side of the packing tape of boxes containing bloodied items?"

"No. I can't remember."

"Do you recall a visit to Dr. Dytham's office in Wan Chai on the morning of November 4, 2003?"

"I have no recollection."

"Do you remember going to the Aberdeen police station to report your husband's assault and handing officers there a copy of Dr. Dytham's report on your injuries?"

"I don't . . . I don't know that."

King handed her a CCTV picture of Ira and her in the tower 17 elevator on November 6. "Do you know why your father came to Hong Kong?"

"I remember speaking to him on the phone. It's not very clear the conversation I had with him. He said he was coming out to be with me."

"Do you remember when he arrived?"

"No."

"Can you tell us anything that you and your father did on November 5?"

"I have no recollection."

"Mrs. Kissel," King said, "do you remember doing anything with your husband's body?"

"No."

"Are you able to tell us when you had the first realization that your husband was dead?"

"I started to remember things, just images, bits and pieces of things that didn't really make sense to me, maybe six months or so later in Siu Lam. They just kind of came back in little pieces; those fragments of memory came back. The first month I was there, I don't really remember much. I don't have a clear memory of the beginning."

"On November 3–at *that* time–did you know your husband was dead?"

"No. I don't remember." She began to shake harder, she put her head in her hands, and she sobbed.

After three days, King finished his direct examination. The moment court recessed for lunch, dozens of people who had been waiting in the hallway all morning surged inside, scrambling for the just-vacated seats. The only way to keep a seat was not to leave during the lunch break. Even that tactic could not assure that you wouldn't lose your seat by going to the bathroom. People pushed past the guards at the door and squeezed into standing-room space behind the gallery and along the side walls. In addition to the sixty seated spectators, thirty standees crowded inside. In the absence of floor space, they stood on one another's toes. Another knot of sensation-starved expats filled the doorway, hoping they'd be able to hear and straining for an unobstructed view. Behind them, in the hallway, all semblance of order had disappeared. The normally straitlaced Court of First Instance was in danger of being overrun.

Peter Chapman, bewigged, cleared his throat and began his cross-examination.

"Mrs. Kissel, there's just one little matter you might be able to help us with. Do you accept that you killed Robert Kissel?"

"Yes." She was sitting up straight, seemingly composed.

"And do you accept that you used the metal ornament that's been introduced into evidence to inflict the fatal injuries?"

"Yes."

Chapman nodded. With that out of the way, he could proceed. His manner toward Nancy stopped well short of being disdainful, but Alexander King's solicitousness was notably lacking.

"Mrs. Kissel," Chapman said, "I've noticed that throughout the trial you've been taking notes as witnesses have testified and that you've made it a practice to pass these notes to your attorneys. May I ask, with your knowledge of the prosecution case, can you help us, please? Which portions of the evidence do you dispute?"

"I've heard a lot of people talk about what they participated in, what they saw, and what they said," she replied. "I'm not sure it's about disputing, but trying to understand what's been said. So many people are saying things of which I don't have any recollection. I'm not sure it's about being right or wrong."

"Oh, come now, Mrs. Kissel, of all the witnesses who have testified so far, surely *someone* has said *something* with which you disagree."

"My maid said I was hot tempered. I disagree with that."

"Anything else?"

"My husband's sister said he was a loyal, protective husband. That's not true."

"Anything else?"

"I didn't believe Connie when she said she'd never heard Rob and I fighting."

"And anything else?"

She'd had enough. "There have been weeks of evidence," she said. "I'm not going to try to pinpoint anything else."

"Mrs. Kissel, other than your two visits to Dr. Fung to obtain sleeping pills, have you ever seen a psychiatrist?"

"No."

"You've never been diagnosed with or treated for any form of mental illness?"

"No."

"And prior to killing your husband, had you ever experienced any memory loss?"

"No."

"Where did your husband get his cocaine?"

"Excuse me, I don't–"

"The cocaine that your husband was constantly abusing, along with alcohol while he was in Hong Kong, where was he getting it from?"

"I don't know."

"You never asked?"

"No."

"Did he ever take any with him on business trips?"

"I don't know."

"I would have thought that might have been a concern. Did you ever remind him that countries in this part of the world take a pretty dim view of hard drugs?"

"No."

"Well, he's not much good to you busted in Malaysia on drug charges, is he?"

Nancy agreed that he would not have been.

"I believe you've testified that the frequency with which your husband demanded anal sex increased significantly after your arrival in Hong Kong. Is that correct?"

"Yes. Especially towards 2002."

"How often each month did you have forced anal sex with Robert Kissel?"

"I never counted."

"Give us a number, Mrs. Kissel."

"It wasn't about how many times. It was a progression of how we were together. Starting in different positions. The ability to move into those positions. Progression of sexual activity. There were times when he got very frustrated by my changing, moving into ways he didn't want. It was a period in which things developed into something different. There was force involved. He used force because that's the way he chose to have that kind of sex. He knew I didn't like it."

"And cocaine was involved?"

"Sometimes."

"And alcohol?"

"Sometimes. Sometimes both, sometimes neither."

"Did Robert Kissel ever wear a condom?"

"No."

"Did he ever use any lubricant or gel?"

"No."

"Yet he never had a problem effecting anal entry throughout this period?"

"Yes, it would hurt. Sometimes I'd bleed."

"From the anus?"

"Yes."

"How often would this occur?"

"A couple of times a year, for a day or two each time."

"When your husband was away on business trips, you couldn't know whether he was sleeping with other women in other countries and having anal sex with them, could you?"

"No."

"I believe one of your closest friends contracted HIV and died of AIDS–Alison Gertz, the maid of honor at your wedding."

"Yes."

"Did her fate ever cross your mind while you were passing blood as a result of forceful sodomy? After all, Mrs. Kissel, you say your husband had a cocaine habit and an appetite for sodomy and he traveled frequently. Don't you think that would have made him high risk?"

"I never thought he was high risk."

"In relation to these activities, the cocaine- and alcohol-fueled violent anal sex that hurt so much and made you bleed, did you ever tell anyone about it?"

"No. It was something that was happening gradually. It was my responsibility to deal with it. It's not something you talk about with the girls."

"Well, during the more violent episodes that involved your hair being pulled, your ribs being broken, and pain from penetration that was making you bleed, did you ever scream out?"

"Did I scream out? I may have."

"Did anyone ever hear you? Over five years?"

"I don't know. A lot of the time I was facing down. A lot of the time I just cried."

"So neither of your two live-in domestic helpers ever heard you scream? Never, during the entire five years?"

"They were off duty after seven p.m. They'd be back in their room at the other end of the apartment."

"Did you ever consider going to your friends to say, 'I can't take it anymore?' "

"No."

"Why not?"

"Because people only hear what they want to hear."

"Have you ever been examined in relation to the results of forceful anal sex over this five-year period?"

"No, it's humiliating."

It was a long weekend at Parkview. Reuters reported that Hong Kong's expat community was "shocked and riveted" by proceedings in the

Court of First Instance. That was an understatement. Titillation spread like SARS throughout the towers. More than a few Parkview wives were rallying to Nancy's defense: some because they believed her story of Rob's abuse, others because they felt their sense of privilege threatened. Surely, vast wealth and expat status should insulate one from the petty concerns of a foreign country's legal system.

On Monday morning, the normal contingent of court officers was reinforced by special crowd-control marshals. As early arrivals hurried down the hallway to claim seats, the marshals lined them up single file. They imposed new rules. Only one person at a time would be admitted. When the last seat was taken, the next ten people in line would be admitted as standees. Then the doors would close. No one else would be allowed into the courtroom until someone came out. For those inside, there was to be no saving of seats for any reason. If you went out to the bathroom, you'd go to the back of the line. If you left your pocketbook on your seat in order to save it when you went to lunch, it would be confiscated and you could reclaim it at the court property office downstairs.

Nancy appeared, still clad in black. Behind her wire-rimmed glasses, her eyes darted to every corner of the room. At least half a dozen members of her growing cadre of supporters had managed to find seats near her mother. Nancy smiled quickly at them. She avoided eye contact with Bill Kissel. All rose as Mr. Justice Lunn took his place. The jury entered, expressionless.

Implacably, relentlessly, Peter Chapman resumed. He pointed out that Nancy's application for bail in November 2004 had been accompanied by numerous affidavits–including one from her psychiatrist at Siu Lam, Dr. Yuen–to the effect that she suffered from no mental illness.

"Mrs. Kissel, the affidavit filed by counsel representing you at the bail hearing said, 'She is acting, behaving and sounding perfectly normal. She is visited monthly by a psychiatrist and there has been no suggestion by him that she is in need of any help.' My question to you is this: a person with dissociative amnesia doesn't need help?"

"I can't comment on psychiatric terminology."

"Well, in his first report–from November 19, 2003, your first day at Siu Lam–Dr. Henry Yuen, chief of service at Siu Lam's Department of Forensic Science, describes you as 'mentally stable, good reality testing, not morbidly depressed.' He says you were conscious and alert, that you spoke relevantly and coherently, and that you denied you had any thoughts of suicide. Was that true? Did you tell Dr. Yuen about the cocaine, the sodomy, the suicide attempt?"

"No, he was mostly interested in my medication and my day-to-day life in Siu Lam. He would ask me specifically if I'd had any suicidal thoughts while I was in prison."

"But you'd only been there for a day."

"I don't know if I said that or not after being there for one day."

"I suggest to you, Mrs. Kissel, that you have absolutely no psychiatric problems. Do you agree?"

"Yes. There's nothing psychiatrically wrong with me. I'm not suffering from a mental illness. Depression–yes. Feeling sad, feeling remorseful–yes. Suffering from something tragic–yes."

"But according to Dr. Yuen's report, you never suffered from, quote, 'amnesia or memory loss.' "

Suddenly, Nancy erupted. *"They have no idea! They have no idea of what you've been through in your life! You can't just go in there and say, 'Hey this is what happened to me!' "*

She began choking and coughing. But she wasn't finished.

"You have no idea, you have no idea! You have no idea of the grieving process I went through! Yuen was there as a prison doctor, without having any understanding of what it's like to be there."

She collapsed in tears again. The judge declared a recess.

———————————

Chapman asked Nancy why—if she'd been regularly battered for at least four years, and especially as the beatings had worsened in 2002—no one had noticed so much as a bruise.

"I wore a lot of makeup, wore sunglasses, long sleeves. I put on a good face so people wouldn't know."

"Mrs. Kissel, you were a prominent figure in the Hong Kong International School community. Indeed, you've been referred to as an 'ambassador' for the school. Given all the people with whom you had such frequent contact, didn't it ever occur to you to tell anyone about these terrible injuries being inflicted on you as a result of this sexual abuse and escalating violence?"

"I couldn't. I had to talk about how *great* my life was. I never, ever let anyone know what was really going on. I never once complained to anybody. I didn't even think about approaching anyone, because—"

"Because it wasn't happening, Mrs. Kissel," Chapman interrupted.

"No, because it was something I was very ashamed of. Because it was something I chose to accept for a number of years. It's something I am still ashamed of. That's why I could never tell anyone."

"The alternative, Mrs. Kissel, is that there was nothing to tell." Chapman paused, waiting for Nancy's response. There was none. She only trembled and looked away.

"To briefly refer back to something we touched on last week, Mrs. Kissel, you said you never had yourself tested for AIDS while you were married, is that correct?"

"Yes, this fascination—gay anal sex, prostitution—it's something I was not aware of in our marriage. I'm only putting it together now. It puts things in perspective: why he did what he did with me. It's quite shocking to find out he was somebody I didn't really know."

"Well, this shocking and horrific revelation—has that triggered an impulse to seek medical advice? To get an AIDS test? Even now, after all you've recently learned, have you had yourself tested for AIDS?"

"No."

"No. Because you don't believe it yourself, do you, Mrs. Kissel?"

She did not reply.

Toward the end of the afternoon, Chapman said, "You've told us so much about how your husband mistreated you. You've also cited instances where you say he used force to discipline your daughters. Are you trying to paint a picture of Robert Kissel as having been abusive to his children, too?"

"There were isolated times when he was very rough with the children. There were times when he would terrify me because I had no control of him. But I didn't try to paint a picture of him. I—" She rose halfway out of her seat at the witness stand. *Do you hear me? I didn't try to paint a picture of him! I still love him! Things happened! I stayed with him! I loved him! And I am not sitting here to paint a bad picture about him. He's . . . he's . . . he's my husband!"* She burst into tears again.

"We'll take a short break now to allow Mrs. Kissel to compose herself," Mr. Justice Lunn said.

She turned and spoke through her tears directly to the judge. *"He's my husband! . . . I still love him! If it weren't for these things, I would still be with him . . . I still love him deeply . . . Oh, it's so hard . . ."*

The effectiveness of histrionic displays in a courtroom, like that of exclamation marks on a printed page, is inversely proportional to the frequency with which they are employed. Nancy's trembling, sobbing, and anguished cries fell on increasingly blind eyes and deaf ears as her cross-examination continued throughout the week. Peter Chapman grew impatient. Mr. Justice Lunn was clearly unmoved. There seemed little sympathy in the gazes of the jurors. Chapman had seized control of the proceedings. His indefatigability, seasoned with ever more overt sarcasm, reduced Nancy's answers to grist. He didn't do Del Priore any favors, either.

"He was the man you loved. He was the man in your life."

"He's a person I had a relationship with."

"You went to New York with your husband when he had back surgery only so you could secretly meet with Del Priore."

"No."

"You sneaked out behind your husband's back while he lay on it."

"Only for about half an hour."

"A hundred and fifty-eight phone calls to Del Priore in September and October."

"He continued to give support."

"Del Priore lived in a trailer, right?"

"No. A stationary mobile home."

"And you represented a potential gold mine to him, didn't you, Mrs. Kissel?"

"No, not at all. He understood what my life was about—the struggle of accepting who I was. He accepted me as a person. He didn't judge me by what I possessed. People assume people with money are so happy with their life. I'm tired of that."

"Fifty-two calls in September. One hundred six calls in October. The pattern was you would tell him you could talk and he would call you back. He spent hours on the telephone with you; he spent thousands of U.S. dollars, which a resident of a trailer park could ill afford."

"He worked."

"I suggest, Mrs. Kissel, he considered it a good investment. The day you searched the internet for 'sleeping pills . . . drug overdose and medication causing heart attack' you spoke to Del Priore for more than three hours."

"I never talked to him about drugs."

"On the day you were prescribed Rohypnol by Dr. Dytham, you called him seven times, before and after seeing the doctor. What were those calls about, Mrs. Kissel?"

"I don't remember."

"You were on a shopping spree for drugs that week. And before and after every visit to a doctor to ask for drugs, you called Del Priore. Do you remember any of those calls, Mrs. Kissel?"

"I never told him I was getting pills."

"You had ten tablets of Rohypnol provided on October twenty-third and twenty tablets of dextropropoxythene provided on the twenty-eighth—that's ten pretty good nights of sleep. Then on thirtieth October, off you go to Dr. Fung and you end up with Lorivan, amitryptyline, and some more Stilnox. Three days after that, those three drugs end up in Robert Kissel's stomach, along with the Rohypnol. In relation to those four drugs, Mrs. Kissel, how were you supposed to take them?"

"As directed."

"All together?"

"I'm not sure."

"Well, Robert Kissel seemed to have taken them all together on second November with two as an added bonus, didn't he?"

"I don't know."

"You used the milk shake to conceal the drugs. And *you* didn't bring the milk shakes to your husband and Mr. Tanzer. You used the girls because you knew Robert Kissel wouldn't take it from you."

"No. He continued eating with me. He continued drinking his scotch."

"By November 2003, there was absolutely no way Robert Kissel was going to take a drink from you, Mrs. Kissel. But Mr. Tanzer's visit suddenly presented you with an opportunity. You could tell the girls it would be fun to make milk shakes. You could put the drugs in the milk shakes. And you could ask the girls to deliver them."

"No, no! That's not what happened!"

"And later you delivered—from above—five accurate, fatal blows, grouped together. You were able to deliver those accurate blows because Robert Kissel was unable to defend himself, because you had rendered him defenseless by drugging him."

"No! We had a horrible fight and he used a bat! He was telling me he was going to kill me with that bat. He kept repeating it and I defended myself from him. *He was going to kill me and I fought for my life!*"

"You just forgot to mention that to Dr. Dytham, thirty-six hours later. You forgot to mention this furious life-or-death struggle, which nobody heard."

"I can't remember that visit."

"The account you gave to Dr. Dytham is significantly different from the account you've given here as evidence. As well as depicting a different version of events without mention of a life-or-death struggle or a dead husband, there's not a single reference in that report to you having any difficulty recalling events."

"I didn't know then that I was suffering from memory loss."

"At seven forty-one a.m. on November third, you called Del Priore and talked for twenty-four minutes. By that time, you didn't need a sympathetic ear about an abusive husband. What did you talk about in that call, Mrs. Kissel?"

"We always spoke about a lot of issues."

"Did you tell Del Priore that you had solved the problem with your husband?"

"I can't remember that call."

"Your claim of memory loss is a lie, isn't it, Mrs. Kissel? What Dr. Dytham's report records is an attempt by you to embark on a process of deception, isn't it?"

"No, it's not. I don't have a memory of that day, nor the visit."

"But you *did* have a memory on November fourth. That's your problem, isn't it, Mrs. Kissel?"

"No. I don't know what happened to me after that night. I still don't know. It's a part of my life that's been taken from me."

"The person who has had a part of his life taken from him is Robert Kissel—because you killed him."

It was 4:30 p.m. Chapman indicated to the judge that he'd reached a point suitable for overnight adjournment.

Suddenly, Nancy screamed her loudest scream yet: "*He was going to kill me; he was going to kill me! Oh God, he was going to kill me!"* She laid her head on her arms on the lectern of the witness stand and shook convulsively and wailed.

"Thank you, Mrs. Kissel," Mr. Justice Lunn said drily. "Please return to the dock."

32. AUGUST 13–SEPTEMBER 1

TROPICAL STORM SANVU, THE FIRST OF THE SEASON, BLEW
into the South China Sea on the morning of August 12, the day Nancy
ended her testimony. Sanvu intensified into a severe tropical storm the
next day and made landfall near Shantou in Guangdong province, 187
miles north of Hong Kong. Sanvu's outer rainbands inundated the island with almost six inches of rain.

Nancy viewed the rain from her new cell in the maximum
security Tai Lam Centre for Women. At the close of proceedings on
August 12, Chapman had asked for a conference in chambers. There,
he argued that Nancy's accusations against her husband and her
claims of memory loss were clearly lies and that someone capable of
such deliberate falsification must be considered a flight risk. Mr.
Justice Lunn concurred, revoked Nancy's bail (out of the presence
of the jury and with orders that the press not report her change of
status), and remanded her to Tai Lam. She left court that day—after
the jury had been dismissed, so as not to prejudice them—not
with her mother, but handcuffed and shackled and surrounded by
guards.

From Tai Lam, she wrote to Michael Del Priore:

Thursday, August 18, 19:40

Hello my love . . . I don't know where to even start . . . I finished my eight days of giving testimony on the 12th of August . . . and the judge immediately revoked bail . . . and tonight, believe it or not, is the first pen and paper I've received . . .

It's been raining here so I've really been able to feel you–I love the rain–especially now–it has this magical way of bringing me right to you . . . My Baby . . . my love . . . my Michael . . . I pray that you can feel me . . . feel me loving you, needing you. I want so desperately to come to you . . . to come home to you to be in your arms again–to touch you, smell you–take all of you in . . .

We're another day closer, you know, another day closer–that's what I say out loud every day when I wake up . . .

———————

As a trough of low pressure edged toward the south China coast on August 19, almost eight inches of rain drenched Hong Kong as the wind felled a banyan tree that had stood in Central for more than a hundred years.

———————

Hi my love . . . I'm back from court–long day . . . and guess what . . . it's pouring outside so your right next to me . . . I love the sounds–the wind– everything about the rain . . .

Today you and I went to our favorite local diner . . . we go every
Wednesday . . . same booth in the corner so we can sit together side by
side . . . everyone working there knows us . . . knows our table–so they
hold it every Wednesday–no menus . . . and always a slice of pie is put
aside for you . . . we take a walk after we eat and hold hands . . . when we
get home we get ready for bed . . . you help me get undressed . . . we're
making love to one another . . . so beautifully . . .

We're another day closer my love . . . one day we'll wake up and this
nightmare will be over and once more you'll be able to look into my eyes
and see them loving you . . . tonight we can fall asleep together listening to
the rain . . . make love to me Michael . . . hold me in your arms until I fall
asleep . . . don't let go . . .

The storm battered Hong Kong even harder the next day. As winds
grew stronger, the weather service issued an amber rainstorm warning, a strong monsoon signal, a landslip warning, a thunderstorm warning, and a special announcement on flooding in the New Territories.
Almost twelve inches of rain fell, causing widespread flooding and
more than a hundred landslides.

Good morning Beautiful–how was your night? Mine was wonderful with
you by my side . . . it continues to rain . . . actually it's pouring . . . even
better . . . I feel you so strongly when it's raining like this . . .

I love the way you touch me . . . something so new to me . . . that's
why I have this incredible need to be touched by you . . . something I've

fought against throughout my marriage . . . always associating touch with
pain and humiliation . . .

   I know it must be so hard for you when I talk about my marriage
and my past experiences but I have this need to tell you because of
how you changed my life . . . I struggle constantly to get closer to
you . . . struggling to feel you flowing through me . . . I can't seem
to get enough . . . a sense of peace and trust from a man for the first
time . . .

In the Court of First Instance, the trial was winding down. Doctors
Fung and Dytham testified. Ira and Ryan testified. And Nancy's friends
from Parkview, the Aberdeen Marina Club, and the Hong Kong International School testified.

Parkview neighbor Nancy Nassberg recalled an occasion at the
club when Rob had spoken sharply to Nancy about letting the children
run wild. She said Nancy wanted to let the children express themselves
and have fun, while Rob demanded good behavior.

Nassberg also recounted asking Nancy why she was wearing sunglasses indoors in February 1999. Nancy had moved the glasses to reveal
a bruise around her right eye and had said, "Rough sex."

Another neighbor recalled seeing a bruise around Nancy's right
eye sometime in 2002, while a friend from HKIS remembered seeing a
bruised right eye in October 2003. Everyone said Nancy had always
been friendly and cheerful. No one said they'd ever heard her complain
about being abused, but as neighbor Geertruida Samra said, that wasn't
surprising, given that "the expatriate community in Parkview was very
gossipy."

The last witness called by the defense was Bernard Pasco, the computer forensic expert who had discovered Rob's use of search terms such as "wife is a bitch," "twinks," and "gay anal sex in Taiwan."

Pasco testified that he'd used NetAnalysis and EnCase Forensic software to examine the Kissels' computers. He said the two programs enabled him to determine exactly what search terms had been entered at a given time on a given date, what results had been obtained, and which sites the user had then visited.

He said Nancy's lawyers had told him to explore the time period between January 2002 and November 2003. They'd given him a list of keywords to search for. These "focused primarily on the homosexual area," Pasco said.

He'd examined both Rob's laptop and the family desktop and had discovered extensive activity in "the homosexual area" on both computers on April 4 and 5, 2003, just after Nancy and the children had left for the United States and just before Rob traveled to Taiwan.

On cross-examination, Chapman asked Pasco to estimate the total number of hours Rob had spent searching for and viewing gay and pornographic Web sites during the twenty-two months covered by his investigation.

An hour and a half on April 4, Pasco said, and an hour and a half on April 5.

"And that's it?" Chapman asked. "A total of three hours over two days?" Had that really been the extent of Rob's exploration of "the homosexual area" of the Internet?

That was all he'd been able to document, Pasco said: three hours over two days during a period of twenty-two months.

Good morning Beautiful—how was your night? Mine was wonderful
with you by my side . . . I want to write a book about my life . . . abuse-
wise . . . so many women are afraid to come forward—that's what I want
to write about—my denial for so many years . . . my choice to stay in the
marriage as long as I did . . . the reasons . . . I want to help women who
feel trapped . . . I was sort of feeling like God chose me to be a spokes-
person to speak for women in trouble . . .

No one believes that shitty things happen to women driving a
Mercedes and living the life of luxury . . . I always blamed myself for
what I allowed to have happen . . . I was so weak . . . but on the outside
portrayed what I knew everyone wanted to see—great life, great marriage,
etc . . . bullshit really . . . and then came you . . .

I still haven't been able to remember everything about that night and
I don't know if it will ever come back . . . it's incredibly unsettling having
to sit through weeks of prosecution witnesses that say things about me
during that week—all of which I have absolutely no memory of so I can't
even say whether it is true or not . . .

Other than Nancy's testimony, the linchpin of Alexander King's
presentation was the baseball bat that Simon Clarke had found on
the bedroom floor and kept in his office until the trial was well under
way. Specifically, the barrister wanted to persuade the jury that an
indentation on the base of the lead ornament had been caused not by
Rob's skull, but by the barrel of the bat—the implication being that
Nancy had used the ornament to defend herself against Rob's murderous attack. It was a case, in other words, of "If the bat fits, you must
acquit."

Good morning Beautiful how was your night . . . mine was so wonderful
with you by my side . . . we're another day closer . . . today should be a
good day for us . . . we have a very strong case with this new evidence of
the baseball bat and statue . . . it's the best thing to close with . . . showing
the jury that the baseball bat caused the statue to be curved—it is our entire
case really . . .

The prosecution, however, called two rebuttal witnesses: DNA expert
Dr. Pang Chi-ming and forensic expert Wong Koon-hung. Pang testified
that the only DNA found on the bat was that of an unidentified female—
not Nancy, but possibly Min. This indicated that Rob had not been grip-
ping and swinging the bat on the night of November 2, 2003, Pang
said.

"You would agree, would you not, that not everyone that touches
the end of the baseball bat will leave human DNA material that is de-
tectable by testing?" King asked.

"If I touch this microphone with my finger, it's possible my human
material will not be left on it. But if I held it tightly, and moved it around,
I don't believe that my human material would not be left on it."

Having made it harder to conclude beyond a reasonable doubt that
Rob had handled the bat on the night he was killed, Peter Chapman
asked Wong if the bat had caused the dent in the ornament. It was
"doubtful" Wong said. He then drove a stake through the heart of the
defense linchpin by stating, "It's conclusive that the piece of metal had
not been struck with the baseball bat with significant force."

After seventy-seven days, the presentation of evidence was concluded.

I just want this over with . . . I can't take it anymore . . . I wanna soak in a bubble bath . . . a hot bath . . . I'm sorry I blew my chance that day . . . but too much of my self-stuff was in the way . . . I know it's ridiculous but when you spend years of someone telling you how horrible your body looks . . . well . . . I still can't shake it—and I'm not sure I ever will . . .

Sometimes I find myself in this dream state . . . "is he real . . . or am I dreaming" . . . I'm so scared, Michael . . . I'm sorry . . . I can't stop crying I just can't . . . I'm so fucking afraid of losing you . . .

The trial was in recess on Thursday, August 25, as Peter Chapman and Alexander King prepared their closing arguments, but the line of would-be spectators formed early Friday morning. By the time the courtroom doors opened, well over a hundred people had been standing in the hallway for more than an hour. The clamor for standing room began the moment the seats were filled. The two crowd-control marshals were no match for the throng that pushed its way toward the doors. Dozens of the avid crowded inside as if boarding a Tokyo subway.

Mr. Justice Lunn was not impressed. "I will tolerate no more than ten standees," he said. Proceedings were delayed as marshals funneled the overflow back into the hall.

Peter Chapman was in no hurry. In truth, he didn't know if the case he'd presented was strong enough to overcome whatever innate sympathy the jury—especially its two women—might feel for a mother of three who had sobbed her way through the summer.

"This was a cold-blooded killing," he began. Making a rare gesture, he pointed his finger directly at Nancy Kissel. "The defendant struck five fatal blows with murderous intent. There is no basis for a claim of self-defense. The injuries sustained by Robert Kissel did not result from a life-and-death struggle. There was no shouting, screaming, yelling. There was no baseball bat. There was no provocation. This was a cold-blooded killing."

Dressed, as always, in black—newspapers had begun to call her "the Woman in Black," never a good sign for a defendant—Nancy stared at the floor, expressionless.

"These were not five fatal blows struck in self-defense. Any one of these blows would have been sufficient to kill. These were blows struck with murderous intent while Robert Kissel was unable to defend himself.

"She didn't want him alive anymore. Michael Del Priore was the man in her life. Her perspective and outlook in life had changed considerably when Michael Del Priore had entered it. The seed of murder was planted firmly on August twentieth, when she searched the Internet for 'drug overdose,' 'sleeping pills,' 'medication causing heart attack.' She decided to remove the obstacle in her life that Robert Kissel had become. And on November 2, 2003, Nancy Kissel would do exactly that. Nothing can possibly be clearer."

Chapman was speaking deliberately, not forgetting that English was a second language for the jurors.

"She knew divorce was looming. Nancy Kissel, and perhaps Michael del Priore, felt somewhat vulnerable. She knew the messy divorce proceedings could last a long time. She wanted her children, yes, but above all, Michael was the man in her life. And Michael regarded Nancy as a gold mine—as a way out of his life in a trailer park. And so she planned—possibly with Michael del Priore's tacit encouragement—to remove the obstacle in her life.

"She acquired four drugs in seven days in her various visits to doctors in late October—Stilnox, Lorivan, amitriptyline, and Rohypnol. There was no possible medical reason for her to need them all. Whether the drugs were intended to kill Robert Kissel or to subdue him is an open question, but they were employed successfully.

"Her show of normality, her suggestions of an abusive husband to counselors and doctors in the days leading up to the death of the victim, was evidence that she was attempting to lay the groundwork for the events that followed.

"And afterward, she set about a cover-up in the most calculating and determined way possible. Her actions during those days speak so loudly and so incriminatingly that Nancy Kissel now claims to have no recollection of those events."

Chapman shook his head slowly.

"This case is not about a battered wife doing away with an abusive husband. Her allegations that her husband was abusive are a self-serving act of deception and lies, part of an assassination of the character of Robert Kissel done solely in an attempt to avoid criminal responsibility for what she has done.

"Acts of forced and injurious sodomy committed against the accused by her husband over many years are a similar fabrication. She claimed she was the victim of five years of humiliation, of raving sexual abuse and violence at the hands of Robert Kissel, who abused cocaine, sleeping pills, and painkillers.

"But she never sought medical attention. Why not? It never happened. The years of physical and sexual abuse were invisible to friends and family, including those who guaranteed her bail, and her own father, Ira Keeshin. The reason for this? It never happened."

There was more. Chapman's presentation lasted three hours. But in the end it came down to a single proposition. "The evidence of the prosecution case points conclusively to her guilt on the count of murder."

Chapman could have gone longer. But he was no slouch as a tactician. By wrapping things up at three thirty on a Friday afternoon, he placed his adversary in the most unenviable of positions. Sandy King could only argue for an hour. Then he'd have to pause until Monday. Notwithstanding that they knew more would follow, the jury would have the whole weekend to reflect on Chapman's forceful and fully rounded statement, compared to which King's preliminary remarks might well seem inadequate.

"This is the worst time to start," King began. Perhaps a juror or two would sympathize with his plight. "Before our very eyes, the summer has disappeared." He asked the jury to consider his remarks as only a prologue to the argument he would deliver on Monday.

"We say she is not guilty, because in the course of events Mrs. Kissel acted in lawful self-defense. Circumstantial evidence points conclusively in the direction of the defense. Like a rope, when you put all the strands together, it's strong enough to rely upon. Common sense will show that there is no basis for the theory of premeditation. And when you look at the evidence carefully, you will see the prosecution has failed to prove beyond reasonable doubt that she did not kill in self-defense. The only true verdict according to the evidence is 'not guilty.'

"The prosecution case has been flawed since November 6, 2003, when police went to the Kissel residence. At that time, they thought there was nothing to investigate, because they were already convinced of her guilt. Since then, flaws in the prosecution case have continued. The question to ask yourselves is, 'Was the prosecution done to a standard that I can be sure of?' The answer is no."

King said he would elaborate on Monday. For now, he only wished to warn the jurors to "resist the temptation to come to a collective decision. It is the individual view that matters." He also cautioned against forming a prejudice against Nancy "because of her lifestyle."

Mr. Justice Lunn declared the court in recess until 10:00 a.m. Monday.

Just got back from court . . . wow . . . what a day . . . Chapman's closing took only 3 hours . . . pretty pathetic . . . 75% of his closing was about you! . . . he based his entire closing on you and I premeditating to do . . . well . . . you know . . . I can't even write it it's so absurd . . .

Then Sandy started . . . I wish you were here to listen to him . . . the way he speaks to the jury . . . he's captivating . . .

On Sunday, August 28, Nancy wrote:

I just came back from seeing Simon—the prosecution is so weak . . . and the defense is so strong . . . the only obstacle is the Judge in providing provocation for an out for the jury—a murder conviction is not at all in the cards—way too many holes in the prosecution case.

And before leaving for court on Monday morning, she wrote again:

Good morning Beautiful how was your night . . . mine was wonderful with you by my side . . . my stomach is in knots . . . even if the jury comes back with what I want . . . my fear is this prejudicial judge will overrule their decision . . . he's the absolute worst judge in all of Hong Kong . . .

———————————

Because Alexander King had chosen not to make an opening statement, Monday marked the jury's first sustained exposure to his rhetoric. And it was sustained. He spoke from dawn to dusk and said he'd be back in the morning for more. He pursued three lines of argument: Rob was such a perverted, reprehensible control freak that he deserved to die; the police had investigated like Scotty the Clown; and if she *had* murdered Rob, Nancy would never have behaved so stupidly.

"The truth about Robert Kissel's character is unpleasant, is brutal," King said. "He was a paranoid, suspicious, manipulative man, who abused his wife sexually and wanted to be in total control at all times. His ruthless competitiveness in work and play, his detailed supervision of household finances, his installation of spyware and hiring of private detectives: these are all evidence of the paranoid, controlling nature of a violently abusive husband.

"When he suspected that their marriage might be in trouble, did he use his usual energy to say, 'Right, let's go to marriage counselors and sort it out'? No. What did he do? He installed spyware, so that six times a day, he could check on his wife. And that was even before her relationship with Michael Del Priore had begun.

"What kind of man, in advance of traveling to destinations, is looking to procure gay sexual services? What kind of husband, when his wife is away, starts searching out for male prostitutes?"

That was enough for Bill Kissel. He hadn't listened to the testimony about Rob's search for gay anal sex Web sites and he wasn't going to listen to arguments derived from it. He strode angrily out of the courtroom.

"Records show that his first search term on Google in April 2003 was 'my wife is a bitch.' He would refer to his wife in that way again, on November 2, 2003. That was payback time. He was going to finally tell her that he was divorcing her, not her divorcing him. He had controlled every other aspect of her life. The one thing left in her life was her children. When he realized that she had hit him, he was enraged. Robert Kissel had never been hit before by his wife. It's always been him doing the beating. So he lost his temper. He said: 'I am going to fucking kill you . . . you fucking bitch!' "

What had happened after that? Because of the bungling of the Hong Kong police, King said, no one would ever know.

"A chief inspector, a senior inspector, and a superintendent, along with a large team of officers, descended upon Parkview and told the stupid and ridiculous story about investigating a missing person. That was rubbish. That simply doesn't make sense. Could it be any clearer that their intention was to investigate murder, not a missing person or an assault?

"There was a six-minute period in the master bedroom when

Nancy Kissel described to police how she had been assaulted by her husband. But the most senior officer at the scene, who says he is investigating an assault or missing person, can't remember a single thing she said. They thought this was an open-and-shut case. They made only cursory glances around the apartment. The result is that the jury has been deprived of a confirmatory record of the true events.

"If it just stopped there it would be bad enough. But it doesn't stop there, it gets a whole lot worse. When the police were notified on November 8 that they had missed a black bag of bloodied items in their initial search, they should have thought 'We better search every room.' But they didn't. As a matter of fact, if it were not for the accused's solicitor, there would not even be a baseball bat available for examination in this trial."

Whether or not the baseball bat was relevant was, of course, open to question. Only the jury could decide.

"The prosecution theory of this case is like something out of a movie script—a colliding of the universes. The prosecution would have you believe that the cheating, ungrateful, plotting, scheming wife links up with a lover who lives in a trailer park in the New England state of Vermont—someone living a wretched life, eyeing up wealthy people, and then tacitly encouraging a premeditated plan to kill. The motive? A classic: money, love, lust, and sex. That is pure speculation. It simply defies common sense.

"Despite all the evidence that has been based upon e-mail correspondence captured by eBlaster spyware, nothing suggests that she was planning a future with Del Priore. Where is the e-mail that says, 'Oh my darling, we will soon be together?' She had already set up a home with her three children in a lovely house in Vermont. She could have said, 'Sorry, Robert, I'm not coming home, I'm filing for divorce.' Instead, when he called her, she quickly packed up to go home.

"And it simply does not make sense that she would choose to kill her husband on a busy Sunday afternoon, when their three children and maids would be going in and out of the flat. She's planning to kill her husband and get away with it? Where was the planning? Nothing shows any planning. The theory of premeditation goes out the window.

"All the evidence in this case shows that Nancy Kissel was a very good organizer. Where was the organization for the disposal of the body before November 2? There simply is none. She must have spent at least two nights in the bedroom with the body of her dead husband. If she had a premeditated scheme, she certainly did not rely upon it. What happened afterward is she melted down. Isn't it clear that Nancy Kissel suffered from dissociative amnesia after the killing? Her behavior could almost be described as bizarre. She almost went on living as if nothing had happened."

King proposed an alternate scenario. "Robert Kissel had been searching for an excuse to have divorce proceedings go in his favor, hence his obsessive spying on his wife. He knew that if Nancy Kissel filed for divorce on the grounds of spousal abuse and sexual violence, the ensuing proceedings, as with all divorce suits, would be ugly, dirty, and messy. His whole world—and career—would come crashing down.

"Given the solid evidence of Robert Kissel's controlling nature, the true scenario is one where the husband confronts his wife with the threat of removing the children from her care, and it escalates into a furious struggle in which she fears for her life. The alleged murder weapon is a family heirloom. What's more likely? That being chosen as the murder weapon, or that being picked up in self-defense?

"Too much force? In the middle of a fight, how could someone of Mrs. Kissel's size turn around and decide how many blows are necessary to make sure her husband didn't get up again? Adrenaline and fear take over and you do what you can to defend yourself."

King said he would finish the next morning.

My body is so exhausted but my mind is racing . . . are you alright? I ask Simon every day if he's heard from you and the answer remains the same: no. I hate that . . . it worries me so much . . .

I'm not at all looking forward to this weekend . . . it'll be the longest most painful weekend of my life . . .

Let's go for a drive . . . we'll pack some blankets and a nice lunch . . . find a nice spot somewhere to spread the blanket . . . I'll lay my head in your lap . . . looking up at you . . . your hand is stroking my head . . . playing with my hair . . . your telling me your version of seeing me in my "those ain't goodbye pants!" . . . and we both laugh . . . I get up . . . I need to get closer to you . . . so I sit on your lap . . . facing you . . . my legs wrapped around you . . . I need to kiss you . . . I feel your hands under my shirt . . . you've placed them both on my back . . . we've never made love outside before . . . on a blanket . . . on a cloudy day . . . maybe it'll start to rain . . . but neither one of us will care . . .

The usual crowd tried to pile into the courtroom on Tuesday, August 30, for the conclusion of Sandy King's argument. A steady rain fell. It was the nineteenth rainy day in three weeks. Almost forty inches of rain had fallen during August, compared to the norm of fifteen inches. For the year, rainfall was almost 50 percent above normal: perfect weather for Nancy's romantic fantasies.

King hammered away again at the alleged incompetence of the police investigation: "This evidence is put before you as expert evidence, and the reality is that there is nothing expert about it at all. . . . You should be very concerned why a proper investigation was not done and why the full picture was not put before you."

But his primary goal was to leave the jury feeling that Nancy was incapable of having committed such a heinous crime. "She was trying everything she could to make the marriage better," King said. He told the jurors that in determining whether Nancy had the "propensity" to commit murder, they should rely on character testimony such as that given by Gabriel Ip, former bus director of Hong Kong International School. In testimony that was "straightforward, honest, truthful, and heartfelt," Ip had said he'd always found Nancy to be "very kind, pleasant, always helpful to kids."

Nancy sobbed her way through King's comments, and during the morning recess she became so upset that both her mother and King were needed to calm her down.

In conclusion, King said, "Is Nancy Kissel the sort of person who would commit the type of crime the prosecution alleges? Was she someone who was shown to be violent? Does she have it in her to shop for drugs, serve them in a milk shake to her husband, and then bludgeon him to death while he lies defenseless, with five lacerations to the head, each one of them fatal? The answer is no."

In the United States, a judge instructs the jury on relevant points of law before sending them to deliberate. In Hong Kong, in addition, the judge summarizes the evidence, offering the jurors a presumably more objective and authoritative view than that presented by counsel from either side during closing argument. Obviously, the judge's summation carries great weight.

Mr. Justice Lunn wasted no time starting his. Although Sandy King had taken up almost the full morning, the judge launched into his summary even before breaking for lunch.

He told the jury they had three options: guilty of murder, guilty of manslaughter due to provocation, not guilty. He explained that they could find provocation if they believed that Rob's conduct had provoked in Nancy a "sudden and temporary loss of self-control."

He reminded the jury that Nancy had killed Rob by "smashing his skull with five separate blows to the upper right side of his head, each one of the blows fatal. Fractured skull bone was driven into his brain, causing massive spillage of brain substance. Did the defendant believe it was necessary to use force to defend herself? If yes, was the amount of force she used reasonable?"

He reminded jurors that each of the five blows "required a great amount of force" and that there were no defensive injuries on Rob's upper limbs, indicating that Rob might have been "sufficiently impaired by a cocktail of drugs" so as to be capable of "little or no motion at the time the blows were dealt to his head."

He also reminded jurors to bear in mind Nancy's "amorous relationship with U.S. resident Michael Del Priore" as well as Rob's estimated US$18 million estate.

But he told them to also bear in mind the defense contention that Nancy had "killed in lawful self-defense when her husband, following taunting and provocative statements, attempted to force anal sex upon her while threatening her with a baseball bat" and that "fearing for her life, she killed him with the metal ornament, originally used to fend off blows from the bat."

"Another element to note in the defense case," he said, "is the allegation that Robert Kissel had a controlling nature that developed into paranoia." The jury could also consider whether "homosexual pornographic Web sites found on the family computer supported the defendant's testimony that Robert Kissel routinely forced anal sex upon her."

Mr. Justice Lunn said he would conclude his summation in the morning and that the jury would be able to start deliberating after lunch.

The judge began summarizing the case. I knew it was going to be biased but had no idea just how far he'd go until today. He's basically presenting the entire prosecution case all over again . . . piece by piece . . . speculation by speculation with his opinions . . . every time he says the word murderer . . . he looks right at me . . . it's bullshit . . . but the jury sits there and listens . . .

I know what's ahead . . . I think it just hit me today in a way that's never been clearer . . . I think things are gonna get a whole lot worse from this point . . .

Before leaving for court the next morning, Nancy wrote:

> *I play this image in my mind all the time . . . your coming home from work*
> *and you pull in the driveway . . . its pouring . . . I run out to you as your*
> *getting out of your truck . . . you say, "Baby it's pouring, what are you*
> *doing" . . . I don't say anything . . . I just press up against you . . . my*
> *mouth on yours . . . kissing you hard . . . needing to feel you . . . all of*
> *you . . . as the rain falls down on both of us . . . we're soaking wet–but all I*
> *feel is you and how warm your lips are . . . we both run into the house*
> *peeling off our wet clothes as we make our way to our bedroom leaving a*
> *trail of bunched up wet clothes along the way . . .*

———————————

The judge concluded his summary of the evidence by focusing on the claim that Nancy had experienced a "meltdown" in the aftermath of having killed her husband in self-defense.

"These claims must be considered in light of the manner in which she carried out what the prosecution has called her 'cover-up' activities." He drew the jury's attention to still pictures taken from closed-circuit television footage that showed Nancy dragging a large suitcase, carrying a rug, and carrying shopping bags on different occasions. He reminded the jury that the salesperson at Tequila Kola had described Nancy as "normal, but a little bit loud."

He said, "The accused bought a chaise lounge, two cushions, and a small carpet before returning the next day to buy two more large carpets at a total price of twenty-seven thousand dollars. The defendant also on the morning of November third ordered twenty cartons from Links Relocations. The police later found bloody items, including the three-point-seven-kilogram lead ornament in the boxes."

He reminded the jury of Bryna O'Shea's testimony that on the day after the killing Nancy was not crying on the phone and was "forcing herself to sound upset."

Concluding at midday, Mr. Justice Lunn said, "I would invite you to consider these facts, in respect of whether or not the defendant had gone into a meltdown." He reminded the jury that a unanimous verdict was not required: five to two would suffice, either way.

———————————

The jury deliberated for eight hours, returning a verdict at 8:30 p.m. They did not look at Nancy as they entered the courtroom. Although it did not need to be, their verdict was unanimous: guilty of murder. Not manslaughter due to provocation: murder.

Nancy stood, silent, head bowed, not crying. Mr. Justice Lunn said, "As I am required to do by law, I impose a sentence of life imprisonment upon you." Still dressed in black, she was led away by four officers of Hong Kong's Correctional Services Department. She was not given a chance to embrace her mother.

———————————

Outside the courtroom, seventy-eight-year-old Bill Kissel said to the assembled reporters, "Justice has been served. My son is resting in peace now. All the allegations against him have been proven false. Rob was a wonderful father. He tried his best to be a wonderful husband. His children can go on with their lives now, knowing how much he loved them."

Nancy's mother, Jean McGlothlin, said, "Right now, I'm just going to try and get by."

Simon Clarke and Alexander King said they would appeal.

———————

September 1, 2005 11 PM or so . . .

hi my love . . . I don't have a clock . . . so I'm guessing what time it is . . . I'm back at Tai Lam . . . and by now you know why . . . I'm pretty speechless really . . . especially with you . . . I don't quite know what to say . . . sorry doesn't really work . . . does it . . . Forgive me my love . . . I'm in shock . . . I certainly didn't see this coming . . .

I can't write anything that can explain what's happened . . . How can you ever forgive me . . . your precious heart has been shattered into a million tiny pieces . . . and every night I pray that one day I can put them back together to make you whole again . . .

Tonight like every night I'll whisper your name . . . it still belongs to me . . . I'll cherish saying it and hope that you can hear me . . . I love you Michael Scott Del Priore . . .

PART FIVE

THE IMMUTABILITY OF HATE

Hatred is in my brain, not in my stomach or my skin. It can't be removed like a rash or an ache.

—GRAHAM GREENE, *The End of the Affair*

33. NANCY

This is, indeed, a story of domestic violence, power and greed. Nan was "over her head" in many respects. She also made unwise choices along the way . . . as we all do . . . She, however, fell through that thin gauze that supports most of us above the pit of irretrievable consequences.

    —Nancy Kissel's mother, Jean McGlothlin, in an e-mail to the author

SIMON CLARKE MADE THE FORTY-FIVE-MINUTE DRIVE FROM Central to the Tai Lam Centre for Women in the western New Territories the next day. He'd already been assured that Nancy's guardian angel from Goldman Sachs would pay the full cost of all appeals, and he'd decided to hire Hong Kong's preeminent appellate barrister, Gerard McCoy. He knew Nancy would be heartened by knowing that she'd continue to be represented by the best.

But he also knew Nancy wouldn't want to talk about appeals, or even about the verdict, which had come as a shock. Both Clarke and Alexander King had been prepared for manslaughter due to provocation. Nancy had resisted having that option presented to the jury because she'd felt it would give them an easy way out. She'd been able to prevent King from arguing it, but she'd had no such control over Mr.

Justice Lunn. In any event, it had been an obvious option, and no one would have been surprised if the jury took it.

But a unanimous verdict of murder, after less than eight hours of deliberation, following a trial that had lasted almost three months and in which the evidence had been entirely circumstantial? A unanimous verdict of guilty against a multimillionaire expat investment banker's wife?

It was sobering, to say the least. Although Nancy had consistently refused to take advice from him, and King had insisted that everything be done her way throughout the trial, Clarke would not have blamed her for ranting that it was all his fault that she might spend the rest of her life in a Chinese prison. But he didn't expect that to happen. He knew that, odd as it seemed, she was going to rant at him not because of the verdict, but because in the sixteen hours since then, he'd not been able to reach Michael Del Priore with the news.

The mystery of Nancy's enthrallment with Del Priore had only deepened for Clarke after he'd met him the previous winter. The man had not struck him as either a romantic charmer or evil schemer. It could well have been his very blandness that lay at the root of his appeal to Nancy. He'd been a blank canvas on which she'd been able to paint her own portrait, born from a lifetime of neediness, neurosis, and insecurity. His chief attribute may have been his willingness to let Nancy direct every aspect of their time together. With him, she'd never have to fight for control. He certainly had been her husband's opposite in that respect.

"Had been" were the operative words, and not only because her husband was dead. "Had been" because of a short item and photo in the new edition of the *South China Morning Post*.

During the trial, Hong Kong newspapers and magazines were

prohibited from publishing anything about the case except courtroom testimony. Now the gag was off. The caption under a picture of Del Priore opening his car door read:

> This is Michael Del Priore, the muscular TV repairman and notorious ladies' man . . . The 41-year-old with piercing eyes is known as a man with a colorful past . . .
>
> The trauma of Kissel's arrest no longer seems to bother him, as he now lives with a blonde woman called Tracey who drives a red Ford GT sports car. She moved into Mr. Del Priore's tiny home in Hinsdale, Vermont, in January . . .

Nancy was not going to be pleased about Tracey. Clarke hoped to get in and out of Tai Lam before she had a chance to see the story. He'd be subjected to tirade enough for having failed to reach Del Priore. He didn't want to be anywhere near her when she learned the reason for her ex-lover's elusiveness. He mentioned the story but emphasized how handsome Michael had looked in the picture.

Nancy wrote to him that night, before she'd seen the newspaper:

> Simon and I spent some time alone . . . started to cry uncontrollably . . .
> my first words were "Where is he . . . find him for me . . ." He said
> the arrangement was that you were to call him . . . you still haven't
> called him . . . call . . . please call . . . I need to know that you're
> alright . . .
>
> Don't go anywhere . . . I won't let you . . . I'm begging you to stay . . .
> can I do that . . . to give up years of your life really . . . that's what I'm

asking . . . begging really . . . praying . . . can I ask you to do this . . . stay
exactly where you are in your mind, in your heart, do not falter from
that . . . don't give in to anything . . . I won't let you . . .

. . . I ask God to let you feel the love I have for you . . . I ask God to
outstretch His arms that possess so much power, and take you in, and
rescue you . . . outstretch your hand to His . . . let Him take you to
me . . . let Him guide you inside my soul and I'll do the same, until we
meet . . . let Him join our spirits together . . .

The next day, the Chinese-language magazine *Eastweek* published its
story:

EVIL FOREIGN WOMAN MURDERS HUSBAND–LOVER SCOTFREE IN AMERICA

The chief case investigator Ng Yeung-yuen, chief criminal inspector of
the Hong Kong Western district, said that although the main culprit in
the case has been convicted and sentenced to life in prison, the investigation has not ended. The possibility that more arrests will be made
cannot be excluded.

The additional person indicated by the police is believed to refer to
Nancy Kissel's lover, 41-year-old Michael Del Priore. If sufficient evidence is gathered, the Hong Kong police will go through the Interpol to
arrest Michael Del Priore, who is presently in the United States.

Michael's younger brother Lance Del Priore said that Michael was
tall and handsome with attractive blue eyes. The ladies like him and he
has lots of romances . . . he locked onto the married Nancy Kissel. In

January 2003, he divorced his wife in order to win this rich woman who can "lay golden eggs."

After the Nancy Kissel murder case broke, Michael did not concern himself about that and found a new lover. He is presently living with a blonde woman who drives a sports car.

Then the Chinese-language magazine *Next* published the story it had been sitting on:

Our reporter met the lover Michael in the United States. He was an ordinary middle-aged man. When our reporter asked if he had contacted Nancy or if he still thinks about her, Michael shook his head and said that he did not want to talk about it.

Michael lives in a mobile home . . . there is a woman who stays overnight at this house. On a weekend night, the reporter observed him and his blond girlfriend. Outside his house is the silver sports car of his girlfriend.

At around midnight, the girlfriend changed into a singlet and shorts and stepped outside to smoke a cigarette. According to his brother Lance, the blond woman moved in with Michael a month ago. Michael is a lady's man and had many partners before. During short conversation with the reporter, he was somewhat blunt but at least he was quite gentle in tone. With his attractive smile, it is easy to see why he is a lady's man.

One afternoon, the reporter observed Michael in sunshades coming back from shopping at a supermarket, bringing bags of grocery back into the house. After about half an hour, he came back out of the house and then he used the lawn mower to mow the lawn. At the time, the sun was high in the sky and the temperature was about 30 degrees Centigrade. The sweating Michael took off his shirt and walked around with his fat belly bouncing around.

The stories and pictures would have disabled many denial mechanisms, but Nancy's was sturdier than most. She wrote to Del Priore:

> *My entire body . . . it's completely wasted . . . drained of all energy . . . I can't eat . . . this pain in my heart is destroying me physically . . . every day . . . my mind . . . starting to convince me of something I may not be able to recover from . . . my constant battle of facing the reality of letting you go . . . I've refused to accept this . . . I just can't face ever letting you go . . .*
>
> *Maybe I'm living in a fantasy world . . . I know the reality . . . you're human . . . and you have needs . . . but my selfish side wants to keep you all to myself . . . not ever wanting you to share yourself with another . . . never wanting your heart belonging to another . . . never wanting your hands to explore another . . . I want to keep you all to myself . . . forever . . . my heart refuses to give up on this extraordinary once in a lifetime love . . . I refuse to give up on my dream . . .*

Nancy still did not write to her children. Two weeks after her conviction, Jane filed suit in New York State Surrogate's Court, seeking custody of them. New York courts had jurisdiction because Rob's last legal address in the United States had been in New York. In an affidavit accompanying the suit, Jane said, "Hayley has represented to me that her and Andrew's legal problems have left her in a desperate financial situation and that she intends to fight for custody of Robbie's children—even though she admits that it is not in their best interests to remain with her—in order to benefit from their considerable assets. Hayley told me that Andrew had leveraged everything, including their house in Vermont, and that he had left her with nothing."

A week after the suit was filed and three days before a hearing in Surrogate's Court, *The New York Times* published a lengthy story about the suit and all that had precipitated it. Bill was quoted as saying, "Andrew is in deep trouble and it wouldn't be appropriate to have the children in a house without a mother and a father, where the wife needs the children to support her lifestyle."

The story also said, "Back in June, Ms. [Chandler], a co-executor of her brother's estate, testified during the murder trial that the estate was worth $18 million. That estimate has now been lowered to $15.5 million. Some of that gap can be attributed to investments that Robert Kissel had made in apartment buildings in New Jersey, which Andrew Kissel is now accused of having secretly sold out from under his own partners."

The day after the story ran, Andrew called Jane and left a blistering message on her voice mail: "Jane, it's your ex-brother. You're famous, you're on the front page of *The New York Times*. You should get it. You're quoted. You've managed to do what Dad has tried to do for seventy-five years: tear this family apart. You've done that. And we're going to bury you, Jane."

Hayley called the same day. Her tone was more restrained, but she left no doubt that in the matter of custody—if in nothing else—she and Andrew would present a united front: "The betrayal I have gotten from you is of a magnitude that I never thought possible. But obviously I underestimated you."

Convinced that Bill lurked behind Jane's bid for custody, Hayley left him a somewhat less restrained message: "You're an evil man, and I would say that you'll get what you deserve except that you already got what you deserve."

——————————

The Kissels were at it again. New York Surrogate's Court judge Eve Preminger expressed her disgust from the bench at an October 2 hearing: "This isn't a game here. These children aren't property," she said. In a new filing, Jane's lawyer said, "Hayley Kissel has demonstrated blatant financial self-interest in seeking to maintain custody of the Kissel children and a disregard for their best interest." Judge Preminger seemed to agree. "If one has to speculate" about Hayley's motive in seeking to retain custody, "the speculations aren't pretty," she said.

Hayley hired Nathan Dershowitz, the brother of Harvard law professor and author Alan Dershowitz, to represent her, which suggested she had not yet reached the point of applying for food stamps. The phase of dueling press conferences began. "It's not right for the court to suddenly swoop in and take these children off," Nathan Dershowitz said. "I just don't understand the rush to get in there and pull them out. There is a very strong bond between Hayley and the children."

Alison Leigh Cowan wrote in *The New York Times* that the children "have endured nearly as much tragedy in their short lives as the waifs of the Lemony Snicket stories."

During the first week of October, even as his lawyer was trying to negotiate a plea bargain on the federal charges, Andrew was indicted in New York on charges of grand larceny, forgery, and falsifying business records in relation to the $4 million he'd stolen from his co-op. In order to turn himself in for arraignment on the New York charges, Andrew had to get permission from federal authorities to leave his house in Greenwich. Because he was already wearing an electronic surveillance device, he was released on minimal bail on October 6, but the grand larceny count alone carried a penalty of up to twenty-five years in prison. *The New York Times* said he looked "dazed" at his court appearance.

Jane's lawyer, Randy Mastro, of Gibson, Dunn and Crutcher, said the new charges against Andrew made it "even more apparent that these three children who've been through so much need to be in a stable supportive environment, and that's what Jane Kissel [Chandler] and her family offer." Nathan Dershowitz replied that the new charges had been expected and should not affect Hayley's attempt to maintain custody.

———————————

Nancy didn't write *to* her children, but she wrote about them in a manner that suggested she actually still knew how they were. She did not, because she continued to refuse letters from them, photos of them, or news about them, explaining to her mother that the emotional toll of such communications would interfere with her ability to work on her appeal.

In October, she sent a letter to Judge Preminger of Surrogate's Court urging that Jane not be given custody of the children. "I have been overwhelmed by Hayley's unconditional love, support, and her exceptional skills as a devoted mother," Nancy wrote from Tai Lam. "The fact of the matter is my children are not in harm's way emotionally or physically right now. Children understand love. They don't understand change. Loving families don't turn on each other. They support one another." She added that Jane was only after the trust fund money.

Judge Preminger was bemused. On October 17, noting that Nancy was "the lone voice for that position and would seem to have forfeited my belief in her good judgment based on the actions she was convicted of" and that in his will Rob had said he wanted Jane to raise the children if Nancy was unable to do so, the judge granted custody to Jane.

Outside court, with her husband, Richard, by her side, Jane tearfully said she was "thrilled." Bill, who had flown up from Florida for the hearing, said, "Robert's children can now go and have a wonderful life." Hayley was not present in court. Nathan Dershowitz said she would have no comment.

34. ANDREW

ALTHOUGH SHE'D FILED FOR DIVORCE A YEAR EARLIER, Hayley and her children continued to live with Andrew in their rented estate at 10 Dairy Road in the Greenwich backcountry through February.

On February 28, 2006, her divorce lawyer filed a motion in Connecticut State Superior Court in Stamford, seeking to have Andrew evicted. The motion charged Andrew with having forged Hayley's signature on a $2 million promissory note, as well as on a document that transferred ownership of their house in Stratton from her to him. The motion also said Andrew "has resumed drinking alcohol, consumes alcohol on the property, and has been belligerent and argumentative especially when intoxicated including in the company of the minor children." Appended medical records showed that at various times Andrew had been diagnosed as suffering from alcohol dependence, bipolar disorder, cocaine abuse, impulse control disorder, post-traumatic stress disorder, and antisocial personality disorder.

He'd also stopped paying the $15,000 per month rent for the Greenwich house. The owners had begun eviction proceedings, and Andrew and Hayley had promised to vacate the house by April 1. Hayley's father bought her a $2 million house two miles away. Andrew would be going to a different sort of house. He was due to be sentenced on the federal bank fraud charges on April 6, and prosecutors estimated that he'd be given ten years. He'd also changed his plea to guilty on the state charges in New York related to his theft from the co-op and faced sentencing for that crime in May.

Hayley didn't call movers until Friday, March 31. When she did, she said she wanted everything cleared from the house the next day. The owner of the moving company went to the house to give an estimate. There was a lot to be moved. Three trucks would be needed. He couldn't understand why Hayley had waited so long to make arrangements and why she was suddenly in such a hurry to get out of the house.

The next day as the movers packed and hauled, they could hear Hayley and Andrew screaming at each other. The worst fight seemed to involve Andrew's demand that Hayley leave at least a bed behind, so he could stay in the house over the weekend. Federal marshals were due to take him to White Plains, New York, on Monday for sentencing. From that point forward, the United States government would decide where he'd live. Hayley finally agreed to leave a bed, a nightstand, and a chair. The movers said they'd come back Monday morning to get them. Andrew said he'd be waiting for them at 8:00 a.m.

Hayley had not spoken to Bill for almost two years. Nor had she let Rob's children speak to him when he phoned. Nonetheless, Hayley called Bill in Florida on Saturday to warn him that Andrew might be suicidal. She left a message that said, "I moved out of the house last night and Andrew stayed behind. I'm afraid he might do something stupid with his life." Bill got the message but did not contact his sole surviving son.

At 6:00 p.m. Sunday, Carlos Trujillo, a Colombian handyman who'd worked for Andrew for years, stopped by the house to say good-bye and to wish his old boss luck at the upcoming sentencing. The men from JB Moving arrived at 8:30 the next morning, but found the black metal gate at the end of the driveway locked. When they phoned the house, there was no answer. They called their office in Stamford and asked what to do. The office manager called Hayley. She gave him the security code that would open the gate.

The movers backed their truck to the front door, then got out and rang the bell. No one answered, but they found that the door was unlocked. Calling out repeatedly, they entered the house and set to work. No one seemed to be home, but the movers knew they were supposed to load the few pieces of furniture from the bedroom and anything else that had not been moved on Saturday.

One of them went down to check the basement. He found Andrew. His body lay on the floor in a huge pool of blood. His hands and feet were bound with plastic flexcuffs and a T-shirt was pulled over his head. He'd been stabbed many times in the back.

"This was not a random act," Greenwich police chief James Walters told the media the next day. "We believe Mr. Kissel was the intended target." He said Andrew's BlackBerry cell phone and e-mail device had been taken. He added that the absence of signs of forced entry indicated that Andrew had probably known his killer, or killers. Suspicion immediately focused on Carlos Trujillo, the Colombian houseboy and the last person known to have seen Andrew alive.

Bill expressed a different point of view. "Andrew did bad things," he told the press. "He took money from a lot of people. He was killed in an extremely vengeful, angry way. If somebody just wanted to kill him they only had to put a bullet in his head, not tie him up and stab him to death with a shirt over his head. And someone got in there in a very narrow timeline. Someone had to know something." Then he talked about Hayley. "She's driven by money," he said. "She's not a nice person." Was he suggesting that Hayley might have been involved in Andrew's killing? "You can't rule it out," Bill said.

On the day of Andrew's burial service in Lodi, New Jersey, Bill had guards posted at the entrance to the cemetery. They were instructed to prevent Hayley from entering, if she tried. She didn't.

There were only seventeen people at the graveside service on a gray and drizzly April afternoon. Only Jane had come primarily to mourn the passing of Andrew. Bill told the rabbi who conducted the service to speak only about Andrew's childhood. "Once he grew up, he turned bad," Bill said. "There's nothing good to say about him as a man."

A week later, the e-mail in which Hayley told Jane she had fantasized about killing Andrew with her bare hands was leaked to the press. Hayley's lawyer, Nathan Dershowitz, said he believed Bill and Jane had arranged the leak.

"Things between my client and the Kissels have been rocky," he said, "and that family is feeling very guilty about what happened with Andrew and not being available to provide him with the emotional support he needed."

Dershowitz called attention to the message Hayley left for Bill only a day and a half before Andrew was killed. "Andrew was despondent and she was reaching out to his family hoping that they would reach out to Andrew and help him. What's shocking is that his family, particularly Bill, never responded and never tried." He said Bill must have had "a sense of guilt . . . for not helping his own son in the first place. All Hayley was doing was letting them know this guy's alone, he is having trouble, help him. And no one from his family ever did."

In regard to Hayley, a few days later the Greenwich chief of police said, "We wish she could be more cooperative." The chief "would not discuss whether she was a suspect," the Associated Press reported.

There was never an implication that Hayley herself had committed the murder—though she was a strong, athletic woman with a fierce temper, whose rabid anger at her husband two days before he was killed had badly unnerved the movers she'd called to the house—but police seemed interested in pursuing the possibility that she'd hired the killer or killers.

But not a shred of evidence that Hayley had been involved was ever found, and suspicion remained focused on Trujillo. He was interviewed repeatedly by police, as were members of his extended family. He voluntarily took a polygraph examination. Chief Walters announced that he had failed it. For months, the police made it seem that Trujillo's arrest was imminent. Then they backed off. Eventually they fell silent. Bill denounced them in the press, calling them "Keystone Kops." He continued to tell friends that the police should question Hayley more aggressively. "What does Hayley know and is hiding from the police?" Bill wrote in an e-mail to an acquaintance.

Time passed. Rumors swirled. The Greenwich police did not seek help from state or federal investigators. The focus of the investigation shifted to former business partners of Andrew's, whom he had swindled. The list was long. Particular attention was paid to an olive oil importing venture that had linked Andrew to businessmen in Sicily. But the Greenwich police department was not about to start messing around in Palermo or Catania.

After sparking an initial flurry of sensational headlines, the story of the unsolved murder of an unloved con man who'd been about to start serving a long prison sentence lost its grip on the public imagination. Only tabloid television continued to pay attention.

In midsummer, Hayley watched a *Nancy Grace* show that was devoted largely to the question of whether she might have been involved. Afterward, she sent a long e-mail to an acquaintance:

It was surreal watching a TV show where the topic of discussion was whether or not I murdered my husband. Hate is a word that is thrown around pretty loosely and my e-mails are no different from what many women write when they are unhappy.

My god, two months after he took in three kids, and after we discussed that he would have to help me or at least support me emotionally so I could do the job, he goes off and has an affair. I couldn't believe that this is where my life ended up as I sat and watched in horror.

I always believed that Bill gave Elaine cancer (I believe that stress breaks down the immune system—another reason why I divorced AK). I feel like they are the insidious cancer. I guess in the end for deciding to divorce Andrew, I will be better off than Elaine, who died at a young age, but it sure feels like crap now.

There will be a time that I will look back at this period with some clarity and I hope that I will have greater self-esteem, perhaps be less trusting and less willing to sacrifice my own happiness. I will certainly feel like a survivor and you know what—my girls and I will have a relationship that is so incredibly solid, that is built around mutual respect, love, an appreciation for our collective inner strength and for the bond that was created through this adversity. My kids will be fine because they have a wonderful support system both through friends and family, I will impart good values in them, and they know they are loved and respected; I just need to convince them that they are safe.

Back to Nancy Grace, I also enjoyed her command of the law and Andrew's legal entanglements when she stated that, with his death, I now get all the money because he never pleaded. Okay well let's see, there are about $25 million of liens on all his assets, liens in place thru judicial order all part and parcel to civil cases. Do they just vanish?

And my personal favorite is when people call him a millionaire . . . He could've been a millionaire. The jerk had great instincts in real estate and was very smart. That is what I'll never understand. He could've made a really nice living and he had two beautiful kids and a wife he loved. Why couldn't he be happy with that? It should have been a perfectly fulfilling life . . .

———————

Throughout the summer, Bill remained isolated in his mansion on the grounds of a Florida country club. His seventy-ninth birthday arrived. He e-mailed an acquaintance:

It is so hard to get Robert's murder, and then Andrew's out of my mind, and the poor children.

I am going to sleep. It is 8:45 PM, and I am exhausted. I wake up at 2 or 3 in the morning, and there it is: Robert and Andrew . . .

More months passed. The Greenwich police reported no progress in their investigation. On the first anniversary of Andrew's death, Bill told the Stamford *Advocate*, "The police have hunkered down and closed the investigation. It's going nowhere."

In May 2007, both Chief Walters and his assistant chief announced their resignations. Walters had served only four years as chief and they'd been turbulent. The department had faced charges of racism in hiring and promotions, twice Walters had received votes of no confidence from his force, and he'd been reprimanded by Greenwich officials for granting special privileges to Diana Ross during her forty-eight hours in a Greenwich jail cell that had followed her arrest on drunken driving charges.

When asked if he had any regrets about unsolved cases, Walters mentioned the 1984 strangling of a thirteen-year-old boy. "That's really the only case that still bothers me," he said. He expressed no regret about having failed to find whoever murdered Andrew Kissel.

Television commentators remarked that while Greenwich police were quick to pounce on anyone found waterskiing after sunset, the town was a great place in which to get away with murder.

Hayley lost her hedge fund job as a result of the brouhaha surrounding Andrew's murder, and she couldn't find a new one. Eventually, she started working part-time for her father. She appeared in civil courts frequently as she battled creditors for any scant funds that could be salvaged from Andrew's estate. She resisted attempts by banks to

foreclose on the house at Stratton Mountain. She broke off all contact
with Rob's three children, but poured much time and energy into helping her own two daughters maintain equilibrium. Hayley told friends
she had a new boyfriend who treated her well, but socially she kept a
low profile.

She sent an e-mail to an acquaintance in the spring, saying Andrew might not have been murdered if Bill and Jane had not ignored his
cries for help.

Perhaps if Andrew's family had come to his rescue . . . No, instead they all
turned their collective backs and let him rot. Nary a visit. And what do I
hear after the fact, "I always thought that when Andrew got out he could
live with me and I would help him." Perhaps something that could have
been shared in the months leading to his conviction. But no, revisionist
history is so much more, well downright easier to deal with. Heck!

I don't know—if your son was under house arrest, heading to jail for 8
years and had extensive emotional problems, you were in your 70's, would
you rise above it all and try one last time? Make a heroic attempt—haul
your tush on that 2½ hour plane ride and knock on the door and just
steamroll your way in? "Goddamnit Andrew, it's time we put this behind.
You've done bad things and you deserve what is coming but heck I am your
dad and I may have done some things wrong but you are my son, my only
remaining son." . . . you just get on the plane and if you don't get past
the door you just write it off and know that in your heart you tried. That's
what you do for your kids and you do it for things far more trivial than
this . . .

No, but Bill spent his summer in HK mourning the only son who ever
mattered, retrospectively of course. The good son. The one he was so close

to. Who achieved greatness when he moved to HK (as measured in wealth) . . .

And then it was even more enjoyable to turn his rage on me. I don't know—lose one son, losing a second that you would likely never see again because he was going away for 8 years or so. Try and make amends, heal the wounds that have been festering. Nah.

Festering was what the Kissels did instead of breathing.

35. MICHAEL

IN HINSDALE, NEW HAMPSHIRE, 166 MILES NORTHEAST OF Greenwich, Michael Del Priore was keeping a low profile, too. He refused all requests for interviews and turned down a $25,000 offer from the *National Enquirer* to tell his story.

No one from Interpol ever came calling. There was insufficient evidence for extradition. He was never charged with any crime.

He married Tracey in June 2006. She was the blonde whose picture had appeared alongside his in the Chinese magazine. He continued to operate his one-man business, installing home security systems. He and Tracey lived together in the stationary mobile home that Peter Chapman had called a trailer. It sat on a hill, just down the road from the dog track. He saw his daughter on alternate weekends.

Every day during the spring and summer of 2006, the mailman would bring a new letter from Nancy. Most were at least five pages long, packed on both sides with her handwritten words and ellipses. She wrote as if she still didn't know there was already a new woman in Michael's life. In letter after letter, she'd spin out detailed fantasies of the life together she and Michael would share as soon as her appeal set her free. Many of the fantasies involved rain. A surprising number involved washing dishes, with the lovers' hands coming together among the pie plates and cereal bowls in the hot, soapy water. They all ended with her drifting off to sleep after making love as Michael murmured, "I'll never leave you, baby doll . . . I'll always be here for you . . . You'll always be safe in my arms."

She told him she'd begun to study the Bible. She'd also taught herself to play the guitar, and at night she would perform the new love songs she was writing about Michael for the twelve other lifers in her maximum-security ward. She said their response was gratifying, especially considering that none of them understood English.

Her mother still came to visit, as did a few remaining Parkview friends. Rob's former colleague from Goldman Sachs continued to pay her legal fees and continued to insist on anonymity. A man wanted to make a movie about her life. Although no hearing of her appeal would be held until 2008, she was sure it would prove successful. Once she was freed, she planned to travel the world, establishing retreats for battered women. "In the mountains, where it's peaceful," she wrote. She was sure that Michael would want to travel with her. She knew they'd make a great team.

Michael and Tracey would read the letters together and shake their heads. But as time went on, the letters began to rankle Tracey, and there got to be too many to keep in the trailer, so Michael boxed them up and took them to a locker he'd rented at a storage facility located on the side of the road that led to Brattleboro.

He started to put off reading the new ones as they arrived. Then he stopped reading them altogether. Eventually he stopped even opening them, just tossing them in a carton instead and taking the carton to the storage locker when it was filled.

At the start of September 2006—almost a year to the day after Nancy's conviction—Michael wrote to the superintendent of the Tai Lam Centre for Women, 110 Tai Lam Chung Road, New Territories, Hong Kong, and asked him to stop sending her letters.

For Del Priore, at least, there was such a thing as enough.

In order to protect their privacy, the first names of the three children of Robert and Nancy Kissel have been changed, as has Jane Kissel's married name.

ACKNOWLEDGMENTS

MANY PEOPLE PERSONALLY CONNECTED TO AND IN SOME cases deeply affected by the murders of Robert and Andrew Kissel sought to help me understand the complex and destructive dynamic of the extended Kissel family.

I am especially indebted to those family members who shared their recollections, insights, and feelings at no small personal cost in terms of heartache. I would like to thank in particular Bill Kissel, Ira Keeshin, Jean McGlothlin, Hayley Kissel, and Brooks (Ryan) Keeshin for their candor and their trust.

I would also like to thank, in particular, Frank Shea and Bryna O'Shea for their patience in the face of my persistent and no doubt annoying questions about myriad details.

Michael Del Priore spoke to me at length and shared with me hundreds of Nancy Kissel's letters to him, for which I am grateful.

Michael Paradise, Cris Parker, Charlie Dolan, Carol Horton, Susan Povich, Lee Smith, Doug Darrow, and Liz and John La Cause were particularly generous with their time and recollections, and I thank them.

In addition, I'd like to express gratitude to those individuals, both in Hong Kong and elsewhere, who spoke to me on the condition that their identities not be disclosed.

I remain blessed by the confidence and enthusiastic support of

Simon & Schuster publisher and executive vice president David Rosenthal and my exceptionally gifted editor, Kerri Kolen. Amy Ryan's copyediting and fact checking were superb. Elisa Rivlin and Emily Remes provided legal counsel in the most supportive manner imaginable.

The least of my debt to Dennis Holahan arises from his extraordinary labors as my lawyer and agent. More important, he is as caring, unselfish, and inspirational a friend as any man could hope to have.

Finally, the one person whom I don't even know how to start to thank is Nancy Doherty, the best editor I've ever worked with and, for so many years, so much more. This is the ninth of my books over which Nancy has waved her editorial wand and, as always, she has helped me to make it several orders of magnitude better than I could have made it myself. Her eye is unerring, her ear pitch-perfect, her surgical skills superb, and her insights both original and profound. I don't know what I'd do without her.